MATERIAL
PHENOMI

Other titles in the series:

Posthuman Glossary, edited by Rosi Braidotti and Maria Hlavajova
Conflicting Humanities, edited by Rosi Braidotti and Paul Gilroy
General Ecology, edited by Erich Hörl with James Burton
Philosophical Posthumanism, Francesca Ferrando
The Philosophy of Matter, Rick Dolphijn

Also available from Bloomsbury:

Philosophical Chemistry: Genealogy of a Scientific Field, Manuel DeLanda
Philosophy and Simulation: The Emergence of Synthetic Reason, Manuel DeLanda
A New Philosophy of Society: Assemblage Theory and Social Complexity, Manuel DeLanda

Intensive Science and Virtual Philosophy, Manuel DeLanda

MATERIALIST PHENOMENOLOGY

A Philosophy of Perception

Manuel DeLanda

BLOOMSBURY ACADEMIC
LONDON • NEW YORK • OXFORD • NEW DELHI • SYDNEY

BLOOMSBURY ACADEMIC
Bloomsbury Publishing Plc
50 Bedford Square, London, WC1B 3DP, UK
1385 Broadway, New York, NY 10018, USA
29 Earlsfort Terrace, Dublin 2, Ireland

BLOOMSBURY, BLOOMSBURY ACADEMIC and the Diana logo are trademarks
of Bloomsbury Publishing Plc

First published in Great Britain 2022
Reprinted 2022 (twice)

Cover image: Molecules Concept of Neurons(© Pavel_R / iStock)

A catalogue record for this book is available from the British Library.

A catalog record for this book is available from the Library of Congress.

ISBN: HB: 978-1-3502-6394-9
PB: 978-1-3502-6395-6
ePDF: 978-1-3502-6396-3
eBook: 978-1-3502-6397-0

Series: Theory in the New Humanities

Typeset by Deanta Global Publishing Services, Chennai, India
Printed and bound in Great Britain

To find out more about our authors and books visit www.bloomsbury.com and
sign up for our newsletters.

CONTENTS

INTRODUCTION

Traditionally, communication between philosophers of the materialist and phenomenological schools has been minimal. The former have tended to either reduce the mind to the brain or declare it a mere epiphenomenon, and once the mind loses its autonomy, or is rendered causally impotent, any common ground between the two schools disappears. But is it really impossible to recover the insights that a methodical analysis of phenomenal experience has produced, without having to import the idealist ontology in which the expression of those insights was originally casted? Is it not viable, for example, to consider the human body as it is lived subjectively, without rejecting the physical body that can be harmed by bullets or crushed by torture? The lack of interest in bridging these two worlds may be explained by the fact that materialists fear that a commitment to an autonomous and causally powerful mind is incompatible with a rejection of *substance dualism*, the idea that the body and the mind are literally made out of different materials, one physical, the other spiritual. The routine antidote to this dualism has been to eliminate the nonphysical substance and to eliminate all properties but the physical ones. But this is not our only option. We can affirm substance monism while retaining *property dualism*.[1]

More specifically, there exists today several varieties of *non-reductive materialism* that can be used as an alternative. This philosophical school can be roughly defined by three basic ideas: first, that there are mental properties that are different from physical properties; second, that the existence of mental properties depends on the existence of physical properties; and third, that mental properties can confer causal powers on mental events.[2] The second idea is what makes this school a materialist one, while the first and the third are used to block reductionism and epiphenomenalism, respectively. These three ideas, however, define only an abstract schema, because they are compatible with many actual philosophical positions depending on how we conceive what mental properties are, how they depend on physical ones, and how mental events acquire causal powers.[3] This book is an attempt to flesh out the formal schema with substantive accounts of each of these three subjects. On the other hand, unlike other studies carried out within this framework, our project here is not to explain cognitive behavior in general but only visual experience. But is not the latter entirely subjective, and as such, beyond the reach of a materialist approach?

Any coherent form of materialism must be a species of realism; that is, it must be ontologically committed to assert the existence of an objective world that does not depend on our minds. This requirement, however, can be understood in two different ways: we can believe that there are entities which are independent of the *existence* of our minds, like the geological, climatological, and ecological processes that shaped the planet on which we evolved; and we can believe that there are entities that are independent of the *content* of our minds, that is, entities that have a definite nature, which does not change when our beliefs about it change. This is the kind of objective existence we will assume the visual field has: as a mental entity it cannot exist without minds but its nature is what it is regardless of the theories that our minds create in order to understand it. To be a realist about the phenomenal content of vision in this way, however, comes at a cost. In particular, it prevents us from accepting that this content is made intelligible by the mental use of concepts. If we agreed with this, then we would also have to accept that when our concepts change visual content also changes. So another theme running through the pages of this book is that human beings can make sense of what they see without the help from any conceptual machinery. This is not, of course, to deny the role that concepts, beliefs, and explanations play in our cognitive life, but only to assert that cognition comes in many different forms, and that in the particular case of visual perception, cognitive activity is mostly nonconceptual.

In addition to restricting our approach to visual perception, we will also downplay the role of social factors. This does not imply any commitment to an "individualist" conception of the mind, only a rejection of any approach that dehistoricizes the human species, assuming we have always been language users. We spent hundreds of thousands of years as part of hunter-gatherer communities, with a material culture of stone tools and bound by egalitarian social norms, but without linguistic abilities.[4] If the content of the visual field was structured by language, how are we supposed to explain our survival in those conditions? We can acknowledge that our lives as hunter-gatherers did produce adaptations that are social in nature, such as the evolution of neurons specializing on the recognition of human faces, but most of the brain machinery that underlies visual perception evolved prior to our becoming humans. There is no deep discontinuity between animal and human visual experience, as there would be if linguistically expressed concepts shaped perception. And it is that continuity that explains the homologies that exist between our brains and those of the animals (macaque monkeys, cats) from which we have learned most of what we know about the role played by the brain in perception and action. Some of those animals have a social life, and some do not, so we can expect the evolutionary effects of living in a community to be very specialized. Viewing the history of our species as connected to a deeper past also has the advantage of reducing the appeal of some old philosophical fantasies, like the brain in a vat. Our own mental life is so rich that it may tempt us into thinking that it could go on if we were fully disembodied. By placing the human mind in the context of animal minds we are reminded that its operation requires a body that can perform causal interventions in the world: perception in the animal world evolved as an aid for action and it must always be understood in the context of the bodily activity that it guides.

Chapter 1 begins where any materialist approach should begin: in the world of structured matter and energy. The majority of objects that populate the world have a solid structure, this being a contingent fact about our planet, and they interact with each other emitting *natural signs* as they do. We may refer to these signs as "information" but only as long as we use this term to refer to the content of the signs, not just to their material vehicle, as it is routinely done in the theory of information. The light that conveys those signs to our eyes, in turn, should also be conceived as being structured by its interactions with the surfaces that bind objects. Structured light not only stimulates our retinas, undergoing a transformation into other forms of energy as it does, but it also informs them. When light is viewed as a mere stimulus the content it conveys is assumed to be highly impoverished, needing concepts and inferences to become enriched into something that can be plausibly related to phenomenal experience. But an analysis of the optical events taking place on any slice of structured light reveals how rich the content can be, and how it could have affected the way in which our sensory organs evolved. In addition to discussing the material and energetic preconditions for our evolution, this chapter also introduces several topics that will be further developed in the rest of the book: how the use of natural signs by the brain should be conceived and how to think about the neural agency required to transform natural signs into intentional signs.

Chapter 2 investigates the role of embodiment in action and perception. When approaching the question of causal interventions in the world, the body must be viewed as an object among others, the main difference being the much higher degree of control that our brain has over joints, muscles, and tendons. How we think about the way this control is achieved has important consequences for our conception both of internal signs and of the neural agents that use those signs. On the other hand, treating the body as an object that can affect and be affected by the world does not shed light on questions about phenomenal experience, except to the extent that successes in taking advantage of objective opportunities and avoiding objective risks leave behind a subjective residue. Capturing the various effects of embodiment on perception requires that we approach the body as it is lived by a subject. The lived body has many dimensions, the most basic ones of which are related to the way we experience its internal environment as well as to the way we experience its state of movement, its posture, and the possibilities for action open to us from a given position. This chapter will analyze the two forms of internal perception that are behind these elementary bodily experiences, interoception and proprioception, and explore their involvement in the generation of the visual field.

Chapter 3 takes us on a journey through the brain, starting at the retina and following the different streams of information it produces as they make their way through different parts of the cortex. While previous chapters dealt with the question of neural agency in a mostly metaphorical way, here we confront this thorny issue head on. Taking inspiration from artificial neural nets, a cognitive technology that clearly displays the difference between agents and signs, this chapter is an attempt to draw a principled distinction between the kind of agency displayed by the cortical areas involved in visual perception and the intentional signs these areas produce and consume. Although the argument that these signs are not symbolic (or otherwise conceptual) runs through the entire book, it is only when we finally focus on the brain itself, and on the way in which it maps both the retina and the body, that the temptation to speak of conceptual representations enriching stimulation recedes into the background. We have acquired so much knowledge about retinal and somatic maps over the last decades that the nonconceptual role that these iconic signs play has become impossible to ignore. In addition to representing how the world appears to an embodied subject, the brain must also plan and implement the bodily activities undertaken on the basis of that representation, so this chapter must also deal with the way in which the brain controls the body, as well as with how it relates to the body's visceral environment providing it with the elementary biological values it uses to automatically select appropriate responses in urgent circumstances.

Chapter 4 considers the enormous gap between what we know about the way in which the brain represents the world and the way in which we visually experience it. A sharp distinction will be made between sensory inputs and motor outputs, on the one hand, and perception and action, on the other. Visual perception is not an input from the world to the mind, and voluntary action is not an output from the mind to the world. Between inputs and outputs and the resulting phenomenal experience there is an explanatory gap that must be bridged. But, it will be argued, the required bridge should not be conceived as linking brain and mind in a single step, but as requiring several intermediate steps of increased sophistication. The perception of properties, such as color or brightness, requires nothing more sophisticated than neurally implemented measuring devices and the transformation of their output into a lived property. For peripheral portions of the visual field, in which objects appear in an undifferentiated state, this may be enough. But in those parts we are attending to at any given moment, the empiricist conception of objects as mere bundles of properties is clearly inadequate, because objects are rendered there as integrated wholes with an identity that goes beyond their possession of those properties. And when what we are attending to is not single objects but groups of them interacting in complex ways, we need an even more sophisticated kind of perception to understand the different kinds of situations into which objects can enter. The task of demonstrating that the content of the visual field is not conceptually structured grows in difficulty as we move from properties to objects and then to situations. In particular, the kind of situations that can be grasped without concepts is limited to those experienced directly, in which the interacting objects are all present at once, and in which the subject is actively involved. This chapter must, therefore, clarify the nature of the different forms of perception and then attempt to bridge the explanatory gap for each of them separately.

The overall message of the book is that only by taking into account the contributions of the material world, the body, the brain, and the mind, can we make any progress in understating the nature of phenomenal experience. But to get this project started we need to get rid of our past baggage. On the one hand, we must reject all theories of direct perception and the naive realism that these theories imply. Not all materialists believe that we see reality as it is, but many do, and to adopt this position is not to dissolve a false problem, but to abandon any hope of solving a true one. On the other hand, we must reject accounts in which the visual field is generated from the intentional acts performed by a unified central subject. Once we multiply the kinds of agency at work in the construction of this field, a process in which populations of unconscious agents must work in parallel to produce basic content, and layers of progressively more conscious ones must elaborate and integrate that content, any privileged center of intentionality disappears. Between the two extremes of perceiving objectivity directly and being trapped in a world of pure subjectivity, there are, of course, many possible philosophical positions, some of which we will consider in detail in the following chapters before offering a novel alternative. Or more exactly, before bringing together the existing pieces of a puzzle that could be solved if not for the fact that its pieces are widely dispersed in a hundred different places. What follows is, therefore, more a synthesis of what already exists, rather than the creation of something entirely new. Just a first step but in the right direction.

1 THE CONTRIBUTION OF THE WORLD

Biological evolution is opportunistic. Natural selection must work with what is available at the moment, taking advantage of existing opportunities, unable to favor an adaptation due to its potential future benefits. It follows that when sensory organs began to evolve, the world had to already possess something they could exploit: the water, the air, as well as the ambient light that bathes the planet's surface had to be *populated by signs*. But what kind of signs could these be? Certainly not symbols, since these can stand for something else only through an arbitrary social convention. But there are two other kinds of signs that do not depend on human communities to exist and could, therefore, be candidates for the natural signs we require: *indices and icons*. Roughly, an index is a sign that stands for an object by being a causal effect of it, while an icon stands for an object through a relation of similarity.[1]

The most obvious illustration of an index is smoke, which indicates the presence of fire. Other examples include a hunter who tracks his prey by following footprints, droppings, broken branches, pieces of hair trapped in the bark of trees, smells, and sounds, using these signs as indicating the presence of the prey; and a forensic doctor who uses fingerprints, the shape of a wound, blood spatter patterns, the presence of gun powder in a corpse, or even the DNA contained in hair or fingernails left in the crime scene, as indicating the identity of the criminal, as well as the nature of the crime. The same point applies to doctors linking external symptoms to a disease, analytical chemists using a reagent to reveal the presence of a given substance, and ordinary people using the spontaneous facial expressions of others as indicators of their emotions.[2]

The second candidate for natural signs varies depending on whether the icon can stand for an object by virtue of being similar to it in appearance, in which case a realist drawing would be a good illustration, or by possessing *similar relations* among its components, like the spatial relations between cities preserved in most geographical maps, or the functional relations between electronic components in circuit diagrams.[3] There are, however, two problems with this characterization. The first problem is that it incorrectly suggests that an icon is a visual sign. A good example of a nonvisual icon are the grooves in an old fashion vinyl record that may be said to stand for a particular piece of music. The record has a spiral groove that guides a needle, the groove having a specific pattern of changing depth. As the needle follows the groove, it moves up or down, and its motion is transformed into a pattern of electrical impulses that preserves relations. When this pattern reaches the speaker through a wire, it is transformed into yet another similar pattern of vibrations, which as they travel through the air and reach a human ear are finally transformed into a musical pattern. The second problem is the very concept of similarity or resemblance. As is well known, similarity must always be relativized to a particular aspect, since any pair of entities, regardless of how different they may be from each other, are similar in some respect, such as being located on planet Earth or moving at less than the speed of light. For this reason, instead of the word "similarity" a more technical term, *isomorphism*, is often used when icons are discussed, a term that refers to a one-to-one mapping between two sets of things. If we map not the items in each set into each other but the relations between items in each set, we get what is called a *structure preserving mapping*.[4] This, however, does not solve the problem of the indefinite number of ways in which two things can be similar to each other, because mathematical isomorphisms are equally abundant, so we must restrict the term to mappings that are performed on natural sets, such as the sets of groove heights, voltage peaks, and speaker vibrations, in the example just given.[5]

Both icons and indices have been recently proposed by philosophers as serious candidates for natural signs.[6] They existed prior to the evolution of sensory organs, but they merely possessed a disposition to be used as signs, a disposition which, to be actualized, had to wait until a living creature came along and *treated the natural signs as signs*. In the examples earlier there is always a user: the hunter or forensic doctor, but also the person using the map or playing the record. In the original formulation of this classification of signs the relation involved was *triadic*: a relation between a sign, what the sign stands for, and a user or an interpreter who connects the two.[7] We need an entity who can treat an effect as being about its cause, an entity who can follow the direction from effect to cause; and we need an entity who can treat an isomorphic map as being about what it maps, as oriented toward what it maps. In both cases the directionality or orientation is referred to as *intentionality*, a property traditionally taken to be a mark of human mentality. In these terms, what the user does is to transform a natural sign into an intentional sign. This transformation is performed by giving the sign a *function* to play in a specific task—tracking prey, investigating crime scenes, playing recorded music—and in examples involving human beings it is relatively easy to understand how an index or an icon may be assigned a role. But what of the use of signs by animals? In this case, we can argue that the function was selected through an evolutionary process. All we need to do to back this conclusion is to show that connecting a sign to what it stands for, and doing so regularly and over many generations, improved the reproductive success of animals of a given species.

This classification of external signs has been revived, and its extension to nonhuman creatures worked out, not only to explain the conditions allowing the evolution of sensory organs but, more importantly, as a prelude to using these ideas in a theory of *internal signs*. However, as some philosophers have argued, this step is anything but unproblematic. All these ideas supply us with is an intuition of how a *whole person* (or whole organism) can transform natural signs into intentional ones by employing them systematically as part of a task, but how can this intuition be applied to what is basically a part of a person? Can a theory that works for an embodied, situated subject also work for the subject's brain? What is required here is a well-formulated *job description* of external signs, so that the intuitions we have about how they operate can be used for internal signs.[8] There are several items in this job description. The first item uses a distinction that has been part of the philosophy of signs for centuries: the distinction between the *vehicle*, or sensible component of a sign, and the *content*, or its intelligible component.[9] The best-known example of this distinction is that between the signifier, or phonological vehicle of words, and the signified, or their semantic content. But the distinction applies to all signs, indices and icons included, the vehicle being what allows a sign to interact causally with other material entities, including animals and humans, the content being the referent assigned to the sign by its function in a task. The first requirement in the job description can then be expressed in the following way: for internal signs to be real signs, they *must interact with each other through their content*, not only through their vehicles.[10] In other words, their interactions must be not only causal but also intentional.

How do external signs achieve this double interactivity? By the fact that they are being used by a cognitive agent who interacts causally with the vehicles and intentionally with the contents. So the most obvious objection to imposing this requirement onto our treatment of internal signs is that we would need to postulate the existence of a small version of the full subject inside the head, a homunculus. But this is clearly not a viable solution, since this homunculus would need a smaller homunculus in its head, and so on. This threat of an infinite regress looms large, however, only if what we postulate to exist in our brains is an *exact replica* of the whole subject. But that is not the only alternative. We can also envision an entire population of homunculi of different complexity, the simpler ones serving as component parts of more complex ones. Thus, starting with the whole subject we can imagine that it emerges from the interactions among a set of less cognitively capable homunculi, which would, in turn, emerge from the interactions among homunculi possessing even more meager cognitive capabilities. This would remove the danger of infinite regress, since the bottommost layer of homunculi would be mindless, the kind of homunculi that could perform their tasks in an entirely mechanical way.[11] Armed with such a multi-homuncular model we could meet the first requirement of the job description because these cognitive agents could, if properly designed, make signs interact through their contents: all they have to do is to causally manipulate vehicles in a way that takes their content into account.

To get started we will need a clear example of a mindless cognitive agent, ignoring for the time being the question of how it could be implemented in our brains. All we need to show is that such an agent would indeed be capable of using nonsymbolic signs as part of its mechanism. A widely discussed example is that of *artificial neural nets*. Unlike digital computers a neural net does not acquire its capabilities by being programmed using logical operations on symbols, but by being trained: it is taught by example and learns by doing. The simplest neural net consists of two layers of simple computing units, each unit capable of computing its own degree of activation. Each unit in the input layer is connected to all the units in the output layer by connections that can vary in strength. The training consists in presenting the neural net with many pairs of input and output patterns until it learns to map one into the other, that is, until it is capable of *associating* inputs and outputs. The training rule can be as simple as this: when two units in different layers are active simultaneously, the strength of their connection should be increased; when they are inactive at once, the strength should be decreased.[12] As the training proceeds, a pattern of connection strengths begins to emerge, reflecting regularities in the input-output pairs used as examples. Finally, when the training is over and the neural net is ready to operate, we can feed into it a new input and the pattern of strengths in the connections will shape the transmitted activation in a way that ensures that the output associated with it is produced.[13] It could be argued, therefore, that this device can perform a simple cognitive task (a pattern association task) in a purely mechanical way. But can it also be said to be *using signs* as an integral part of this performance? The answer is probably negative, because in most cases it is the human user of the device who assigns semantic content to the input and output patterns.[14] In a sense, everything that pertains to content has been added by the human user in his choice of training examples.

This limitation, however, can be lifted by adding an extra layer of units in between the input and output layers, and by using a more sophisticated training rule. The extra layer, called a *hidden layer*, can augment the capabilities of a neural net, eliminating to some extent the need for a human user to assign content, because its units can learn to extract statistical regularities in the input and output training pairs. These regularities are not provided by the human users and are often not obvious to them.[15] We can characterize the ability with which the additional layer endows a three-layer neural net as the capacity to *map relations of similarity* in its inputs *into relations of proximity* in the space of possible activation patterns of its hidden layer.[16] In other words, if two inputs have similar characteristics they will be mapped into two nearby points in the space of possible activation patterns, with the consequence that the neural net will treat the two as if they were the same *kind* of pattern, responding with the same output for both. This analytical operation can be considered to *extract a statistical prototype* (not an essence) from the training examples. If we imagine that we are training the neural net to recognize zebras, for example, and if the images used for training contain average zebras, then the prototype will include properties like being a quadruped and having a camouflage skin pattern. But if the training set contained unusual zebras with no skin patterns, then the prototype would lack any sign for camouflage. Hence what the hidden layer does is not to extract an abstract universal for "zebrahood" but only whatever regular patterns exist in a given population of actual zebras.

This improved design would be a better candidate for a mindless cognitive agent, since the signs it generates do take into account the content of the inputs. But these signs do not yet meet the conditions specified in the job description because the signs are not usable by other neural nets. Because the prototype is extracted after a process involving teaching by example and learning by doing, the recognition abilities with which it endows the neural net resemble a manual skill with inaccessible content. In other words, the content is only a disposition of the connections between the input and hidden layers, a disposition actualized only as part of the task of matching an input to an output, and not part of an explicit sign that can be used as such by other neural nets.[17] But this limitation too can be lifted by a new design, such as a *self-organizing map*. In its simplest version, this type of neural net consists of two layers, an input layer and output layer, the units of the latter arranged in a specific spatial pattern, such as a rectangular array. This design can be trained to map relations of similarity into relations proximity, except that now the mapping is not between inputs and a space of possible activation patterns but between inputs and an *actual location* in the rectangular array.[18] Hence, what used to be a sign that was implicit and usable only by the neural net that produced it is now explicit and usable by other neural nets, as long as they have acquired the function of treating a location in the output layer as standing for a prototype.[19]

We may conclude from these brief remarks that, given an appropriate design, artificial neural nets can serve as temporary representatives of the kind of mindless agents capable of using internal signs. We will replace them in time once we discuss more anatomically plausible models. What kind of internal signs are these mechanical devices using? The answer is that they are using neither indices nor icons but *a hybrid of the two*. A good example of an external sign displaying this hybridity is a modern GPS map: the layout of streets and landmarks in the map is isomorphic to the real layout, so it is an icon, while the dot informing the user where in the map he is currently located is an index, since the dot is causally linked to his actual location.[20] So what in a neural net plays this double representational role? The outcome of the training process is an iconic classification of *types* of inputs, the similarities between tokens of a type mapped into locations of a self-organizing map, for example. But when the training is over and the neural net is presented with an object to recognize, the stable activation pattern caused by the object is an index of a *token of a type*.[21] So the full sign being used has an iconic part standing for types or kinds, and an indexical part standing for tokens or members of that kind.

A different question worth asking at this point is whether a device using these hybrid signs displays intentionality. To the extent that the device is oriented toward external inputs, its acts of recognition will also be so oriented, and in this sense, it displays a minimum of intentionality.[22] Since we are using neural nets to represent the bottommost layer of the homuncular population, this minimum is all we need. Stronger forms of intentionality, more recognizably human, could be expected to emerge as cognitive agents increase in complexity, so our concept of intentionality must allow for *gradations*.[23] Nevertheless, and however weak the intentional relation may be, it must be explained by the (evolutionary, cultural, or training) history of its users.[24] And this brings us to our next question. If the job description demands that the signs produced by one neural net be usable by other neural nets, what insights from the use of external signs can we deploy to think about what internal agents must do in order to share signs? Are there examples of the *cooperative* use of external signs by many organisms that we can use as a source of inspiration to properly conceptualize what goes on in our brains?

Let's imagine an animal searching for food, vigilant to any indication of its presence. Such an animal is *consuming* natural signs by transforming them into intentional signs. At the same time as it conducts its search, it is *producing* natural signs: carving footprints on soft terrain, emitting odors and sounds, and leaving behind hair and droppings. These natural signs can be transformed into intentional signs by a human hunter who is tracking the animal, but they clearly do not have that evolutionary function: the purpose of those signs is not to guide the hunter. On the other hand, it is not hard to find in ethological literature many examples of animals producing natural signs that do have the function of being consumed by their conspecifics. Territorial mammals and birds, for example, use a variety of signs to mark a territory, signs meant to be consumed as warnings by male rivals, as well as signs meant to attract females and thus be consumed by them. But this implies that rivals and potential mates have evolved the ability to be warned or be seduced by those natural signs. For this condition to be met, the abilities of both producer and consumer must have *coevolved*. And when a cooperative use of signs has emerged through a coevolutionary process, we can say that the natural signs produced by the territorial male have become intentional signs.[25] It can be shown that producer-consumer pairs, like animal warning-animal being warned, or animal seducing-animal being seduced, are stable evolutionary outcomes, as long as *common interests* motivate their interaction.[26] Can we apply this insight about the cooperative use of external signs to internal agents?

The sophistication of territorial animal displays, as well as their complex way to assess common interests, makes it hard to use this case to think about the brain. What we need is an example in which common interests are hard-wired into the animals and in which collaboration is not between pairs of animals but among communities of them. Honey bee colonies seem to fit this description perfectly, since most members have lost their ability to reproduce and their sign producing activities are genetically programmed to be performed in the evolutionary interest of the entire community. Because most cells in the brain also lack the ability to reproduce in a way that can be subjected to natural selection, communication in bee colonies can serve as a better source of intuitions.[27] The best-studied type of sign produced and consumed by honey bees is the so-called *waggle dance*. When a source of nectar has been located, a foraging bee can communicate its location to the other foraging bees by repeatedly moving in a figure eight pattern relative to some reference vertical line and waggling its stomach each time it traverses this vertical. The average orientation of the waggling relative to the vertical indicates at what angle (relative to the sun and the hive) the nectar is located, while the average duration of the waggling indicates the distance of the location.[28] These indices, however, work only by being embedded into an icon. For example, if a particular dance is rotated 45 degrees it will now indicate a location rotated by the same amount. This implies that there is an isomorphism between potential dances with rotational structure and potential locations with rotational structure.[29] Or in simpler terms, the bee dance involves an icon mapping types of dances into types of locations (types differing only in distance and orientation), as well as an index linking a token of dance with a token of a location.

Among the insights that we can import from this cooperative use of external signs is that within a producer-consumer couple it is easier to fix the referent of a sign. To see this let's first consider the single-user case. Everyone would agree that a vinyl disc holds a *record of* a song. The word "of," much like the word "about," marks an intentional relation, so the grooves on the disc are intentionally related to the song. But why should the grooved disc stand for the song and not for any of the intermediate isomorphic patterns produced when the song is played? Because it is the normal function of the disc to be used to produce songs. We could, of course, imagine that someone can make a different use of the disc, as when an engineer is checking for a faulty component in the system and examines not the song but the electrical patterns in the wire or the mechanical patterns in the speakers. But that does not change the fact that the disc was originally created to play songs. This shows that in the single-user case we must invoke some external agency to fix the function, and in so doing, fix the referent of the icon. But once the use of signs takes place within a coevolved producer-consumer pair we need not bother with that: the consumer itself will determine which of the several isomorphisms matters and what intermediate steps are irrelevant to its current activities.[30]

And a similar point applies to indices: between the original cause and the final effect acting as a sign for it there may be many intermediate causal steps, but if the consumer uses only the information that leads to the original cause ignoring the rest, then that cause is the referent of the index.[31] Imagine a novice foraging bee that has just discovered its first stash of nectar. As is well known, bees can learn by Pavlovian association: the licking reflex triggered by the presence of nectar can be triggered by association with floral aromas or colors.[32] Let's imagine our novice bee to have just learned this association. When it arrives at the hive and begins its dance, the learning episode that occurred between finding the nectar's location and performing the dance will indeed be part of the causal process that led to the dance, but it will not be part of what the bee communicates. Even if the novice bee devised a way of making it part of the content, that piece of information would be ignored by the other bees who are only concerned with information about locations. Generalizing this conclusion we may say that whereas a natural sign carries information about all the intermediate steps between its production and consumption, an intentional sign disregards most steps retaining only what is relevant to the current user of the sign, and the user in this case is the consumer: in the cooperative use of signs, *it is the consumer that determines the content*.[33]

To apply this insight to internal signs we need to get a rough idea of the kinds of perceptual activities in which mindless cognitive agents would normally engage. In an influential model of computer vision, for example, the perception of external objects is broken down into three separate stages, each one involving consumers and producers: a first stage, in which discontinuities in the intensity of light in the retina are consumed while intentional signs for the edges and contours of objects are produced; a second stage, in which these signs are consumed to produce intentional signs for surfaces; and a third stage, in which these signs are consumed to produce intentional signs for objects.[34] The process is, in fact, more complex than this and we will describe it in more detail in Chapter 3. What matters at this point is that it can be carried out and that its success depends on the existence of certain statistical regularities, such as those caused by the *relative abundance of solid objects* on terrestrial ecosystems.[35] Let's illustrate this with an example from the first stage. If evolution had managed to internalize the higher frequency of occurrence of solids into the wiring of the brain, this would allow simple agents to guide their consumption of natural signs by assumptions that reflect this fact. Thus, agents can implicitly assume that any sudden change in intensity at a specific location in the retina will correspond, with high probability, to a localized cause in the world, such as a real boundary.[36] This would not be the case if most objects in the world were liquid or gaseous. When signs standing for edges are produced and passed to the next level of consumers, their connection to changes in intensity in the retinal input will cease to matter: agents at the next stage will not be interested in luminance discontinuities but only about line segments that indicate boundaries, since it is by selecting and grouping those linear elements that they can produce intentional signs standing for surfaces.[37] And similarly for the final stage, in which the only thing that matters for the production of signs standing for solid objects are the finished signs for surfaces, all other information produced during the intermediate steps of the process being dutifully ignored.[38]

Let's summarize the argument so far. We cannot take for granted that our intuitions about how external signs work, intuitions derived from a lifetime spent producing and consuming them, will be useful to understand the internal use of signs by the brain. In particular, in order for external signs to stand for anything there must be a user or interpreter, and this would seem to imply that for signs to be used internally a duplicate version of the whole subject (or organism) must be postulated. A solution to this problem is to replace a full-fledged interpreter with a team of sign users that have lesser cognitive capacities (so they are not duplicates) and that can interact with each other to generate, as an emergent result, the full interpreter. Each member of this team of agents must be the emergent result of interactions among even less cognitively capable agents. We can recursively apply this part-to-whole relation between agents as far as needed until we reach a level populated by entirely mindless agents, avoiding the problem of infinite regress. At each level in this homuncular population the signs produced and consumed are postulated to be hybrids of icons and indices. The iconic component is the product of a mapping operation that creates a sign isomorphic with what it stands for, while the indexical component must have a causal connection, however indirect, with what it stands for. Depending on the nature of the isomorphism and of the causal relation, the two components of a sign may have different content. If the icon maps spatial relations in the world, then the function of the index would be to display a current position in that space. But if the icon maps similarity relations, capturing categories or types, then the function of the index would be to stand for a particular token of that type.[39] Other combinations are possible so it would be wise not to try to limit at this point the kinds of content that these hybrid signs can convey. Finally, we need temporary surrogates for the brain mechanisms involved in the handling of these hybrid signs. Neural nets can serve this purpose but only if they make an explicit use of signs and if they are coupled to other neural nets that have acquired the function of using the content of those signs. The complementarity of functions can be achieved by coevolving the neural nets playing the roles of sign producers and consumers.[40]

Having laid out the basic strategy we will be using to deal with the internal transformation of natural signs into intentional signs, let's return to that ancient time when planet Earth was full of natural signs but there were no biological organisms to perform the transformation. The next question we must ask is if this world and its signs had any *statistical structure* that could influence the evolution of sensory organs. We just argued that taking into account the relative abundance of solid objects on terrestrial ecosystems is required in order to explain why some natural signs, like discontinuities in the intensity of light, can be transformed into signs of boundaries.[41] We must now expand on this insight and ask whether other relative abundances have influenced the evolution of neural sensory processing. For a sign-using function to evolve, it must have effects on actual reproductive success, and it is ultimately the behavior of a whole organism that can have that effect. Nevertheless, we still need to consider how external sources of natural signs, such as objects, surfaces, and edges, can be handled by mindless cognitive agents in such a way that the behavior of the whole organism can be successfully guided by the identification of the correct objects, surfaces, or edges.[42] This cannot be taken for granted because the very *projection* of sources of natural signs into the retina introduces ambiguities. Let's start with the case of physical surfaces. In a given retinal image, one and the same projected surface may correspond to multiple possible external sources having different sizes, located at different distances from the point of observation, and subtending different angles relative to the observer. In fact, in a world without any statistical structure a particular projected surface can correspond to an *infinite number* of possible sources.[43] Does the world display any statistical regularities that can be exploited to disambiguate the relation between a source and its projection?

One way of approaching this problem is to view it as involving a three-dimensional space of all possible sources, the dimensions being the orientation, distance, and size of surfaces in a given environment. Within this possibility space, two-dimensional slices represent all the combinations of orientation, distance, and size that could have given rise to a given projected surface.[44] What we need to know is whether the space has any structure, that is, whether some combinations of the three properties are more frequent than others, or whether they are all basically equiprobable. This is, of course, an empirical question that must be answered by collecting data, a task facilitated by the technology of *laser range scanning*, which can link every point on a projected image to its source in the world. By scanning a large number of natural and artificial scenes we can obtain statistical information about the relative frequencies of occurrence of different distances. Further analysis of this data can then yield the relative abundances of different orientations and sizes.[45] What this procedure shows is that the space of possible sources does have structure: not all physical surface orientations, for example, occur with the same frequency. Horizontal and vertical angles are more frequent than others, due to the omnipresence of the ground and the horizon, as well as to the relative abundance of objects like trees.[46] These statistical regularities can be used for disambiguation: if the projected surfaces were *ranked* by the frequency of occurrence of their sources, then when a particular projection can be linked to several alternative surfaces, the one with the highest rank should be the one picked as the most likely to be correct. What is needed to perform this ranking is a record of the history of interactions with surfaces, and the distribution of successes and failures in those interactions. Since it may take many generations to sculpt the connectivity of the brain so that it reflects the statistical structure of the world, it is the evolutionary history of an entire reproductive community that matters. We should, therefore, expect that the internal use of statistical regularities to select the referent of an internal sign is not performed consciously, although we may find traces in phenomenal experience in the form of stable visual illusions.[47]

In addition to its statistical structure the world contributes to the evolution of sensory organs by providing exploitable regularities in the relation between the *structure of light* and the geometry of the objects, surfaces, and edges with which light interacts. What does the phrase "the structure of light" mean? Let's imagine the surface of our planet filled with sunlight that has been repeatedly bouncing of the surfaces of objects. Such a repeated bouncing is called a *reverberation* and it can be shown that reverberating light reaches a steady state at which every point in the planet's surface and the air above it receives light rays from every direction. That is, every single point in space gets a spherical bundle of rays carrying natural signs from the last surface with which each ray interacted. Ambient light in such a state is referred to as the *optic array*.[48] We can imagine that before there were any living creatures in this planet, each point in the optic array defined a *potential point of view*, that is, a position in space from which information about all the surfaces visible from that location could be obtained.[49] We can study the structure of the light arriving at any of these potential points of view by intercepting it with a flat surface, an operation that yields *a section* of the optic array. The retina is not, of course, a flat surface, and we have two eyes, which means that we section ambient light twice. In what follows we will ignore these complications, and deal with an ideal retina: a single surface without any curvature into which the natural signs emanating from all the surrounding surfaces project in a simple way. We should emphasize that the content of the intersecting plane—the projections of objects, surfaces, and edges on it—is as objective and mind-independent as the statistical regularities that we just discussed. Or to phrase this more accurately, the events taking place at the intersecting plane constitute an *optical*, not a psychological, phenomenon.[50]

Let's imagine a subject viewing a single object from a specific point of view and of all the light rays bouncing of the surface of that object let's select only the ones that happen to converge at that point. This operation creates an irregular cone of light, with its apex at the observation point and its base defined by the outer contour of the object. This irregular light cone is referred to as a *solid angle*.[51] We can study how changes in this solid angle depend in a regular way on the object's distance from the observer. As the object recedes from the point of observation, for example, its solid angle becomes smaller, approaching zero degrees as it converges at the horizon. And conversely, as the object moves closer to this point its solid angle gets larger, approaching 180 degrees as it is about to make contact with the observer.[52] It could be argued that the solid angle is a natural sign of distance that, once transformed into an intentional sign, can be used to stand for specific events. As the angle approaches 180 degrees, for instance, it indicates a possible collision. And if the angle is increasing at a very fast rate it indicates an imminent danger that demands an urgent response, like getting out of the way. Both the angle and its rate of change are the kinds of properties measurable by mindless cognitive agents so we should not expect either property to be represented phenomenally. In these terms the structure of light at a particular location in the optic array can be defined by the set of all solid angles converging at that location. The section of the optic array performed by our ideal retina would, therefore, cut through the bundle of solid angles, leaving a well-defined pattern inscribed in it.[53]

The information that this section carries can be substantially increased if we allow the observer himself to walk, creating a moving pattern known as *optic flow*. Let's illustrate this optical phenomenon with the simplest case: an observer located on a vast plane devoid of objects, in which only the horizon and the texture of the ground are visible. As the subject moves forward the texture elements will appear to move toward him in a centrifugal direction until they are left behind and exit the visual field. This centrifugal flow (or outflow) can be part of our phenomenal experience— we do see textural elements getting larger and passing us by as we walk— but the mathematical structure of the outflow is not necessarily part of this experience. This structure can be made more intelligible if we replace each moving texture element by a vector showing its direction. The resulting field of vectors can then be analyzed to figure out what natural signs are conveyed by it. Thus, if the vectors diverge from a fixed point, this is an indication that the subject is moving in a straight line; if the vectors increase proportionally in all directions from the point of divergence, this indicates that the ground is flat; if the point of divergence is at the horizon, this is an indication that the subject is moving parallel to the ground; and the exact position of the divergence point along the horizon is an index of the destination or target of the motion.[54] If the subject moves backward, the flow will be reversed becoming centripetal (an inflow) with the textural elements appearing to converge at a distant point. Thus, the very presence of an outflow or an inflow is an index of the direction of a subject's motion, while the absence of any flow is an indication that the subject is standing still.[55] In this simple situation it would be possible to think that optic flow is part of our subjective experience, but once we add moving objects to the empty ground this ceases to be the case. The moving objects generate their own local flow patterns overlaying the main optic flow. A mathematical analysis of the complex vector field generated by self-motion together with an object's own motion shows that the pattern is quite different from the pattern of motion that is phenomenally experienced.[56] Therefore, we can assert that in the more general cases we do not perceive optic flow as such.

There are other natural signs carried by optic flow, signs that can also help disambiguate projected surfaces. The ambiguity, let's recall, is caused by the fact that many external sources distributed in three-dimensional space can project into the same two-dimensional shape in the retina. But optic flow can *code the missing third dimension into time*, providing us with natural signs of depth. Let's return to the previous example replacing the empty ground with a space full of objects. In this case, depth can be indicated by a relation of *occlusion*, the relation between the projection of a nearby object and the projections of objects located further away. Which objects are partially or totally concealed by other objects depends on the subject's point of observation but occlusion is not a psychological but an optical phenomenon. As the subject walks forward objects increase in apparent size while informative events take place at their occluding edges: objects located behind them are progressively revealed by those edges and then fully displayed the moment the occluding object leaves the visual field. If the subject walks backward new objects entering the visual field on either side will progressively conceal objects located further away, which will themselves be wiped out by even newer objects entering the field.[57] The optical events taking place at occluding edges may be designated in various ways, as revelation/concealment, accretion/deletion, or wiping in/out, but whatever the designation these are events loaded with natural signs that can be transformed into intentional signs by a mindless cognitive agent. These signs can be used, for example, to tell the difference between an object that presents the walking subject with an obstacle and an object that allows him passage through an opening. Both objects are projected on the retina as closed contours, and in both cases the contours get larger as the subject approaches them. But the optical events occurring at the occluding edges will be different: in the case of the object acting as an obstacle its contour will conceal progressively more background texture, whereas the edges of the opening in the second object will reveal progressively more texture.[58] Hence, the deletion and accretion of texture at the occluding edge is an index of a real difference in the world.

These and other ideas promoted by ecological psychologists have had a great impact on philosophers. To take the most obvious example, the static conception of the retinal image that dominated our thinking about visual perception has been replaced by the more dynamic concept of a retinal optic flow. But even if we stick to the case of a motionless observer, a section through the optic array is a much richer object than the unstructured, highly impoverished *raw sense data* that dominated empiricist thinking for centuries. The concept of sense data led to the idea that the external world contributed nothing to perception but stimulation, an idea which was expressed in some extreme cases by saying that the input to the process of perception was merely an *irritation* of the sensory surfaces.[59] But a simple example can dispel this myth. Let's imagine an evenly lit room completely filled with a thick fog. The diffuse light in the room is clearly acting as a stimulus, since it is energetically interacting with receptors in our eyes, arousing them and changing their state. On the other hand, the light in the room is not causing us to be aware of its contents since we are incapable of seeing any object. If we allow the fog to dissipate, the light will continue to be a stimulus but it is now, in addition, something else: it is not just stimulating us but also *informing us* about the contents of the room.[60]

Unfortunately, the discovery of the wealth of information contained in each section of the optic array has led many ecological psychologists to assert that since logical inferences are unnecessary to enrich raw sense data, then postulating brain computations to mediate between light and phenomenal experience is unnecessary. The computer metaphor for the brain is thereby replaced by another metaphor, a radio receiver that can directly detect broadcasted content by being tuned to the same frequency as the signal. Unlike a computer, in which specific contents have a definite location and can, therefore, be said to be stored in it, in a radio receiver it does not make any sense to ask where in the radio's innards is the content carried by the signal located. So what plays the role of the radio's antenna in the case of visual perception? The *retina itself* directly picking up content broadcasted using the optical portion of the spectrum.[61] As we will see, the retina is indeed a highly complex organ equipped with specialized output devices that can perform a preliminary analysis of the content transmitted by light. But practitioners of ecological psychology underestimate the difficulty of transforming this content, rich as it may be, into a phenomenal experience.[62] They are certainly correct to reject the computer metaphor and the accompanying idea that internal signs are symbols operated on by logical inferences. But to replace one faulty metaphor by another does not advance our understanding.

There is one more way in which the world contributes to the genesis of the visual field. Our planet also supplies us with objects and surfaces that are capable of returning to a normal state after being disrupted; that is, it provides us with *stable sources* of natural signs, and it allows us to repeatedly encounter similar objects and surfaces by making their construction repeatable, yielding *recurrent sources* of natural signs. These two characteristics are required if natural signs are to have the kind of evolutionary impact envisioned in these pages. The importance of stability goes beyond its role in yielding enduring sources of indices and icons: anything in the world that persists in time needs an explanation in terms of factors promoting stability. The study of these factors has been important in physics since the eighteenth century. At that time, mathematicians invented a method, called the *calculus of variations*, which allowed them to explore the space of the possible solutions of the differential equations physicists used to model the way a system changes. Because in these models each solution stood for a different state of the system, determining the structure of this possibility space was a way to discover which state, if any, was the most stable. Mathematicians realized that a small set of those solutions, those representing a minimum or maximum of some magnitude, were special or *singular*, and that they indicated which states had the highest and lowest probability of existing in the world.[63] In other words, of all the states in which a system could be, the state corresponding to the minimum would be the most stable, since all the possible states surrounding it were less likely to occur, while the one corresponding to the maximum would be the least stable, since its immediate neighbors were more likely to occur. Stability and instability, in turn, impinge on perceptibility, because the state corresponding to the minimum should be the most frequently observed (in the laboratory as well as in nature) while the one corresponding to the maximum should be observed only rarely.

Most philosophers of science were largely oblivious to this achievement because they wrongly assumed that a scientific theory could be understood as a set of true statements, some general ones expressing laws, some particular ones denoting specific conditions, in which what mattered was the logical connections between statements.[64] And it is true that toward the end of the nineteenth century some theorists managed to cast the content of classical physics in this axiomatic form. But this was not the final form in which this content was expressed, the form that still persists in physics textbooks to this day, for example. Of all the different alternatives it was the variational form that became the standard.[65] Moreover, in the last decade of the nineteenth century, variational methods were extended to a larger set of dynamical systems with a wider variety of singularities: *attractors* representing the most probable and most stable states, and *repellors* standing for the least probable and least stable ones.[66] For those who ignore the actual history of physics, the concept of a distribution of singularities structuring a possibility space may seem fashionably new, but nothing could be further from the truth: the concept is classical and of enduring significance. Outside of physics, the reason why this concept is important is that it provides us with a rigorous way to frame an *ontology of dispositions*. Traditionally this issue has been tackled using logic (modal logic) not mathematics. The logical approach starts with an analysis of the way in which people ordinarily talk of dispositions using *counterfactual* statements like "If this system was disturbed by a shock it would spontaneously return to its original state." But this strategy can lead to the wrong ontological conclusions, such as thinking that we must be committed to the mind-independent existence of *possible worlds*.[67] In the mathematical approach, on the other hand, the ordinary points in a space of possibilities are not assumed to exist independently of our minds. It is only the singular points that demand us to take a realist stance. In other words, as materialists we must be committed to the objective existence of the structure of a possibility space (its dimensionality, connectivity, and its distribution of singularities) not to the possibilities themselves.

Armed with this conception of stability we can explain why surfaces and the solids they bind persist in time and resist being changed, thereby becoming steady sources of natural signs. A crystalline surface, such as the surface of a metallic object, for example, derives its stability from the fact that the components of its crystals exist in a configuration that minimizes bonding energy, a configuration that is more stable than others and which, therefore, will resist being changed into other configurations. We will use the somewhat anthropomorphic expression of a *preferred state* for the configuration that is energetically most favorable, and which will, therefore, be the one most frequently observed. This is a harmless expression that can be replaced by ascribing to a surface a *tendency* to be in that preferred state. The existence of a state that is favored over others explains not only that a particular natural sign will endure through time long enough to have an impact on evolution but also its recurrence: if the causal process responsible for generating the signs is partly constrained by the structure of the possibility space then each time the process occurs again it will tend to yield similar outcomes. In a world populated by inanimate objects, for example, we would observe many of them in a steady state of some kind. Even the reverberating light constituting the optic array is in a steady state like this.

If we include animals as objects to be observed then the recurrent patterns will include cyclic or rhythmic states, as in the periodic repetition of limb positions that constitute a moving animal's gait. The relative abundances of both steady-state and rhythmic patterns as sources of natural signs would be explained by the existence of point and periodic attractors. On the other hand, these mathematical ideas must be used carefully. Singularities are a form of determination that is *complementary* to causality, as was already recognized by mathematicians in the eighteenth century.[68] But many contemporary thinkers erroneously consider the dynamical approach, which by definition is *mechanism-independent*, to be a replacement for explanations in terms of causal mechanisms.[69] This is an error we will correct in the next chapter.

Let's summarize the second part of our argument. If the states (solid, liquid, and gas states) of the objects populating the world were all equiprobable, there would have been no exploitable natural signs for evolution to track as it developed sensory organs. That this equiprobability was broken early on in the planet's history, and then further broken as living creatures began to proliferate, can be ascertained by examining existing populations and the *statistical distribution of variation* in these populations. In the kind of terrestrial environment that we must consider when exploring the evolution of human sensory organs, the variation in physical states is dominated by the solid type, and this must have played a role in shaping our sensory organs. Other distributions of variation, like the variations in orientation, distance, and size of the surfaces that bind the solid objects, can be used to disambiguate their two-dimensional retinal projections. The statistical evidence that states are not equiprobable can, in turn, be explained by the fact that objects possess certain tendencies and that the causal mechanisms which actualize those tendencies have in fact operated. The ontology of tendencies is not at all settled, but it can be clarified by replacing the logic of counterfactual statements with models of possibility spaces defined mathematically, allowing us to verify that the possibilities making up these spaces are not equiprobable. Finally, there is the ambient light that fills the surface of the planet and that has a structure which varies regularly as light interacts with the geometry of objects and surfaces. The regularities present in this relation can also be studied mathematically if we slice through the light's structure to obtain a section in which informative optical events occur. Since the retina performs such a slicing operation, the input to the visual system is clearly not an impoverished set of stimuli (raw sense data), which must be enriched by logical inferences.

At this point we have a rough sketch of the conditions under which natural signs would be exploitable to evolve sensory organs like ours, and the conditions under which they could be transformed into intentional signs by mindless cognitive agents consuming the information extracted by those sensory organs. We should now follow these intentional signs as they become progressively elaborated in the brain by multiple producer and consumer agents operating in parallel. But in order to keep our account of this progressive elaboration on the right track, we need to explore how different conceptions of the visual field can lead to very different explanations of the internal processing of signs. One way to conceive the visual field is as a space in which every bit of content—every object and surface, every light effect and motion effect—has arrived *simultaneously*, like the contents of a motion picture that arrive at the exact same time on the screen on which they are projected. For this simultaneous convergence to occur we would have to imagine the population of producers and consumers organized as a pyramid, in which a large number of agents at one level pass their products to a smaller number at the next level until the apex is reached, at which point a single agent would consume the final product.[70] A different way to think about the visual field is suggested by an alternative metaphor: a computer screen displaying a web page that must be updated continuously with fresh content, like the web page of a newspaper. In this case there is no need to assume that the different pieces of content on the screen arrived there simultaneously, since older content may have been added earlier in the day, newer content later, while the latest news are being added now as we view the page. No one view of the web page would yield a sight of the final draft: there are many drafts, the content of which is being edited, supplemented, changed, and deleted continuously.[71]

This alternative metaphor suggests a very different way of conceiving how visual content is produced. As we said earlier, we can assume for the time being that constructing intentional signs standing for solid objects can be done starting with signs for edges, combining these into signs for surfaces, and assembling these into signs for solids. Objects in the world that happen to project to the center of the retina, corresponding to the high-resolution portion of the visual field, require that this process be carried to completion, but for the low-resolution peripheral parts of the visual field edges may be enough to render how objects appear there, while for areas of medium resolution surfaces may suffice.[72] Thus, the web page metaphor suggests a visual field that is being continuously updated by a population of agents working on different parts of it. And because the content of different locations in the field is built partly sequentially—the conversion of illumination discontinuities into signs for edges happening earlier than the creation of signs for surfaces, for example—a visual field generated this way will not have a uniform temporality. To the subject, everything may appear to be present all at once in his visual field as in a movie screen, but this is an illusion created by an updating process that happens too fast to become conscious. We can express this important point by saying that the temporal order of the activities in which mindless cognitive agents engage does not correspond to the temporal order of events in phenomenal experience.[73]

A good example of the dislocation between the two temporalities is the phenomenon of *apparent motion*. In the laboratory this effect can be elicited by using two lights (or two projected dots) separated by a small distance, then turning them on and off at very short intervals. If the spatial distance between the lights and the temporal interval between flashes are within a certain range the subject will experience not two lights but a single one moving from the position occupied by the first light to that of the second one. This is, of course, an effect very familiar to anyone who has seen an old movie theatre marquee. A more interesting version of the effect can be created if we color the two lights differently, the first one colored red and the second green, for example, in which case we will experience a single light that changes color midway through its movement. The difference between brain time and phenomenal time is clear here. In the brain the effect of a red light changing to a green light cannot be produced until both lights have been detected and processed, so the temporal sequence is: red light—green light—color transition. But in the subject's experience the sequence is: red light—color transition—green light.[74] We will return to the question of different temporalities in the final chapter, when we will argue that the experimental evidence shows that the relation between brain processes and subjective experience takes place at several timescales, which can be rigorously quantified. But for the time being we can simply assert that this phenomenon favors the temporal relations suggested by the web page metaphor over those suggested by the projected movie metaphor.

But this raises another question: If the visual field is constantly being created by an army of cognitive agents, how are these agents controlled? This is, again, a subject that must be analyzed in detail once the neural mechanisms behind these agents have been discussed, but we can settle now for another metaphor derived from the way different programming languages control a computational process. The more traditional way to approach the problem of control is *hierarchical*: a master program defines the main goal to be achieved, and presides over a set of subprograms (or subroutines), each capable of performing a particular part of the overall task. When the master program needs that portion of the task done it surrenders control to the appropriate subroutine. The latter may, in turn, need an even more specialized program to execute portions of its subtask, temporarily yielding control of the process to it. When a low-level subroutine finishes its job it must return control to the subroutine that called it which, in turn, must return control to the master program.[75] If the visual field was like a projected movie then this hierarchical form of control would be adequate, the master program being the counterpart of the topmost homunculus watching the movie. But there is a very different way to control a computational process that does not involve a master program. It proceeds by encapsulating every subtask into an autonomous software object that is *invoked into action* by changes on a shared workspace in which data representing outside events, as well as the results of intermediate operations, is deposited. We can picture the software objects as constantly checking the common workspace for the data patterns that would trigger their activity: when a pattern activates one object the latter responds by executing its subtask and placing the results back in the common workspace, creating new data patterns that trigger other objects into action. In this scheme there are no commands or delegations of authority, not even messages exchanged between objects. All messages are broadcasted, and control is always captured.[76]

In its original version, the multi-homuncular model makes use of these new metaphors to counter the influence of the old metaphors, preparing the ground for a nonmetaphorical treatment of the subject. But the original model incorporates an additional claim that is highly problematic: that the cognitive agents populating the brain are not capable of handling the content of signs. The argument in defense of this claim has two premises: first, that the properties of the vehicles of signs do not determine the properties of their contents; and second, that the relation between the brain and phenomenal experience can be characterized by saying that the former is all vehicle and the latter all content. The first premise is correct: we should always keep apart the properties of what is doing the representing from the properties of what is being represented.[77] But the second one amounts to postulating that the brain is a mere syntactical machine that knows nothing about semantics. If we accepted this we would have to grant that agents in the multi-homuncular model can interact causally with vehicles, but not intentionally with contents.[78] But the job description defining a legitimate use of signs requires agents that can interact with vehicles and contents, producing and consuming signs both causally and intentionally. This implies that the brain is not a mere syntactical machine but a machine endowed with an *iconic-indexical semantics*. Moreover, accepting both premises leads to the conclusion that the content of the visual field cannot be created from the content of the brain, because the brain has no content.[79]

But if phenomenal content is not produced from brain contents then where does it come from? The answer given is that it does not really exist, that it is created retrospectively by verbal reports pretending to be actual descriptions of how things appear to be.[80] We can illustrate the main thrust of the argument used to defend this conclusion using the lab phenomenon just discussed: two differently colored lights, turned on and off at short intervals, that appear to move and change color. In this case, the argument goes, we cannot decide whether the subject reports that the lights moved because he saw them move, or whether he reports to have seen movement because he believes that there must have been a movement. If the first alternative is correct then the perceived motion must have been a real property of his phenomenal experience, but if the second one is right, if he is retrospectively judging that the lights moved, then the apparent motion was literally created by the verbal report. And similarly for the change of color.[81] Crucially, this is taken to be a problem not only for the experimenter, a problem due to the fact that he is forced to adopt a third-person point of view of the phenomenon, but also for the subject himself despite his alleged privileged access to phenomenal properties. The reason for this is that what the subject is reporting is his memory of what happened in the experiment, and he cannot be sure whether the apparent motion and the change of color he remembers were inserted into his memory pre-experientially, in which case he did see the effect, or whether it was inserted post-experientially, in which case he is merely judging to have seen it.[82] We can agree that there is a real indeterminacy in this case and that neither the experimenter nor the subject can be sure that the apparent movement and change of color of the lights were actually experienced or only judged to have been experienced. But we could argue that this indeterminacy is an artifact of the experimental setup, and of the simplicity of the stimuli. Testing subjects with richer inputs that go beyond mere stimulation could decide in favor of one of the two interpretations. If we ran a similar test but using more complex forms of apparent motion, such as an actual motion picture, for example, would we really be so doubtful that the subject actually experienced seeing characters interacting with one another, and would we seriously consider that his report at the end of the movie created that misimpression? We must refute in detail the two related claims that the brain is a mere syntactical machine and that the content of experience is constituted by our retrospective reports about it, but at this point what matters is to emphasize that both claims are logically independent of the multi-homuncular model.

To summarize: we argued that breaking free from old metaphors was important to prepare the ground for a materialist approach to visual experience. Rather than conceiving the visual field as a screen on which contents are projected, we should think of it as constantly being generated by armies of cognitive agents with different degrees of consciousness and intentionality. These agents must not be pictured as senders and receivers of messages or commands: they all broadcast their signs to whatever other agents are capable of making use of their content, and they are triggered into action by patterns of activity resulting from the consumption of other content. The content itself is fixed by the consumers. While a natural index carries information about every cause that figures in its production, once it is transformed into an intentional sign only one of those causes is picked out as its referent. And similarly in the case of natural icons that may also undergo many isomorphic mappings, only one of which will be treated as its intentional content. Finally, we considered two problematic claims that come packaged together with the multi-homuncular model but that can be rejected without affecting it as long as we treat all agents as capable of interacting with both the vehicles and the content of signs.

We can now advance to the next part of this chapter's argument: exploring the consequences of the requirement that the populations of cognitive agents be able to form temporary coalitions and enter into part-to-whole relations. If the overall effect of the activity of a given coalition were the same as the effects of the activities of each of its members operating separately, then talk of coalitions would not be very informative. And similarly for complex agents composed of simpler ones: if the cognitive capacities of the former were simply a sum of those of the latter, we would not view the higher-level agent as performing a novel function. For this reason, we must assume that the properties of both coalitions and novel agents cannot be reduced to those of their components. The concept needed to block this reduction is the concept of an *emergent* property: a property of a whole that is not possessed by its parts but that is produced by interactions between its parts. The original concept of emergence was born in the eighteenth century in the field of inorganic chemistry, although its name had to wait a century to be coined. Chemists are rare among scientists in that they must perform both analysis and synthesis, a feature of their practice that allows them to routinely observe emergent phenomena in their laboratories.[83] Thus, if a practitioner used chemical analysis to break down a compound substance into its component elementary substances, he would typically check the results of the analysis by re-synthesizing the compound and checking that it recovered its original properties. In the nineteenth century, when philosophers adopted the concept of emergence they typically used chemical examples to illustrate the differences with physics.[84]

Nevertheless, for most of the twentieth century materialist philosophers continued to advocate *ontological reductionism*, according to which chemical phenomena are nothing but physical phenomena.[85] This kind of reductionism must be distinguished from the epistemological variety, according to which chemical phenomena are *explainable* in terms of physical ones. The reason is that in the contemporary version of emergence this idea is already built into the concept itself, since its definition includes the idea that the properties of the whole must be explained in terms of causal interactions between parts, interactions that, in the case of elementary substances, will tend to be physical. In what follows we will use the term "reductionism" to refer exclusively to the ontological kind. Why did so many materialist philosophers subscribe to reductionism? Partly because most philosophy of science tended to focus on physics as the one true science, and that its practitioners uncritically accept physicists' own reductionist claims despite the fact that the evidence supported only a few cases. Thus, the supposed reduction of thermodynamics to statistical mechanics is usually defended with evidence from the simplest possible case: a gas at the limit of low density, the equation of which can be deduced from statistical mechanical principles.[86] Similarly, the reduction of chemistry to quantum physics was defended using the simplest possible case: the hydrogen molecule, which can be shown to be more stable than the hydrogen atom using quantum mechanical principles.[87] Because more complex cases have not been shown to be reducible, these claims amounted to mere promissory notes: we reduced the easy cases but we promise that in the future the complex ones will be reduced too. But the checks were never cashed, and under careful examination most of the reductionist claims in the complex cases fall apart the moment we take into account all the technical details.

Let's examine a prominent example of a contemporary argument against the concept of emergence that derives its plausibility from a deliberate neglect of those technical details. In fact, the argument assumes the existence of different levels of reality, so it is not an argument against emergence itself, but against the idea that an emergent whole can have causal powers of its own. Its proponents could agree, for example, that complex agents composed of simpler ones do exist. But they would deny that they can causally affect anything that their component neurons cannot affect. Emergent entities do not have to be eliminated from existence if they can be rendered impotent, reduced to mere *epiphenomena*. The epiphenomenalist argument proceeds like this. Imagine an emergent whole that exists at one level while its components exist at the immediately lower level. From the definition of emergence just given, it follows that the direction of causality between the two layers must be bottom up, from parts to whole, a requirement expressed in the argument by saying that an emergent property must be caused by the components' own properties. Now imagine that there is a second emergent whole possessing a property which, we would be tempted to say, was caused by the first one. What would justify this assertion? After all, the second emergent property must have been brought into existence by the properties of the second set of components, so why should we believe that it was a property of the first whole that caused it? It seems more intuitive, the argument goes, to say that it was the components of the first whole that caused a change in the components of the second one which, in turn, produced the second emergent property. In other words, the real causal relation is the one that exists between components, not emergent wholes, and this makes the latter epiphenomenal.[88]

Let's illustrate this with an example of emergent wholes existing at a mental level, like perceptions or beliefs, while their components exist at the level of the brain. Picture a subject who has just perceived something dangerous and he now believes that he is in danger. We could explain this situation by saying that the subject is in a vigilant state because he believes he just perceived a dangerous threat. This explanation assumes that a mental event (perceiving danger) caused another mental event (believing he is in danger). But, says the epiphenomenalist, the explanation is that the brain substratum of the perception brought into existence the substratum of the belief, which in turn, caused the belief. This way, proponents of this argument do not have to deny that the perception and the belief exist, or that they are irreducible to the brain, but only deny that the perception has the power to produce the belief and it is, therefore, an epiphenomenon. The reason why this is significant in our current context is that while there is nothing in the argument to oppose the idea that simple cognitive agents can become components of more complex ones, it denies that the latter have any capacity to interact causally with vehicles, let alone intentionally with contents. Hence, we must examine the assumptions behind the epiphenomenalist argument, figure out where it goes wrong, and then offer a counterargument.

So what are the assumptions? The proponents of the argument claim to be materialists so their definition of efficient causality must be a realist one: causality is an objective relation in which one event produces another event.[89] If we accept this definition then there is an immediate problem with the argument: the first premise is that the properties of a whole are caused *by the properties* of the parts, but properties cannot be causes since they are not events. To address this problem, epiphenomenalists argue that the required events are *instantiations* of a property.[90] But what kind of events are these? Certainly not the kind of events studied by scientists. The only way to count instantiations as real events is to believe that essences or abstract universals exist independently of our minds, in which case the *incarnation of an essence* into a material property would be a real event. But can a materialist philosopher seriously believe in the existence of transcendent entities like essences? Or perhaps the problem is that the term "property" as used in the argument refers not to the kind of properties measured in scientific laboratories, such as temperature, speed, or pressure, but to what logicians call a "property," which is anything that can be predicated about a subject, like "is hot," "is fast," or "is compressed." We may think that this is a minor detail since the last three predicates seem to capture what matters about the three physical properties just mentioned, but that would be wrong. Predicates include many things which no physicist (or any other scientist) would consider to be real properties, such as predicates like "is running from danger" or "is thinking of how to escape."[91] So the first assumption in the epiphenomenalist argument is that logical events (or worse yet, essence incarnations) can have causal powers but mental events cannot.

The second assumption is the *linearity* of causality.[92] Linear causality is represented by the formula: same cause, same effect, always. This formula is easy to confuse with a logical implication—if the same cause occurs then necessarily the same event will occur—adding to the problem of treating all properties as predicates.[93] But in science there are many departures from linearity as when small causes produce large effects or large causes produce small effects, the former illustrated by priming effects, the latter by saturation effects, both of which are widespread in the brain. This is referred to as *nonlinear* causality. A second, more radical departure from linearity is when one and the same cause can yield different effects, or different causes produce the same effect. Examples in neuroscience include the *catalytic* effect that some hormones have on the brain, the effect of any one substance depending on the brain area involved.[94] But a simpler example would be a stick of dynamite that can be triggered to explode by a large number of causes: a sudden increase in ambient temperature; a mechanical shock; or even an electrical spark. These ubiquitous violations of linearity create problems for the epiphenomenalist argument because it weakens the apparent law-like necessity of the causal connection needed for its logic to seem compelling. To incorporate departures from linearity into our conception of causality we need to make two changes. First, we must stop thinking about causes as involving atomic events, like collisions, and instead think of these events as being changes in the properties of whole objects.[95] Properties may not be events, but changes in properties certainly are. This way we will not be tempted into thinking that the object acting as a cause brought into existence the object it affected, but only that it produced a change in its defining properties. Second, we must always take into account the first object's *capacity to affect*, as well as the second object's *capacity to be affected*. This can accommodate the case when a target object does not react to the object affecting it until the latter's influence has reached a threshold of intensity, as well as the case of catalysis in which the capacity to be affected by various triggers becomes the most important factor in the determination of the effect.

The final assumption is the idea that the only form of determination that operates in the part-to-whole relation is *efficient* causality. The properties of the whole certainly arise from efficient causal interactions between its parts. But as these components affect and are affected by one another, the entire set may display a certain dynamical pattern. As we saw earlier when discussing the stability of the sources of natural signs, physicists have known for 200 years that these dynamics can have preferred states determined by singularities. Singularities do not behave like efficient causes but rather like *final causes*: the dynamic created by the component interactions has a tendency to seek the preferred state defined by the structure of the space of possible states. Since that state will tend to recur, and since it stabilizes the outcome of the interactions, it constitutes an enduring source of the properties of the whole. Moreover, this dynamic may have several preferred states and while the whole can be in only one state at a time, the other states are always available to it. Depending on the strength of the barriers between these preferred states, the whole can be pushed to switch between them by external causes that need to spend very little energy to produce an effect. To phrase this in the terms we just used, a distribution of singularities endows a whole with a variety of ways in which it can be affected by events that are efficient causes but that have only a catalytic capacity to affect it.

Once we reject the linearity of causes, and the idea that all causality is efficient, the conclusion that one emergent whole cannot cause changes in another emergent whole loses its appeal. The reason is that we are not arguing that the first whole brings the second into existence, only that it can trigger a change in the dynamics of the second whole's components. These components are the ones that produce the properties of the second whole, but since they are now in another preferred state, the resulting emergent properties will also be different. We will argue in the next chapter that this is the way in which the brain controls the actions of the body: it does not issue detail commands capable of bringing a particular action into existence, but rather relies on the fact that the physical components of a bodily activity (the set of joints, muscles, and tendons involved) have several preferred states, and that simple commands can switch the set from one state into another. In the final chapter we will argue that this is also the way in which mental events can affect brain events. But there is a more general conclusion that follows from this: making a list of component's properties and relations, and linking them *logically* to the properties of a whole does not constitute a valid explanation.[96] Rather, a scientific account of a whole's emergence involves showing how the interactions (not the relations) between its components constitute a *mechanism* capable of producing the whole, as well as identifying through mathematical analysis the singularities determining the preferred states for that mechanism. Once this is done, the interactions between emergent wholes can be specified without the need to invoke any form of determination that actual physicists (as opposed to the physicists that exist in the imagination of some philosophers) would reject.

Having restored the capacity of one emergent whole to affect another, we can also restore its capacity to affect its own components. But the concept of *downward causality* needs to be deployed carefully to avoid incoherence: we cannot, for example, claim that the parts bring the whole into existence, while at the same time the whole brings the parts into existence. In other words, we cannot assume that efficient causality operates in both directions. Rather, the whole acts on its parts by *selecting* which of their capacities to affect and be affected are exercised, or which of their preferred states becomes actual. Selection is the least controversial form of downward causation because in one of its manifestations it is widely accepted: natural selection, or more exactly, the properties and dispositions of an ecosystem, can causally determine which genetic materials will remain in a given reproductive community and which ones will be eliminated. This is clearly a case in which changes in macro-properties (climatic conditions, relative abundance of predators) can cause changes in micro-properties (distribution of genotypes). Another uncontroversial form of downward causality comes from physics: the macro-properties of a container affecting the micro-dynamics of what it contains. This effect is incorporated into mathematical models through the concept of a *boundary condition*. A simple example is a gas composed of a population of molecules confined in a container. The relevant properties of the gas are pressure, temperature, and volume. The regularities in the way in which these properties change depends on whether the container can or cannot conduct heat: if it can, then a change in volume will cause only the pressure to change, leaving the temperature constant; if it cannot, both temperature and pressure will change when the volume changes.[97] The effect of these acceptable forms of downward causality can be described this way: the state of an emergent whole at any given time selects which outcome of its component's interactions is compatible with producing the state of the whole *at the next moment of time*. That is, the whole participates in selecting the conditions that lead to its own reproduction.[98]

To recapitulate: the concept of emergence, as a way to block ontological reductionism, has a long history, part of which was conceptually muddled. In particular, the early emergentists misconceived emergent properties as properties that cannot be explained and must be accepted with natural piety.[99] But once the concept was rediscovered its new definition challenged those early misconceptions by explicitly adding that, besides irreducibility, the property in question had to be explained by a mechanism of emergence: the properties of a whole that are not possessed by its parts must be accounted for by specific interactions between those parts. Nevertheless, challenges to the concept continued to multiply, in some cases not by denying the existence of emergent properties but by denying that these properties serve as the basis for causal powers. Emergent properties, it turns out, are not fictitious but only impotent. But we saw that the most prominent argument behind this conclusion is based on many false assumptions: that events like the instantiation of a property are real and can act as causes, that all efficient causality is linear, and that all causality is efficient. Once we correct this error, the argument that makes perceptions (and other mental events) into mere epiphenomena ceases to be compelling.

Let's conclude this chapter by applying these insights to a more specific question: How can a set of interacting cognitive agents generate a whole that is an agent with superior cognitive capacities? After what we just argued we can assume that this is possible, but we still need to provide a mechanism to explain the emergence of the more sophisticated agent. Because at this point we do not have the resources to discuss brain mechanisms, we can answer the question with the devices we have been using as stand-ins for mindless cognitive agents: neural nets. Let's start with a simple three-layer net conceived as a whole composed of both computing units and connections between these units. At any given time, the units and the connections have certain characterizing properties: a certain degree of activation for each unit and a certain degree of strength for each connection. These properties, which are both real and actual, serve as the base for dispositions, which are real but not necessarily actual: the capacity of a unit in one layer to affect units in other layers, the capacity of the connections to transmit activation from one unit to another, and the tendency of a connection to change its strength in response to the state of activation of the units it connects are all real regardless of whether they are presently being exercised or manifested. When the neural net is trained using many pairs of inputs and outputs, those dispositions are actualized. After the training is over the whole acquires an emergent property, a specific pattern of strength in its connections, which serves as the base for an emergent capacity: the ability to classify inputs into categories and to use the categories to produce an output.

That the trained neural net has a new capacity can be verified simply by using it with a specific input and checking its output. But this still leaves many unanswered questions about the mechanism it uses to exercise that capacity as well as about the nature of the capacity. First of all, can we consider this to be a causal capacity? In practice, neural nets exist as software simulations, so whatever causal capacities they may have are simulated. But it is relatively simple to connect the neural net's output to a robot's arm and trigger various responses in this arm by converting the simulated activation pattern into a nonsimulated pattern that can causally affect the robot's arm. Second, if the existence of emergent properties implies some form of downward causality, can the trained neural net be said to affect its own components? The cognitive processing in the neural nets we have been considering moves strictly in a forward direction: from the input layer to the hidden layer and then to the output layer. Because the external input completely determines the activation pattern in the input layer, the latter is not downwardly affected by the whole net, although it does partially affect, via the emergent pattern of strengths in its connections, the activation patterns in the other layers. Thus, the extent to which there is causal influence moving downward is limited. But this can be easily fixed by design. Take for example, *recurrent neural* nets, the design of which involves adding new feedback connections from either the hidden or output layers to the input layer. Basically, a copy of the activation pattern that either of these two layers had in the previous time step is stored, and then it is fed into the input layer together with the external input in the next time step. This design not only makes the state of the input units at any one time depend partly on the state of the whole but, more importantly, when the feedback is recurrent it transforms the neural net into a dynamical system. Whereas a feedforward net basically maps a static input into a static output, and does this instantaneously coming to a full stop when the mapping is done, a recursive neural net becomes a true dynamical system governed by singularities.[100] Thus, after a few iterations of the feedback loop, the whole net may settle into a preferred state and downwardly select the states of its component units that are compatible with that global state.

The different mechanism involved in the operation of recurrent neural nets also determines how they can affect other neural nets. Take for example a recurrent design in which the activation pattern of the hidden layer is copied (into a set of context units) and fed back into the input layer. In the first time step the hidden units are affected only by the external input, but in the second time step they get both the external input plus a copy of their own immediately past state. As the loop repeats the hidden layer is fed more and more episodes from its past activity, in a very real sense getting a *compressed version of its own history* as part of its input. So while nonrecurrent designs may be said to have a long-term memory of the effects of the training process, a memory embodied in the pattern of strengths of the connections, a recurrent neural net has in addition a short-term memory of its own immediate past.[101] This allows recurrent networks to deal with temporal patterns, an ability that would be required to make use of the natural signs contained in optic flow. As we saw earlier, the idea of a static retinal image is inadequate to deal with the retinal content created by an animal that is constantly moving and exploring its environment. A normal feedforward network would be able to deal only with a static retinal image, but to exploit optic flow and other optical phenomena (like motion parallax) that are extended in time, we need feedback.[102] If we assume that there are other neural nets coevolved to use the output of the recurrent net, then the particular type of optic flow it has classified (an outflow or an inflow, for example) will inform those other devices about the overall direction of motion: forward or backward.

This leaves only one more question to be answered: Can several neural nets become the component parts of a larger neural net possessing more sophisticated cognitive capabilities? The devices we have discussed so far exercise their ability to recognize using only the properties of objects as indicators of their presence, but they lack the capacity to use the objects themselves as sources of natural signs. Can a neural net that can represent objects be built out of neural nets that represent only properties? One possibility is to use as components several three-layer networks that interact with each other to produce a single output. Each of the subnetworks must have its own input layer, receiving content about a different external property and a single output unit, the content of which is added to that of the other output units to yield the overall output.[103] As the network is trained the connections of each of its subnetworks are adjusted to become *more like each other*, a procedure that causes the mappings of inputs to outputs in each subnetwork to converge. Because each device inputs a different property, and each one contributes to the overall output, as their connections converge the correlations in their activities become isomorphic with the correlations between the object properties.[104] Let's imagine that we have three-component neural nets, the input for which are color, texture, and motion. If the source of those inputs happens to be a tiger then a yellowish color, a texture of black stripes, and a characteristic gait will tend to co-occur whenever a tiger is used for training. And the training procedure will cause the compound net to track these co-occurrences and to store them in the form of correlations between the patterns of strengths in each component net. In a sense, the compound net may be said to represent objects that possess the correlated properties, an emergent ability that goes beyond those of its component parts.

To summarize the last part of this chapter's argument: Emergent phenomena were first appreciated in a scientific field in which both analysis and synthesis were practiced. Connectionist artificial intelligence is like that: its practitioners routinely break neural nets apart by performing mathematical (cluster) analyses of the spaces of possible activation patterns to check the effects of training. But they also engage in the synthesis of completely novel designs that helps them stay a step ahead of those critics who focus their attacks on the deficiencies of old designs.[105] For those philosophers that take emergent phenomena seriously, this suggests that questions about whether an entity can exist and whether it can have causal powers should be answered by giving a *proof by construction*—proving that an entity can exist by actually building one—which makes logical proofs that they cannot exist or that they cannot have those abilities entirely redundant. Since we can give examples of such constructions, we can conclude that the multi-homuncular model is plausible in principle. But a proof by construction inherits the limitations of what has been constructed. In particular, neural nets have shortcomings, the most important of which is that they are totally *disembodied*. The way in which we have dealt with cognitive agents in this chapter is compatible with the assumption that they model a brain in a vat. Our emphasis on exploratory behavior, and the way it enriches the content of the retinal section of ambient light, does not remove this limitation, since the brain in a vat could simply be placed on a motorized wheelchair to achieve the same effect.

What is needed is to replace the intersecting plane of our ideal retina with two eyes that are *embedded in a head*. Each eye sections the optic array, but the manner in which the intersection is made depends on the way the eyes are located in the head: human beings have them in the front but horses have them on the side. One consequence of this is that while the brain of a human being moving forward has access to the divergence point of optic flow, the brain of a horse moving in the same direction has access to both the point of divergence in front and to the point of convergence in the back. This does not imply that humans cannot have visual access to what is behind them, since they can rotate their entire head giving their retinas the opportunity to sample other portions of the array. But it does mean that the optic array is not sampled by the retinas alone but by the entire complex formed by the eyes, the neck, and the body.[106] One consequence of this is that whereas disembodied retinas can exploit the regularities in the relations between an object's geometry and the structure of light bouncing off that object, embodied eyes can exploit the regularities in the relation between the way in which the eyes, the neck, and the body move and the effects of these movements on the visual field. Let's then proceed to consider the contributions of the body to the generation of phenomenal experience.

2 THE CONTRIBUTIONS OF THE BODY

The brain must command and control, not only represent. And its main target is typically the body within which it resides. How should we alter our notion of the content of intentional signs to accommodate this double duty? We must consider two kinds of content, *descriptive and directive,* involving different responsibilities for producer and consumer agents. The descriptive part places the responsibility on the producer: it must perform the correct transformations to ensure the sign it produces maintains whatever isomorphism the precursor of that sign had with its referent. Only if that isomorphic relation is maintained will the consumer find the interaction useful. The directive part, on the other hand, places the responsibility on the consumer: the producer may command, for example, that something in the world be changed (the direction of the eyes, the location of the body), and it is the task of the consumer to change the world (rotate the eyes, walk forward) so as to make it isomorphic with the content of the command. Only if this isomorphism is achieved will the producer find the interaction useful.[1] So how should directive content be conceived? We may think, for example, that when we intend to raise our arm the brain must specify the exact angle that each different joint (shoulder, elbow, and wrist) must end up having, as well as the precise degree of contraction that the attached muscles must have once the target position is reached. If the directive content of brain commands was like this, the descriptive content would have to be a fully detailed representation of all the forces and articulations of the body. But we do not have to accept this characterization because the field of robotics provides us with an alternative.

It is possible to build, for example, a robot capable of walking while being entirely brainless, a so-called *passive dynamics walker*. Such a robot has neither a motor propelling it nor a control system to guide it as it moves forward. It manages to walk by exploiting the properties and dispositions of its own body as well as those of its immediate environment. Each of the two legs of the robot acts like a pendulum driven by gravity, spontaneously swinging and maintaining its motion through its own momentum. Counter-swinging arms and wide feet contribute to stabilize this spontaneous activity. Yet, for walking behavior to be produced the robot must be placed on a special environment: an inclined plane at the right angle. We can widen the type of immediate environments in which the robot can achieve locomotion by performing small enhancements to it, such as adding an electrical motor to each leg, allowing it to walk on flat surfaces.[2] In principle, we could continue to enhance the design by adding visual sensors and neural nets so that the robot could learn to avoid obstacles as it moves. But each enhancement would continue to take advantage of the spontaneous effects created by the pendulum-like legs. In a very real sense, even after adding motors, sensors, and processors, much of the computational work would still be offloaded to the dynamics of the robot's legs interacting with the ground.[3] A human leg is a more complicated structure than a passive dynamics walker's lower limbs, but some of its morphological features are comparable. The whole formed by a leg's muscles and tendons, for example, can be modeled as a spring with a mass attached. As a human being walks, the legs go through different phases, one of which, the swing phase, is only partly controlled by the brain or the spinal cord: its pendular movement is a result of the properties of the leg's materials (elasticity, momentum) in interaction with properties of its immediate environment (gravity). In addition, the movement of some of the leg's joints, like the knee, is determined with very little neural control by the forces generated when the foot hits the ground.[4] Other muscles, tendons, and joints in a leg play a more active role during walking but they constrain each other in such a way that not all configurations are equally stable. Some of these are, in the terms introduced in the previous chapter, *preferred configurations* for the dynamical system formed by the body and its immediate environment.

If this dynamic characterization of the body is correct, brain commands do not need to specify every anatomical detail but only the information required to select a preferred configuration. To see how this could be achieved let's derive some insights from the graphic representations employed by mathematicians to study dynamical systems. These representations, which we will refer to as *state space diagrams,* define an abstract space in which each point represents a possible state for the system. The dimensions of the space are defined by the properties of the system that are free to change, such as muscle contraction or joint angle. These are the *variables* that define every possible state for the system.[5] A state space diagram also has one or more *parameters,* representing properties that affect the entire system, such as the properties of the immediate environment. Finally, a state space diagram specifies the singularities giving structure to the possibility space, making some configurations of joints, muscles, and tendons the preferred states. How does the state space of a body acting in the world acquire structure? Through a process of learning, taking months or years, that adds new singularities while eliminating others. Thus, a small child learning to walk would be sculpting a state space in which crawling is already a preferred state, while walking would be in the process of becoming stable. As the child grows older other singularities would be added, corresponding to jumping, running, dancing, and so on.[6] When a diagram has several singularities the sphere of influence of each must be defined. This sphere of influence is referred to as a *potential well,* in the case singularities of the minima and maxima type, or as a *basin of attraction* for those of the attractor type. The degree of stability of a given preferred state depends on the "depth" of its well or basin, shallow ones providing less stability than deep ones.

What insights can these diagrams provide? The most important one in the present context is that some parameters, like the degree of muscle stiffness, can be used to select the preferred configuration adequate for a particular activity.[7] This is achieved by the effect of the parameter on a well's or basin's depth. We can, for example, manipulate a parameter to make some wells or basins shallow with the result that the associated preferred state becomes less stable. In this condition, random fluctuations can spontaneously dislodge the system from that state and push it into another state. In the terms we used in the previous chapter, what the parameter does is to select a preferred configuration using final causes, leaving the task of efficiently bringing the selected state into being to the random fluctuations. This kind of indirect control provides an efficient way to control the movements of the body. If we assume that each preferred state represents a different manner of walking, one appropriate for smooth and the other for rough terrain, for example, parametric control would allow the brain to adapt the body's walking activity in real time, without having to perform any calculations to match joint, muscles, and tendons to each type of terrain.[8] More complex action sequences that involve different uses of the legs—start walking on an inclined plane; then leap over a gap; resume walking on a flat surface; then switch to running—can be obtained by using a more complex distribution of singularities and parametrically manipulating their wells or basins.

Let's extend the dynamical treatment of the body to activities other than walking. Much as a human leg can be compared to a pendulum, other parts of the body can be given dynamic counterparts. A bone acting as anchoring for a muscle, for example, acts just like a lever. A lever's dynamics depend on the placement of three components: the load, the force required to carry the load, and the fulcrum or pivoting point. Depending on the relative positions of these components, a lever can perform several specialized kinds of work, like holding the head level or lifting a load with the hand.[9] Muscles are literally motors (more like fuel cells than steam engines) so they are capable not only of carrying loads but of exerting loads on their own. Tendons, finally, function as an interface to link a soft and jelly material (muscle) to a hard composite one (bone). As we just said, groups of muscles and tendons, spanning several joints, can act as a unit, with some configurations having a much higher probability of occurring than others.[10] The preferred configurations may be said to define *special purpose devices* that can be assembled in real time. A hand, for example, can become a grabbing device or a holding device, a punching device or a throwing device.[11] And as the body conducts a particular task, it may have to switch from one special purpose device to another, a switch that can be performed parametrically. Parametric control can also be used to adjust a device to the requirements of a specific task: How hard should a hand hold an object, how fast should it turn it, and how should it orient it so it may be fitted into another object? Finally, as the body interacts with its immediate environment it may do so continuously, the results of its own activity at any one time used as feedback to decide whether, in the next time step, a change of configuration is required.[12]

More complex interactions between the body and its surroundings can be accommodated by extending the dynamical framework to coupled systems. Take for example the activity of returning a ball in a tennis game. To return the ball a player must simultaneously take into account three things: the movement of the approaching ball in order to position his body in the right place, the position of the rival player in order to calculate where the ball should be returned, and his arm's motor components to strike the ball in a specific way. Because the states of the ball, the rival's body, and his own body are changing and affecting each other, this presents the player's brain with a much more complex task than picking the right manner of walking appropriate to a given terrain or the right manner of holding an object to inspect it.[13] But just as in the previous cases, the brain's task can be simplified if it deals with the situation as if it was a *coupled dynamical system*: it can treat the player's body as one dynamical system, the rival's body as another dynamical system, and the ball as a parameter that the player whose turn is to hit it can manipulate to affect his rival. Doing this may involve coupling the perceived variables of the environment (the rival's movements) to a parameter governing the player's own dynamic (muscle stiffness), as well as mapping the variables of the subject's body (the hand holding the racket) to a parameter in the environment's dynamic (the ball).[14] In simple cases, as when we hold a hammer to strike a nail, we can consider the relevant properties of the tool as added dimensions to the state space of the body, and think of the whole formed by the body and tool as a dynamical system that happens to extend beyond the skin. In more complex cases, as in the example of the tennis players, we may need to couple two dynamical systems by linking the variables of one to the parameters of the other.

In order to deal with any of these situations, we need a way to conceptualize integrated wholes, displaying emergent properties, that are easy to assemble and to disassemble. In other words, even when we consider coupled systems we must treat them as capable of being decoupled.[15] In some cases the whole may include only parts of the body (a set of joints, muscles, and tendons) while in others it may add to these body parts a tool, a working surface, or even another organism, but in most cases the emergent whole must be *transient and dissoluble*. These ensembles of heterogeneous components are usually put together for a specific task, and as the circumstances that an organism confronts change it must be able to meet them by rapidly forming a different ensemble.[16] If we followed a subject as he coped with various challenges, the series of ensembles he would enter into would display a persistent core (the subject's brain), various recurrent components (the subject's eyes, hands, and legs), as well as components that enter into the ensemble only for a given purpose but that may change in the course of a single task.[17] The interface between body parts and external objects should also be allowed to change: in some cases the interface may be mechanical (a hand holding a can by its handle), in others it may involve exchanges of energy (a hand bouncing a ball), and in yet others it may require coupling two systems with their own energy sources (a hand on the steering wheel of a running car).[18] But regardless of the complexity of the coupling, or of the entities being coupled, the ensembles should be capable of being dissolved and their parts capable of being articulated into other ensembles.

Let's recapitulate what has been said so far. In the previous chapter we introduced the concept of a preferred state, as determined by the structure of a space of possible states, to explain the stability and recurrence of the sources of natural signs. Here we have extended this concept to account for the fact that some configurations of muscles, tendons, and joints are more stable than others and can, therefore, be expected to occur more frequently than others. We supplemented our previous treatment by adding parameters that can be adjusted to manipulate the structure of the possibility space: the nature and distribution of its singularities, or the "depth" of their sphere of influence. This allowed us to think of the way the brain controls the body not as involving detailed commands but the manipulation of a parameter, such as muscle stiffness, allowing it to rapidly select the preferred configuration that is compatible with the value of the parameter. We also applied this dynamical treatment to the case of a body interacting with its surroundings, distinguishing cases in which the dynamical system is simply an extension of the body from those in which we must consider two separate dynamical systems coupled to one another. But in neither case were we willing to grant that when the body is tightly coupled to external objects, or even to another body, it forms an indissoluble totality with it, so that we would have to accept that the body and the perceived environment co-construct each other, or more generally, that parts and wholes co-emerge.[19]

The dynamical treatment of the body just given provides us with only half of what we need, the half that is mechanism-independent. To say that a possibility space has structure, and that that structure determines preferred states, says nothing about how the properties that define the dimensions of the space causally affect one another. Similarly, to say that an organism is dynamically coupled to a piece of its environment (like the ground beneath its feet) does not explain through what mechanism this coupling is effected. To add the missing half let's recall what was said about causality in the previous chapter. In a materialist ontology causality is defined as the production of one event by another event. In this definition, the term "event" must refer not to atomic events (like simple collisions) but to changes in the properties of entities, so that what is brought into being is not the whole entity but only a modification of the traits that characterize it.[20] We also argued that in order to include nonlinear and catalytic causality, these entities must be viewed as having capacities to affect as well as capacities to be affected. In the current context this refers to the body's capacity to affect its surroundings and to the capacity of the latter to be affected by it, as well as to the capacity of the world to affect a body that can be affected by it. Ecological psychologists use the word "affordance" to refer to the environment's capacities to affect, because they afford, provide, or supply an animal with opportunities and risks for action.[21] And they use the term "effectivities" for the abilities required to affect the environment, and take advantage of the opportunities or avoid the risks.[22]

Both of these terms refer to dispositions that are real but not necessarily actual, since opportunities can be missed, risks avoided, and abilities not exercised. So in this view an animal and its surroundings possess dual dispositions that must be meshed, or made to match, to become actual. Much as the capacity of a knife to cut can only be actualized by interacting with an object that has the capacity to be cut (cheese, bread, paper, but not a block of titanium) so the body's abilities to affect an object in its vicinity can only be actualized if the object has the right capacities to be affected by the body. Ontologically, the dispositions of objects depend on their properties because properties persist through time giving both tendencies and capacities a continuous basis through which they can subsist as potentialities. But perceptually the dependency may be flipped: organisms tend to perceive affordances not properties. This does not imply that the properties of objects, when they are preserved under retinal projection, are not part of our sensory input. They certainly are, and hybrids of icons and indices can be used as signs to represent them internally. But human perception is not reducible to its sensory inputs, and for perception what matters is not that which reaches a subject's sensory organs but what the subject *notices*, what he pays attention to because it makes a difference to him. And similarly for nonhuman organisms: whereas the significance of an object may not be part of the sensory input to an animal, it certainly is part of its perception, and it is important to its survival to distinguish what must be attended to and what can be safely disregarded.[23]

Perhaps the most important factor determining what opportunities and risks a particular object or a particular surface layout affords an organism is the *relative scale* of its body. Take, for example, a hole on the side of a hill, which is basically a concave surface layout: it supplies an animal trying to escape from a predator with an opportunity to hide but only if the hole is large enough to fit the prey's body but too small to fit the predator's body. Another example would be a cliff or precipice which is basically a vertical surface abruptly terminating the horizontal surface of the higher ground. A cliff presents an animal with the risk of falling but only if the animal is large enough that the combination of its mass and gravity's pull causes it to hit the ground with great force. A small insect does not run that risk, even though it is also affected by gravity, because air currents can take away some of its momentum and its low mass makes for a weak impact with the ground. Animals can respond automatically to many of these affordances, a fact that shows that their brains have been sculpted by evolution to incorporate information about recurrent opportunities and risks, given their physical scale.[24] For human beings, affordances and effectivities are often a cultural product. The latter are skills that must be taught by example and learned by doing, and the former are tools that have been created to fit those skills. Examples include medium-sized elongated objects that afford wielding to a human hand, and depending on what is attached at the other end (a rigid flat surface or a pointed ending) afford hammering or piercing; objects of moderate size and weight (like a rock) that afford throwing; long, thin, and elastic objects (a thread or rope) that afford knotting, binding, knitting, and weaving.[25] In these cases too, scale matters. The span of a hand determines the size of an object that is graspable, any object larger than that needs a handle to afford graspability. And of course, an object may be graspable by an adult hand but not by a small child's hand.

In some cases it is not only the nervous system that natural selection has sculpted to fit the affordances of the physical environment but the very bodies of the organisms inhabiting that environment. Let's illustrate this with animals that swim. One and the same lake, for example, presents small and large swimming organisms with very different locomotive challenges. A bacterium has such a small mass that the inertial forces it can exert on water as it displaces it during forward motion are minimal, whereas a large fish has enough mass to move through water effortlessly. The water affords both creatures a medium to swim, but their very different scales mean that the effectivities with which they tackle this task must be different: the higher relative viscosity of the medium for a bacterium demands a locomotive strategy based on keeping the motor (the rotating flagella) going all the time and turning in the same direction. But the much lower viscosity that the fish's body experiences means it can use a strategy of thrust and glide, flapping its tail back and forth to propel itself and then traveling effortlessly up to five times its body length.[26] But if affordances can affect the evolution of the bodies of some animals, the reverse is also true: many animals can intervene on the world around them to change what it affords them. They can affect it through the construction of enduring architectonic structures like dams, nests, webs, and hives, structures that modify the opportunities and risks that their surroundings afford them.[27] This, however, should not be taken as evidence that an animal and its environment are not logically independent entities, or that they are fused into a seamless totality. Preventing this mistake also involves considering questions of scale. Specifically, we need a concept to delimit the scale of the *causal reach* of an animal's activities, because whereas a beaver's dam can affect the flow of a river for several miles downstream, a spider web, a bird's nest, or a bee hive have a much less extensive effect. We may use the concept of an *effective environment* to refer to the portion of an animal's surroundings in which the affordances depend for their existence on the animal's activities.[28]

The most complex effective environments are those created by human beings. A cook's kitchen, a blacksmith's workshop, a chemist's laboratory, and many other spaces dedicated to specific tasks are carefully structured effective environments. The space in which an expert cook operates, for instance, couples the cook's various skills with the affordances of tools (knifes, timers), devices (stoves, refrigerators, blenders), as well as surface layouts (tables, counters). This space is full of indices, some of which are natural, like the smell of vegetables indicating their ripeness; others have acquired their function by design, like the oven light indicating that the desired temperature has been reached. As the cook's activity unfolds, his own causal interventions (slicing, chopping, boiling, mixing, baking) produce their own indices: the consistency of the sauce indicating more flour needs to be added, the melting of the butter indicating it is ready to be mixed, and the texture of the pasta indicating it should be taken out of the boiling water. It is a space full of signs, some of which are important for the task as a whole, others for a particular stage of the task, but all demanding attention to be noticed in the midst of a continuous flow of activity, the execution of simultaneous operations, and the monitoring of intermediate results.

Like the concept of the body as a dynamical system with its own preferred states, the concept of an effective environment also lets us reduce the complexity of the intentional signs we must postulate are used by internal cognitive agents. If experts can offload some of the memory, attentional, and computational loads of their tasks into an external *cognitive scaffolding*, this would simplify the operations that the brain must perform in order to generate coherent activity.[29] The intelligent use of space that yields this scaffolding can also be illustrated with the activities of the expert cook.[30] In preparation for a meal the ingredients and tools he will be using are placed in a salient position, while at the same time items that will not be needed are hidden from view. This simple act reduces attentional effort, since affordances that make a difference to the task are made highly visible while those that are irrelevant are not. Once the task has begun, the structuring of the space to avoid distractions must continue. Even simple actions can allocate attention only where it is needed: as the cook washes vegetables, for example, he may place those already washed in one pile and the ones needed to be washed in another, a simple grouping operation that indicates at a glance to what category a given item belongs to, as well as the overall progress of the task.[31] The intelligent use of space allows the cook to notice the signs indicating that previous steps have been effective and that the task is ready for the next step, or on the contrary, that a disruption has occurred and the next step is blocked, as when an ingredient is unavailable or unusable so a replacement must be found. More generally, the expert cook will tend to allocate space in such a way as to *minimize internal processing:* placing reminders of important steps to avoid the use of internal memory, using groupings that indicate numerical properties (rows of sliced vegetables rather than piles) in order to avoid making internal computations, and deliberately labeling containers to avoid lengthy perceptual search.[32]

To recapitulate: the mechanism-independent explanation of bodily activity supplied by a dynamical approach gives us only half of what we need. It must be complemented by a causal account in terms of mechanisms. In the case of the interactions between an organism and its surroundings, the mechanism in question involves causal interactions between what the immediate environment affords and what the animal can effectively do. Much as the existence of preferred states in the dynamics of the body allowed us to conceive of the content of brain commands as involving not detailed prescriptions but only the specification of key parameters, so the concept of a well-structured effective environment lets us simplify the kinds of internal intentional signs we must postulate. Let's combine the two results in the case of the expert cook. Rather than thinking of the cook's brain as containing a single unified model of the entire kitchen and a detailed plan of the overall task we can think of multiple partial models each specific to a task, or even to a single stage in a task. The interactions with an oven or a blender, for example, can be treated separately, since each device has a single parameter which by design can be controlled by a single knob or dial: the temperature for the oven, the speed for the blender. Unlike the case of the tennis player mentioned earlier, this may not require that the two dynamical systems (the cook and the device) be fully coupled but only that there exist easy-to-recognize interfaces allowing the formation of wholes that are temporary and easy to dissolve.[33]

So far we have focused on the way the brain controls the body without any reference to the way that control is experienced by the embodied subject. To tackle this question let's consider two main sources of somatic information that can have discernible subjective effects: *proprioceptive* and *interoceptive*. Proprioception is a form of internal perception required to keep the brain informed about the body's current posture, limb configuration, and state of movement. It uses signs produced by a myriad mechanoreceptors, distributed in joints, skin, and muscles, serving as reliable indices of properties like pressure, vibration, touch, and skin tension.[34] It also uses signs produced by receptors in the inner ear as indices for gravity and acceleration, which are used to maintain the body's postural balance. Interoception is a second form of internal perception, the function of which is to keep the brain informed about the current state of the body's visceral environment in order to maintain its metabolic balance. Its receptors produce reliable indices for properties like the degree of concentration of oxygen, carbon dioxide, or glucose; the degree of acidity or alkalinity of certain tissues; body temperature and arterial pressure.[35] Proprioception and interoception are the result of the brain *monitoring* different components of the body: the signs emitted by striate muscle, the kind that is under voluntary control, and the signs emitted by smooth muscle, the kind that makes up intestines and blood vessels.

Let's start with proprioception. Why would the brain need to monitor self-movement if the section of structured light in the retina already contains many indices about it? Optic flow, for example, indicates the direction in which a body is moving in a way that can be readily distinguished from the motion of external objects around it. Relations of occlusion among objects also indicate a particular position for the body, while affordances indicate a particular scale for it. We may think of these indices as the raw materials for *visual proprioception*, and stress their importance by noticing how hard it is to reach and grab a nearby object while blindfolded, even though our skin, joints, and muscles are constantly supplying us with information about our own movements. But the opposite is also true: patients who have lost access to *somatic proprioception* can control their bodies only with great difficulty and only if they have direct and constant visual access to the limbs they are moving. They must sleep with the lights on because waking up in the dark makes them feel they do not know where their body is.[36] It is as if proprioception of the visual kind gave us access to our bodies from a third-person point of view but only the somatic kind allowed us to experience our body from a first-person point of view.[37] Nevertheless, it would be wrong to conclude that the function of somatic proprioception is to endow subjects with feelings about their bodies. We do consciously feel where our legs and arms are at any time, or whether we are standing, walking, or running, but proprioceptive information is deployed in the interests of producing fluid body motions from groups of joints, muscles, and tendons. In some cases, like postural balance, we do not even experience a well-defined feeling, except when the effect vanishes and we feel vertigo.

A similar point applies to interoception. The detection of imbalances, the assessment of their degree of departure from the homeostatic range, and the urgency with which remedial action must be undertaken are all part of what we may refer to as an *emotional response*. In ordinary language the terms "emotion" and "feeling" are used interchangeably but the term "emotion" should be used to refer to a motivational state of the body that involves a complex response with endocrinal, neural, behavioral, and subjective components, the word "feeling" referring only to the latter.[38] Take hunger for example. Phenomenally, hunger is identified with a certain feeling in the stomach (pangs of hunger) that correlates with contractions in this organ. But the stomach may be surgically removed causing the feeling to disappear while the drive to ingest food continues to exist. The reason is that the intestines and the liver continue to send messages to the brain informing it about low concentrations of glucose in the blood and directing it to motivate eating behavior to correct the imbalance.[39] Hence it is not as if the feeling of hunger caused an animal to search for food. The causal sequence is rather started by the internal imbalance which produces the seeking behavior as well as the feeling.[40] Nevertheless, and despite the fact that the phenomenal experience is not at the center of the process, the subjective part plays a crucial role in determining our *sense of ownership* of our bodies. The fact that interoceptive feelings begin as imbalances of the internal environment and are experienced as occurring within the boundaries of the skin makes them the property of the subject. And similarly for proprioceptive feelings. Those that accompany the execution of successful causal interventions in the world make us feel that the body is responsive to our willed actions and, hence, give us a *sense of agency*. But it is not as if a feeling of ownership and agency of purely subjective origin caused us to act as if we were aware of our boundaries and capabilities, but the other way around.[41]

Do we need to postulate internal signs to explain the phenomenal effects of internal perception? A well-known candidate for this role are *maps of the body*. The distinction between the iconic and indexical content of these maps can be made clear if we first imagine internal maps of a park with which we are familiar because of our daily walks. Routinely traversing the different places and landmarks in this park slowly builds up knowledge of their locations and of the relations between these locations, until the layout of the entire park becomes known to us and we can effortlessly recognize every part of it. This internal map constitutes the iconic component of the sign. But on any given day as we take a walk, the location of our bodies in the park must also be represented so that we can orient ourselves, a task assigned to the indexical component of the sign. The information needed to create this compound sign comes from visual proprioception, so no concepts are required to fully characterize an embodied point of view.[42] The maps involved in somatic proprioception, on the other hand, are of the body itself, as opposed to maps of places where the body is located. But a similar distinction can be made: the iconic component represents the whole body and the relations between its parts, while the indexical component stands for the body parts currently being used. The first somatic map was discovered empirically, by directly stimulating certain areas of the cerebral cortex and asking subjects to report where in their bodies they felt a sensation. As the experimenter stimulated nearby brain areas the subject reported sensations in adjacent body areas and, by methodically moving the point being stimulated, the entire body surface was found to be mapped in a continuous strip of brain tissue. The graphic version of this somatic map ("the homunculus") is well known, as is the fact that the more receptors a body part has the larger the extent of brain apportioned to it, the maximum area dedicated to lips, tongue, and hands. As part of the same research, a second map was discovered in which body parts were represented by what they do, not by how they feel: when different parts of this cortical area were stimulated, specific parts of the subject's body moved.[43]

It is important to emphasize that these "maps" are not signs but physical structures *capable of holding signs*. The vehicle of the signs would be the pattern of activation that these spatially structured neurons have at any one time, a pattern partly shaped by the physical map's own properties. In the following chapter we will develop this distinction in more detail because, as we will argue, the physical map is a component of a cognitive agent, while the signs are what the agent produces and consumes. Strictly speaking, it is the physical map that is shaped by the experience of the species or the organism, but because it must share structure with the vehicle of signs, the latter inherits the effects of that experience. To keep things simple in what follows we will speak as if the signs themselves were the result of evolutionary or learning history. Another simplification that must be made while we wait for a more precise characterization is the nature of those signs. As we have already noted, the two components of a hybrid sign can play a variety of functions. The icon can stand for a set of types (learned by mapping relations of similarity among objects into relations of proximity in the icon), while the index stands for the token of a type that is currently perceived. Or the icon can stand for the range of values that a perceived property can have, while the index stands for the current value of that property. Or the icon can stand for an entire entity (such as the full body of the observer), while the index stands for the parts of that entity that are presently being controlled. Or, finally, and this is the case that we will examine more carefully in the next chapter, the icon can represent the entire content of the retina at any one time, while the index stands for the part of the visual field that the subject is presently attending to. This characterization of the two components is made in a "functionalist" style, that is, without paying much attention to the neural mechanisms behind them. In what follows we will be addressing questions about neural implementation, but our treatment of the hybrid signs will remain mostly functional.

In the seventy years that have elapsed since the discovery of the first sensory and motor maps, technologies to create detailed images of overall brain activity have flourished, and techniques to probe the activity of single neurons developed, permitting those initial findings to be greatly extended. Skin receptors, muscle receptors, retinal receptors, even interoceptive receptors, all have been found to be mapped into specific areas of the cortex. The iconic part of these maps is slowly developed as sensory experiences accumulate, much as the map of the park is the historical result of many walks. There are, however, differences in the way in which an internal map of a place like a park and a map of the human body need to be conceived. Internal maps of external spaces like a park demand the use of coordinates to specify locations. But a body map used to control the body as it walks through the park must have a different structure. We argued earlier that sets of joints, muscles, and tendons have preferred configurations that can be selected by manipulating a parameter. This model of control requires a map representing the body as an articulated whole, in which each articulated segment (with its joint, tendon, and muscles) possesses its own icon and index. A location in one part of the body would not require a set of coordinates and a fixed origin to be determined, only its distance and direction from the joints that bind that body part: a point in the forearm, for example, could be located by its spatial relation to the wrist and elbow joints. From the point of view of controlling body movements a map like this would keep the brain informed at all times where one part of the body is relative to its other parts, precisely the kind of information it needs to determine the starting position of a limb that it is about to trigger into action.[44] We will see later that there are physical maps in the brain that meet these requirements.

Visual and somatic proprioception involve two different ways of internally representing the body. The former allows us to see parts of our bodies, some entirely out of focus (the nose, the brows) serving to frame the visual field by occluding everything else, some clear and in focus, like our hands and our feet. And using mirrors or other reflective surfaces we can see our entire bodies. This gives us perceptual access to our bodies as one object among others, yielding what we may refer to as a *body image*. But somatic proprioception, as we said, gives us access to information about our bodies from a first-person point of view, creating not a body image but a *body schema*.[45] Both body images and body schemas can affect the way we experience our bodies, but they do so in very different ways: the former can influence how we value our body relative to some standard, the latter how we live the way it is structured in space. The phenomenal effects of a body schema can be clearly illustrated by several well-known *somatic illusions* that take advantage of the fact that the receptors for tension in the muscles, referred to as *spindles*, can be fooled into sending false information to the brain. Normally, when the elbow joint bends the tendon that is linked to it slackens. But if we close our eyes and apply a vibrator to that tendon, the spindles will take this as an indication of loss of tension and produce signs that lead to the vivid illusion that the elbow is bending, when in fact it is not. Applying vibrations to other arm tendons creates the illusion that our arm is becoming unnaturally longer or shorter, while placing a vibrator in the biceps tendon and touching one's nose yields the illusion that our nose has grown several times its length.[46] These illusions show that there is a way of experiencing the spatial structure of our bodies, in the absence of visual information, that is entirely different than the visual experience of our body image.

How are maps of the body's different receptors implemented in the brain? We need to introduce several concepts from neuroscience to answer this question. The first concept is that of the *receptive field* of a sensory neuron. The receptive field of a neuron connected to the skin or the retina is the patch of cutaneous or retinal surface which, if externally stimulated, would cause the neuron to change its spontaneous firing rate. If we arranged a population of neurons in space so that neighboring neurons were connected to neighboring patches of retina or skin, the entire array of overlapping receptive fields would be isomorphic to the array of cutaneous or optical receptors, yielding a physical map capable of holding iconic signs.[47] The size of a receptive field varies depending on the neuron's function. Neurons that operate early in visual processing and that must be tuned to small details like the presence of a luminance discontinuity indicating a possible edge must have small receptive fields; in later stages of processing, when extracting information from optic flow, for example, receptive fields must be much larger to capture patterns of greater extension.[48] In addition to their properties receptive fields have dispositions: they give neurons the tendency to react to *preferred stimuli*. The preferred stimulus for a neuron can be established empirically by directly measuring its level of activity while stimulating the patch of retina or skin into which it is mapped. We can learn much about the way the body is mapped, and about the way these maps are used, from the preferred stimuli of neurons in different areas of the cortex.

When the first two body maps were discovered, the distinction between maps used for sensing and those used for moving was thought to be absolute. But this clearly left out a crucial ingredient: the transformation of one into the other, a transformation that could be simplified if there were neurons that had *visuomotor* receptive fields. In one cortical area a population of bimodal neurons like this has been found, the preferred stimulus for which is either the skin being touched at a particular location or viewing an object approaching that location. In other words, the receptive fields of these neurons are tuned to *anticipated contact*, as much as real contact, and more importantly, they are indifferent to the direction of the gaze. This implies that they do not map the nearby object using its position in the retinal image, but its proximity to a particular body part. The visual component of these receptive fields seems to be a three-dimensional extension of the two-dimensional patch of skin to which they are connected. These volumetric receptive fields follow closely the division of the body into segments, a design which, as we just argued, allows the brain to locate sensations without using coordinates. More generally, the volumes of near space around arms and legs, fingers and toes provide the means to locate objects that are within grasping or kicking distance without the need for a fixed frame of reference. Because the set of these volumes maps both the periphery of the body and the most intimate layer of external space adjacent to it, they are said to define a *peripersonal space*.[49]

Peripersonal maps are used by the brain in conjunction with motor maps, so locations on the former refer not just to body parts but to the potential actions those parts can execute. This raises the question of whether the receptive fields of the neurons composing a peripersonal map could change when the hand is holding a tool. In experiments designed to answer this question the part of the peripersonal map of a monkey's hand was first measured to confirm that it conformed to the hand's contours. Then the monkey was taught to use a rake with a long handle to reach for and retrieve pieces of food that were far from his body. Once the skill had been mastered, the volume covered by the receptive fields was measured again and found to extend all the way to the tip of the rake.[50] It is tempting to imagine that the monkey, although unable to report this, felt making contact with the food not at the handle that its fingers were actually touching but at the end of the rake, where its peripersonal map ended. If this seems like a piece of anthropomorphism, think of the following ordinary experiences: when we walk with a cane, we feel that we make contact with the ground at the tip of the cane, not where we are holding the cane; when we cut a piece of bread we feel the cutting action at the edge of the knife not at its handle; and when we grasp a bolt with pliers, we feel the grasping action with its jaws, not at the place where we are grabbing the tool. Evidence that tools can extend the human peripersonal map has been produced in laboratories, but interestingly some of the experiments show that it is only an active use of the tool, rather than just passively holding it, that leads to the plastic extension of the map.[51] We said earlier that a hand using a tool may be seen as a single dynamical system in which the state space diagram's dimensions include the properties of the hand and the tool. Peripersonal maps show how this dynamic relation could be causally implemented in the brain.

Are there other connections between the dynamic characterization of the body and the use of internal body maps? If sets of joints, muscles, and tendons form preferred configurations that can be selected parametrically, we would expect the required internal signs to be stored in a modular way. Moreover, if an action is composed of several preferred configurations, then these could be stored as part of a *mosaic of zones* defining a basic vocabulary of actions. Each zone in the mosaic would contain information about the parameters that must be used to select the most appropriate variant to act on an object, and be able to interact with other brain areas holding signs standing for that object. In the following chapter we will name these areas and describe their interactions in more detail, but at this point a rough characterization would be useful to emphasize the fact that mechanisms involving the use of internal signs are needed to complete a purely dynamical account. One promising candidate for the mosaic of zones is a cortical area composed of neurons sensitive to both motor and tactile stimuli. The preferred stimulus of these neurons is not just individual motions of the body, such as flexing a finger, but motions that are part of a *goal-directed* sequence, like flexing a finger as part of the action of grasping.[52] This area seems ideal to hold icons standing for an entire sequence of movements and their intended goal, and it works in cooperation with a neighboring area that represents the dispositions of the object to be acted upon. Simplifying somewhat, we may say that the latter represents an object's affordances, while the former represents the matching effectivities. The two areas must work in a loop, because there are cases in which an object affords various actions and the correct one must be selected after various passes through the loop. Thus, picking up a cup of coffee can be done in various ways depending on whether we are drinking from it (grasp it by the handle), washing it (grasp it by the rim), or moving it out of the way (grasp it by the body). Which of these actions is deemed appropriate for a task is worked out within the circuit formed by these two cortical areas.[53]

The body maps discussed so far are used by mindless cognitive agents as part of the process of controlling bodily activity. But they can also have a powerful effect on phenomenal experience. Let's begin by illustrating the kind of effect we have in mind with a laboratory experiment in *sensory substitution*: a congenitally blind subject is equipped with an apparatus consisting of a black-and-white video camera and an array of vibrating pins attached to his skin. The camera's image is isomorphically mapped into the array of pins, by connecting each pixel to the corresponding pin and by making the pin's intensity match the luminosity of the pixel. Without any training, the subject reports feeling only the tactile sensations on his skin and nothing else, but after a while his brain becomes able to extract natural signs from the array and process these into "images" of objects, perceived as being located, not on his skin but right in front of him. For our present purposes the most important feature of the experiment was that the transformation from a complex tingling on the skin to a scene with visual properties occurred only if the subject was able *to control the movement of the camera:* if the camera was under someone else's control the transition from tactile to visual did not take place, but if it was mounted on the subject's head it did.[54] One way of explaining this effect is to argue that his brain used proprioceptive information from his neck muscles and correlated it with changes in the image, allowing the subject to learn that moving his head to the left revealed a different view of the room than moving it to the right or moving it upward. More generally, what the subject learned was the existence of regular and predictable relations between his movements and the resulting visual experiences. We will refer to these relations as *sensory-motor dependencies*.

The phenomenal effect of mastering sensory-motor dependencies should be distinguished from more ordinary relations between what the body does and what a subject sees. We have stressed from the start the role played by active exploration in perception, allowing the optic array to be sampled from many different positions and angles so as to harvest as much information as possible. Thus, if we want to see what a large object hides from our view we simply walk around it to a better position, if we want to see what is inside a room we open its door and walk inside, and if we want to have visual access to far away objects we climb to a high place to find a more favorable angle. In these examples, perception is linked to action but the relation is purely *instrumental*: changes in motor activity are used by a subject in order to cause changes in the information he obtains from the world. In the sensory substitution experiment, on the other hand, motor activity has long-term effects on perception, contributing to the content of phenomenal experience even when the information from the world stays the same: the transformation of a skin sensation into a visual scene remains even if the subject ceases to move his head, so his sensory input remains the same.[55] This noninstrumental effect that action has on perception is also evident in ordinary experiences. When we look at a solid object located at some distance from us it appears to us as if it was bounded by its outer surfaces on all sides. That is, we do not experience the object as a collection of free-floating, front-facing surfaces, despite the fact that the surfaces facing away from us are not contributing to the retinal content, and are, therefore, not part of our sensory input. And a similar point applies to objects located in the periphery of the visual field, which appear as undifferentiated blobs, but are not experienced as if they were actually fuzzy.[56] Once sensory-motor dependencies have become part of the process that generates phenomenal experience, the back surfaces of objects and the undifferentiated peripheral objects are experienced as being *accessible to us*: we can make the invisible side of an object accessible simply by walking around it and bringing it into view, and we can make all the missing detail in our peripheral vision accessible by turning our eyes or heads in their direction.[57]

Accessibility is, of course, a disposition, so this claim amounts to this: just as we can experience objects in terms of their affordances because in the past we have managed to profit from the opportunities, and avoided the risks, those objects afford us, so we can experience all the views that an object can afford us, all the contents that the world supplies us with, and all the detail our eyes are capable of delivering, thanks to our previous history of using our bodies to gain access to this information. What neural mechanism could explain this noninstrumental effect? It is relatively easy to understand how the past experiences of an organism (or of a species) could have generated a map of the correlations between two other maps, one retinal, the other proprioceptive. But these "meta-maps" may not suffice to generate an effect that has a counterfactual nature. What seems to be required here is a way of combining retinal and proprioceptive maps with a way to rehearse or *simulate* certain movements. As we just saw, the cortical areas dedicated to the planning of bodily activity contain a vocabulary of goal-directed actions.[58] Could the brain access these actions to simulate movements and link them to their visual consequences? There is growing evidence that the planning and execution of an action involves the activation of similar cortical areas, the main difference being that during planning the motor component is inhibited or blocked, which suggests that planning an action is much like performing it but with the "inhibition switch" turned on.[59] What we are proposing here is that this mechanism may also be used to generate the kinds of simulations that, combined with "meta-maps" representing correlations between visual and proprioceptive information, could yield the complex icons needed to store information about sensory-motor dependencies.[60]

To summarize the second part of our argument: The brain must continuously monitor the body to inform itself of the current arrangement of its locomotive and manipulative parts as well as of its present state of movement. It also monitors the body's internal environment to maintain homeostasis, check the availability of metabolic resources, and regulate the relations between visceral organs. The steady stream of signs from joints, muscles, tendons, and viscera, organized by a variety of body maps, results in two forms of inward-oriented perception: proprioception and interoception. Both forms of self-perception have conscious and unconscious components, the latter playing a greater role in the control of the body, the former giving us a sense of ownership of our phenomenal experience. The internal use of body maps also yields a very different way of experiencing the spatial structure of the body. When we see our limbs move, or even when we contemplate ourselves in the mirror, the body is seen much like other objects in the world. But mapping receptors in the skin, muscles, and joints in a way that preserves the spatial relations these receptors have with each other gives us a way to experience our bodies in a more intimate way. Finally, by combining different kinds of maps (visual, tactile, and motor) the brain allows us to simulate our actions prior to their execution, or even simulate them without any intention to carry them out. We hypothesized that one use of these simulations is to yield a conscious experience of the visual field as filled with opportunities to access its unobservable or undifferentiated content.

Let's consider some objections to our argument. We argued in the previous chapter that the recognition of the wealth of information contained in the slice of structured light had led ecological psychologists to underestimate the complexity of generating phenomenal experience without the use of internal signs.[61] In a similar way, the rediscovery of the body's potential to influence perception has caused various theorists to make the same mistake. Take for instance the anti-representationalist arguments of the influential *enactive approach,* in which the synthesis of phenomenal experience is explained as the result of skillful activity performed by the whole organism.[62] The philosophical approach to the nature of skills begins by drawing a distinction between two types of knowledge, referred to as *knowing that* and *knowing how.*[63] Knowing that something is the case involves a form of knowledge that is verbal and that is taught using lectures or books, while knowing how to do something involves embodied knowledge that is taught by example and learned by doing. While the content of the former is exhausted by a proposition following the "that" clause, and it is easy to report, the content of the latter is typically inaccessible in the sense that most people could not describe what knowing how to swim or knowing how to ride a bicycle consists of. It is, therefore, easy to conclude that if knowledge of sensory-motor dependencies is a type of know-how, then its content is inaccessible, involving no internal signs at all.[64] But the enactivists' argument does not stop here: it involves two very specific claims about what goes on in our heads when we experience something, as well as about the kind of relationship that exists between phenomenal experience and bodily activities.

The first claim is that the brain does not perform information processing: what it does when we perceive and act in the world is to *construct meaning.*[65] The exercise of abilities creates meaningful couplings with the world and it is these meaningful couplings, together with the sensory-motor dependencies they reveal, that generate the content of phenomenal experience.[66] Yet, this claim involves a conceptual mistake that is widespread in the philosophy of mind: it confuses two meanings of the word "meaningful," as illustrated by the phrases "meaningful sentence" and "meaningful life." In the first phrase the term means *signification*, referring to the semantic content of a sentence, while in the second it refers to the *significance* of a life.[67] Something lacking signification is "nonsensical" while something without significance is "trivial." Thus, we are dealing with two entirely different concepts, one about content the other about the value of this content.[68] If we conflate the two then the action of evaluating visual content for its significance and the synthesis of what is to be evaluated (the semantic content of visual signs) become one and the same thing. If we add to this conflation the idea that, to be properly exercised, skills must be matched to the opportunities and risks we value, and that what we perceive is not properties but affordances, we may wrongly conclude that the phenomenal content of experience can be *identified* with the exercise of skills.[69] But this identification can be resisted by simply keeping the two meanings of "meaning" separate, and by giving different explanations for the processes that generate value and content.

The second claim is about relations. For visual content to be reducible to skillful activity there must be a specific kind of relation between the body and the world as experienced: the relation must be *intrinsic*, the kind of relation that *constitutes the very identity* of the terms it relates. The conventional relation between relatives provides a good illustration: the event of my sister giving birth to a boy and the event of my becoming an uncle are not logically independent of each other. Their identity is fully determined by the intrinsic relations expressed by the predicates "is a sister of," "is the son of," and "is the nephew of." This is the only legitimate use of the concept and, it must be stressed, even in this case the intrinsic relation constitutes the identity of the roles (sister, uncle) not the identity of the incumbents to the roles. Extending intrinsic relations from this valid realm to any other case, such as the relation between parts and wholes, has the unfortunate effect of yielding what we may refer to as *seamless totalities*, that is, wholes made out of parts that have no independent existence, since their very identity depends on their relations within the whole.[70] The alternative to this are *extrinsic* relations, relations that do not bring into existence that which they relate. Causal interactions are a good example: a change in an object's properties is an event that produces another event, a change in another object's properties, but the identity of the two interacting objects is not constituted by their interaction. Extrinsic relations must be deployed carefully, because on their own they do not yield an irreducible whole but a mere agglomeration of components: perceived objects are reduced to mere bundles of properties. But if the concept of an extrinsic relation is supplemented with that of an emergent property, the resulting wholes are both *irreducible* and *analyzable*.[71]

The enactivist argument can be summarized like this: the world experienced by an animal is not a prespecified external realm, characterized by properties that can be represented internally. Rather, it comes into being as the activities of the animal endow the animals' perceived surroundings with "meaning."[72] The animal and its phenomenal world are inextricably related because in totalities defined by intrinsic relations the parts cannot preexist the whole. Enactivists use the example of bodily organs like the heart or the kidney that do not preexist the body as a whole but are created simultaneously during embryonic development. We would, of course, agree with this but still argue that the example misses the mark in two ways. First, while hearts and kidneys may not preexist the body they are not fused with it into a seamless whole: both can be detached and transplanted into another body as fully functioning components. And second, this example locates the preexisting parts at the wrong scale: the components of chromosomes (nucleotides), those of structural proteins and enzymes (amino acids), and the building blocks for a bacterium's membrane, did preexist the emergence of life in this planet. And, of course, water and the chemical gradients exploited by the earliest bacteria also had to preexist. We can agree that many dispositions of these life precursors would not become actual until bacteria evolved to take advantage of them, but the properties that serve as a basis for those dispositions were not created by the skillful activities of microorganisms.[73] Rejecting the preexistence of an objective world with its own properties forces enactivists to create their own theory of evolution, one in which selection pressures are not external to organisms but in which organisms and environment define and select each other.[74] Yet, as we saw, an organism may be able to affect its surroundings by constructing dams, nest, and webs, which may act as additional sources of selection pressures partly shaped by its very activities, but there will always be other sources of selection (e.g., the climate) that are outside its causal reach.

The second anti-representational school of thought is known as *radical embodiment*.[75] It also argues that a tight coupling between an animal and its environment makes internal signs unnecessary, but its holism derives from an incorrect ontological analysis of mathematical models, and of the state space diagrams based on those models. The latter are simply graphic versions of a differential equation capturing the way in which a property of the system being modeled changes when other properties change. These equations tell us *that* changes in one property result in changes in others properties, but not *how* one change causes the other. In other words, the differential equations that define a state space diagram say nothing about causal mechanisms. In this book we have used the distributions of singularities that characterize these diagrams as a way to understand the ontology of dispositions, or more exactly, of the type of disposition referred to as a *tendency*. The somewhat anthropomorphic expression "preferred state" was just a convenient way to refer to regular tendencies. The ontological status of a non-actualized tendency, that is, a tendency that is not currently being manifested, can then be clarified: it is a possible dynamical outcome that has a much greater probability of becoming actual than other outcomes. Hence, we did not use dynamical concepts to derive insights about any actual process or event. It may be objected that state space diagrams can, in fact, represent actual systems by using *curves or trajectories* that stand for the recent history of changes in a system.[76] This is, in fact, entirely correct, but it does not make a difference: the shape of these curves is determined by the equations and, for the reason just given, the curves do not contain any causal information. They do represent something actual—an actual series of states that a real system passes through—and they do lead to predictions about the most probable state at the end of the process, the preferred state, but they do not tell us by what mechanism one state follows another.

How are these ideas handled in the radical embodiment approach? As we saw earlier in this chapter, the equation at the basis of a state space diagram has variables (representing the properties of the system) and parameters (representing the properties of its immediate environment). We can couple two such equations by connecting the variables of one to the parameters of the other and vice versa. Thus, in the case of an animal actively changing its surroundings, we can model the animal as one dynamical system, its construction (dam, web, nest, hive) as a second dynamical system, and then couple the two. From a mathematical point of view it does not matter whether we view the result of this coupling as involving two entities, or as a single, more extensive entity. In other words, it is just a matter of convenience whether we view this as two coupled dynamical systems or as a single dynamical system.[77] But advocates of radical embodiment, confusing what is actual with what is not, wrongly conclude that the animal and its surroundings have thereby become inseparable, fused into an unanalyzable whole.[78] Bringing causal mechanisms to complete the dynamic explanation, however, avoids this holistic conclusion. We can agree that when an animal's activities are tightly coupled to its surroundings, a new dynamical system emerges that has its own preferred states. But this does not imply that, causally speaking, an actual fusion has taken place but only that the animal in interaction with a piece of the world has acquired new tendencies. There is a new whole, and it is irreducible to its parts, but as an actual entity it remains analyzable and dissoluble.

Let's take a closer look at the standard example used in these discussions, a control device originally designed for steam engines: the *centrifugal governor*. The problem that this device was designed to solve was how to get uniform power from a steam engine. This could be solved by mapping the up and down motion of its pistons into the rotary motion of a *flywheel*, and using the rotation of the latter to control the intensity of activity of the engine. To do this, a computer programmer today would write a computer program that would explicitly represent the value of the flywheel's speed and compare this representation to one of the desired speed; if there is a discrepancy, then the program would use a valve to change the pressure of the steam until the desired speed is reached.[79] However plausible this may seem to us, the actual solution reached by nineteenth-century engineers was different: they created a device made of a vertical spindle with two hinged arms, each with a metal ball attached at its free end. The device was connected to the flywheel and the valve. When the flywheel rotated rapidly the balls were moved upward by centrifugal force, and as the arms raised they closed the valve. Conversely, if it was rotating too slow, the arms fell and the valve was opened. This way, without explicitly representing speed, pressure, or the state of the valve, the centrifugal governor was able to maintain a uniform engine speed.[80] The entire machine can be viewed as composed of two coupled dynamical systems: one system is the governor itself, a system for which the angle subtended by the arms is a variable and the engine's speed a parameter; the other is the engine, in which the speed as determined by the valve is a variable, and the arm's angle is a parameter. The resulting uniformity in performance is due to the fact that the entire coupled system tends toward a stable steady state defined by a singularity.[81] Thus, unlike the computer program, the centrifugal governor uses no symbolic representations to achieve control of the engine's behavior.

Two things should be emphasized at this point: that this argument is valid only relatively to one kind of internal sign (symbols) and that as an analogy to the case of an animal coupled to a part of the world, it aims only at explaining the control of its *behavior*. That is, unlike the enactive approach, radical embodiment does not pretend to explain phenomenal experience. But even in this restricted area, the argument fails to make its case, because there are other kinds of signs it does not take into account. We could argue, for example, that the angle that the spindle arms subtends at any one time is an indicator of the engine's speed. And because the range of angles that the arm can subtend is also mapped into the range of speeds it can control, this supplies the iconic component of the sign.[82] The standard objection to this counterargument is that the engine works in a continuous *causal loop* so the direction of intentionality (from arm's angle to speed) cannot be fixed: in this loop the speed of the engine is also an indicator of the arm's angle.[83] This is the problem we analyzed in the previous chapter when we said that the grooves in a vinyl record are an icon for the recorded music but not for any of the intermediary (electrical, mechanical) isomorphic patterns required to play the music. The argument we gave there is that, *by design* it is the function of the disc to be a record of the music. And a similar point applies to the engine's case: the valve is designed to use the arm's angle as an index of speed, not the other way around. To this, proponents of radical embodiment reply that the mathematical model fully specifies the preferred state for the whole engine, and that using the model we can *predict* what this state will be. Since the point of explaining the engine's behavior is to predict what it will do in different situations, then adding that it is using the arm's angle as an index of speed is idle or redundant.[84] But this assumes that prediction is the only cognitive task performed by explanations, an assumption deriving from a now obsolete philosophy of science. We also need to supply the actual mechanisms through which the predicted outcomes came to be to get a full understanding of a phenomenon. This implies that, when analyzing an organism and its surroundings we must keep separate what is actual and in need of a causal explanation and what is dispositional and can be explained dynamically.[85]

To summarize: The anti-representationalist philosophies to which the concept of an embodied subject has given rise do not present insurmountable problems for the stance taken here. In the end, they both rely on arguments from holism that can be boiled down to this: if an embodied subject and the environment in which he is embedded form an unanalyzable whole, if they are so inextricably related that we cannot tell them apart, then there is no need to postulate any signs that stand for mind-independent properties, objects, and situations. The different strands of anti-representationalism use different tactics to reach this conclusion. The enactive approach relies on the notion of an intrinsic relation, a relation that constitutes the very identity of what it relates. These relations do exist, but they are limited to those in which social conventions, like the conventions that determine kinship relations, are involved. But even in this case, what intrinsic relations bring into existence are social roles, not the incumbents of those roles. And once we leave the realm of arbitrary conventions to deal with the causal interactions that a subject has with his surroundings, what we are dealing with are extrinsic relations, regardless of whether the causes are linear, nonlinear, or catalytic.[86] The radical embodiment approach, on the other hand, arrives at its holism by assuming that because we can fuse two coupled dynamical systems mathematically, this means that the actual systems the dynamical models stand for can also be so fused. But this misunderstands the way these models work. The equations behind the models capture only regularities in the way in which changes in one property depend on changes in other properties, but do so without providing a mechanism to explain how one change causes the other. It can be argued that this is an epistemological virtue because the regularities of behavior revealed by a dynamical model can be generalized to other systems using different mechanisms. And this is, indeed, true. But this does not obviate the need to complete a dynamical characterization with a causal one when considering each particular case. And once we complete it, the holistic conclusions reached by the advocates of radical embodiment are rendered untenable.

So far we have concentrated our discussion of the phenomenal effects of embodiment mostly on proprioception. But the body as lived by a subject needs to be considered from the interoceptive point of view as well. We mentioned earlier that in the case of hunger the motivational state, with its endocrinal, neural, and behavioral components, should not be reduced to the subjective feeling of hunger. And similarly for emotional responses caused not by internal imbalances but by external events.[87] A few seconds after we detect an object that affords us grave danger, for example, a visceral response ensues: our heart rate, blood pressure, breathing pattern, and the state of contraction of our gut change, while cortisol is secreted into the blood stream to prepare the body for an anticipated higher rate of energy consumption. In addition, a configuration of facial muscles is adopted, one that could be recognized as an expression of terror, while at the same time a couple of potential locomotive behaviors are readied for action: flee in an attempt to escape or freeze in an attempt to hide. The feeling of fear, finally, is also produced and begins to color our visual perception.[88] It is because the emotional response to fear involves the same complex co-occurrence of endocrinal, neural, behavioral, and psychological events, that we can compare it to hunger. The external event may be seen as causing an internal imbalance that the emotional response then corrects. The main difference is that while signs indicating hunger are easy to detect and do not need an elaborate appraisal, those that indicate a dangerous situation are much more ambiguous and demand to be evaluated case by case: the presence of a predator and the occurrence of an avalanche may be both perceived as affording danger, but the kind of response that they require need not be appraised in the same way.

The central place that evaluations have in an emotional response points to the main evolutionary function of emotions: to encode *values* that guide successful action in the world. The neural circuits that underlie emotions are like ancestral memories helping organisms react unconditionally to challenging situations.[89] The evaluations need not be performed consciously by the animal as a whole, but can be done in an entirely unconscious way by the brain. We can use the relatively vague term "neural circuit" to refer to the brain structures that act as evaluators, leaving for the next chapter the task of describing the actual subcortical organs and their interactions. Mapping the brain areas in which these neural circuits are located was also achieved using direct stimulation to trigger specific emotional responses. Among the areas that have already been mapped are those for rage and anger, lust, and fear, all of which exist already in reptiles, and a few more that are important to mammals, like separation-anxiety and play.[90] The evidence gathered using this method established the *discrete nature* of the emotional responses in animals. In addition, by allowing the animal itself to control the stimulation, the *valence* of the emotion could be established: if the animal found the stimulation pleasurable it would continue to perform it, if displeasurable it would cease.[91] One interesting circuit found as part of this research controls an emotional response common to hunger, thirst, and other appetitive states, in which the behavioral component is a *seeking behavior*. This finding adds to the differences noted earlier between fear and hunger: the latter may not be an emotion but rather a sensation that causes an emotional response (seeking food). And similarly in the case of pain. The sensation and the emotion that pain triggers are in fact different and may be dissociated by lesions or drugs.[92]

It is important to emphasize that the values we are presently considering are *biological values* encoded in the most basic emotional responses: fear, enjoyment, sadness, anger, disgust, and surprise. There are, of course, many other emotions, some of which (shame, pride, love) are specifically social and must be treated separately.[93] The maps of neural circuits for the basic emotions resemble the ones we discussed earlier in relation to motor activities. In both cases we find a modular design and a mosaic of brain areas which, if stimulated, triggers the right pattern. In addition there are important similarities in the way the patterns are represented in the brain. As we saw, the ability to efficiently store motor patterns depends on the fact that the set of joints, muscles, and tendons targeted by a motor circuit constitute a dynamical system with its own preferred states, so that the brain can simply manipulate parameters to select and trigger one of those stable states. In the case of emotions there are also dynamical approaches that meet our conditions: the basic emotions are discrete but can enter into complex combinations, the parts retain their identity in these combinations, and the combinations have irreducible emergent properties and preferred states determined by singularities.[94] And much as the selection of a particular motor configuration is determined by an evaluation of what the immediate environment affords, the selection of a particular emotional response is determined by a process of appraisal. Imagine a small carnivore that feeds on a prey species but that is preyed on by a larger carnivore. The moment a suspicious sound is heard nearby, the animal must start appraising the situation: Is it a predator?, in which case fear should be selected; or is it a prey?, in which case curiosity and searching should be selected; or finally, is it a conspecific of the same gender affording competition for mates?, in which case anger should be selected. The three possible outcomes are all a possibility when the evaluation begins, but as it proceeds and new information indicates that one is more probable than the others the animal eventually responds with fear, curiosity, or anger. Thus, a dynamical process guided by appraisal leads to the preferred configuration that matches the circumstances.[95]

Roughly, what an emotional evaluation involves is an assessment of the relation between perceived events and the animal's current goals and needs. If there is a mismatch in this relation, if the perceived situation frustrates or otherwise impedes the attainment of the goal or the satisfaction of a need, the emotion will have a negative valence; otherwise, it will have a positive valence.[96] Because the assessment is made unconsciously, we should not imagine that the internal signs involved represent in detail how conducive the situation is to achieving the goal; how ready the body is to cope with what's coming; or what actions are required to adapt. Rather, the internal signs must be very simple, involving coarse descriptions in which only the most relevant information is highlighted, and subjected to fast and rough processing: an emotional response may be triggered before a complete analysis of the contents of the visual field is done.[97] In conditions demanding an urgent response, the phenomenal component becomes relatively unimportant: things happen much too fast for feelings to play an important role. But this should not be taken to imply that feelings are a mere epiphenomenon. To see why, let's consider the effects feelings have on learning. Innate neural circuits for emotional responses have evolved over many generations and should, therefore, be considered a product of learning by the species. But values acting as guides for action can also be learned in the lifetime of an organism. Instrumental conditioning, for example, involves the learning of new habits, using positive or negative rewards to increase or decrease the frequency of spontaneously occurring behaviors. But in order for this type of learning to take place, the rewards *must feel* pleasurable or displeasurable to the animal. In ecologically realistic situations—that is, if we rule out the use of direct stimulation to cause conditioned responses—the psychological component of the emotional response is an indispensable link in the learning process.[98]

One final source of values to guide action should be mentioned: *attention*. The act of attending, involving as it does directing or orienting oneself toward something in our experience, is one of the most basic intentional acts performed by a subject. Attention can be grabbed by an unexpected event or an unfamiliar object, as well as by intense feelings. And, indeed, one of the functions of feelings may be to give an organism an incentive to attend to its emotions.[99] Attention can also be deployed voluntarily, in which case it enters into processes of evaluation since, when not distracted or daydreaming, we tend to attend to objects that matter to us, or to situations that make a difference in our lives. Voluntary attention is both selective, allowing only a few items in the visual field to be processed fully, and a limited resource that demands justification to be used.[100] The valuations of objects and situations performed by attention are relevant at timescales that match the duration of a task, and in that sense, they complement emotional responses that operate at shorter timescales and sustained habitual behavior extending over an organism's lifetime. Attention has many other effects on phenomenal experience: we typically *notice* what we pay attention to and fail to be aware of what we are not heeding. An object could have been present in the visual field of a subject for an extended period of time, the light bouncing off its surfaces reaching his retinas and going on to be processed by his brain, and yet he may honestly report he did not see the object.[101] There is a sense, therefore, in which to be truly conscious of something we must pay attention to it. Moreover, combining the acts of attending and of foveating yields full awareness of the highest image resolution: the most vivid form of consciousness of the contents of the visual field.

Finally, the phenomenal effects of attention may throw some light on an old problem. Philosophers have often wondered about the *transparency* of the visual field, the fact that we normally see right through it, ignoring appearances and seeing only the world behind them. In the final chapter we will argue that this way of framing the problem is wrong because the visual field is not like a screen standing between us and the world, but we can ignore this for the time being since the question of why we tend to ignore the perspectival content of the field in favor of its factual content is a valid question. And the answer may be provided by attention: we do see the perspectival content, *we just don't notice it*.[102] Given that perception evolved for action, is it any wonder that we tend to focus on what's relevant for action and disregard what is not? On the other hand, human beings can engage in all kinds of activities that have no survival value whatsoever, and in those cases we can train our attention to focus on anything we want, including appearances. It could be argued that this is what realist painters do, deliberately attending to how shapes look from their point of view;

how light bounces off objects; how shadows play with each other; and how colors and textures appear to someone who stands at their location.[103] These artists are trained to direct their attention away from the factual content and to carefully examine the perspectival content, but the fact that training is required shows that in ordinary circumstances attention is focused on the world itself endowing the field with its supposed "transparency."

This concludes our analysis of the role that proprioception and interoception play in phenomenal experience. In both cases we are dealing with processes that involve the detection of many bodily properties belonging to the musculoskeletal and visceral systems, the use of somatotopic maps to organize these sensations, and the production of a response involving simple commands to select one among various preferred states for those systems. And in both cases there is a subjective component: proprioceptive information is transformed into a way of living the spatial structure of the body, of feeling its different parts as articulated with each other and as working together to achieve a goal; interoceptive information, in turn, is transformed into lived hunger, thirst, and sexual arousal, or into a primordial feeling of anger, joy, sadness, or fear. How the transformation is achieved remains, of course, unexplained. So our next task, to be performed in the following chapters, will be to tackle the thorniest of problems. We have already suggested how this will be attempted: in addition to the population of mindless cognitive agents that, working in transient coalitions, can produce the required descriptive and directive content for a proprioceptive or interoceptive response, there are others enjoying progressively higher gradations of consciousness and intentionality that can transform those signs into lived experiences of different degrees of complexity. It will prove useful, therefore, to close this chapter with a brief introduction of the strategy we will follow to think about these other agents.

Proprioception and interoception give us a simpler way to introduce the topic than visual perception does, partly because in self-perception we do not need to account for the synthesis of objects or the grasping of situations in which many objects interact. On the other hand, while there seems to be general agreement that between the basic unconscious circuitry of emotions and the subjectively lived feelings that accompany an emotional reaction, there must exist several levels of emergence, these intermediate levels are conceived as composed of signs, each level *re-representing* what the previous one represented.[104] In the approach taken in this book, however, there are no signs without a user—we entirely reject the suspect notion of a self-interpreting representation—so the levels must be made of cognitive agents that use those signs in progressively more elaborate ways. Hence we must adapt an existing re-representational account of phenomenal effects to work within a multi-agent hierarchy. Let's begin with the simplest kind of agents that can be said to already experience something: *protoselves*.[105] Cognitive agents like these have been postulated to exist in the case of interoception, operating in the periphery of emotional responses but responsible for their phenomenal content. A consequence of including this kind of agent in our account is that we cannot consider primordial feelings to be lived by the whole "subject" as a unitary center of consciousness and intentionality. Protoselves *voluptuously consume* signs of properties of the internal milieu, but their limited experiences do not need to wait until the contributions of all other agents are gathered in one central place: they can be felt immediately right where the right kind of sign consumption occurs.

The emergence of protoselves in the course of evolution may be due to the fact that the internal milieu displays a greater degree of constancy than the body as a whole: the body changes drastically as we grow from newborn babies to adults, while metabolic needs vary within a much tighter range. Continuously monitoring the internal environment may be done by mindless agents, but as we just argued, the motivational function of emotions can be greatly expanded if the organism can be made to notice those emotions as they impinge on its experience. The overall effect of many protoselves consuming internal signs as feelings yields a subjective state we may refer to as the *feeling of being alive*.[106] Agents at the next level of sophistication emerge when the experience of the body provided by protoselves is combined with biological valuations of the external world: valuing what we see according to what we deem significant gives us a sense of *ownership* of a scene. In addition, as we take advantage of the opportunities and avoid the risks that external objects afford us, we get the feeling of being the *protagonist* of our actions. We may refer to agents that can be both the protagonists and the owners of a scene as *core selves*.[107] There are other feelings that belong to this level, such as those generated by the activities of getting to know an object when we explore its appearance from different locations or when we observe how it changes as we perform causal interventions on it. These range from the feeling of uncertainty we experience when the object is unknown, to feelings of surprise as we discover new properties or capacities, to the feelings of satisfaction, and eventually familiarity, produced by a continued interaction.[108] The overall phenomenal effect may be described as the *feeling of what happens* around us. But this feeling is only about what is happening to us here and now, the temporality of core selves being limited to the present moment.

Depending on the complexity of what is presently occurring there may be more than one core self contributing to our overall phenomenal experience. As in the previous case, there is no need to wait for all the subjective components of an experience to be gathered in a single place: the feelings of ownership and agency generated at this level become part of the experience right where the consumption of the appropriate interoceptive and proprioceptive signs occur. On the other hand, those feelings and the ones generated by protoselves do form part of the experience of a more complex kind of agent, one that can live beyond the present moment to have a life shaped by memories of its past and projects for its future. This agent is referred to as the *autobiographical self*.[109] Unlike the other two, this kind of agent can report how it feels, and for this reason may be the only agent encountered in laboratory experiments in which verbal reports are taken to be the main form of evidence for the existence of a conscious state. Access to language allows this kind of agent to create a coherent narrative of its past, using causal inferences to fill explanatory gaps, as well as the means to define and express its expectations for the future. However, as part of its life story, it fabricates a unity of phenomenal experience that is not there: its unifying narrative is the way it explains to itself all the sensations and feelings in which it is immersed and the sense of agency and ownership it gets from its body in action. As philosophers, however, we should never take these reports at face value, or conclude that consciousness can be reduced to reportability.

This rough sketch of the kinds of mental agency that emerge above the basic layer of mindless cognitive agents needs to be worked out in detail, a task we will undertake in Chapter 4. The special way of consuming signs displayed by the three levels of agency must be defined in a way that goes beyond the metaphor suggested by the term "voluptuous" and specify the kinds of temporality and attention characterizing each level. But before we can do that, we need to clarify the nature of the agents populating the bottommost layer. In the previous chapter, we illustrated mindless agents using artificial neural nets. In these devices it is possible to clearly distinguish the properties and dispositions of the agent from those of the signs that it produces and consumes. We make assertions about the agent by saying that a particular neural net has a certain number of layers, or that each layer has a certain number of units. On the other hand, when we say that the iconic content of the signs a neural net uses is stored in the pattern of strengths of the connections between the input and output layers, or that the indexical content is stored in the current activation values of its hidden layer, we are asserting facts about the signs. We need to draw the same distinctions in the case of cognitive agents in the brain. Because vision is our main subject, we will start the journey at the retina and follow the parallel processing lines that depart from there and eventually reach the areas at which perceived objects can be matched to perceived affordances, using emotional values to select an appropriate course of action. Along these parallel lines we will need to specify what an agent is and what the nature of the signs being produced and consumed is. Only after we have done this will we be able to return to the question: how can a population of protoselves, core selves, and autobiographical selves explain the continuous construction of the visual field?

3 THE CONTRIBUTIONS OF THE BRAIN

The retina is filled with natural signs. It takes a slice of the impinging structured light to obtain a two-dimensional array of light intensities that is rich with information. We have already noted how wrong it is to think of structured light as providing only raw stimulation, and of the events happening in the eye as being reducible to the transduction of light into other forms of energy. Both of these physical processes are, of course, real, but they constitute only part of the story. On the other hand, it would be equally wrong to think of this information as being about the size or shape of objects, or about their color or three-dimensional orientation. The slice of structured light contains only intensities defined by their positions, wavelength, time, and whether they belong to the right or left eye. But from this flat array of light intensities the retina can extract further information about contrast, two-dimensional velocity, orientation, and (if we considered both eyes) disparity. Nevertheless, the phenomenal properties that characterize the fully formed visual field are entirely absent, since they are produced much later after many processing steps.[1]

Our first task in this chapter will be to clarify the nature of the earliest processing steps that map the retinal array into cortical structures so that natural signs like luminance discontinuities can be transformed into intentional signs standing for boundaries.[2]

So far we have used the term "map" in the way that neuroscientists use it: a physical map of the retina is a population of neurons, each of which responds preferentially to stimulation of a small patch of that sensory surface, and spatially arranged so that neurons that are next to each other are connected to patches that are next to each other. This use of the term is straightforward, since it refers to a real isomorphism between retinal receptors and the brain.

But it also obscures the distinction between a *mapping device* (or a physical map) and the iconic signs that the device produces and consumes. So let's begin by clarifying this important distinction. At the end of the previous chapter we argued that in an artificial neural net the distinction between the mapping device and the signs can be readily made. The neural net itself is a device for mapping an input activation pattern into an output activation pattern. Its properties (number of layers, number of units per layer) are what they are regardless of whether the neural net has been trained to produce any signs with iconic and indexical content. Once the training is over, and a specific pattern of strengths in the connections has been created, the mapping device can produce signs if given an appropriate input. The vehicle of those signs is the pattern of activation that the units of the hidden layer have at any one time, while the content is what this pattern stands for, as determined by the training history. Thus, in the case of neural nets the vehicle of the sign is *a state of a component* of the mapping device, which implies that this component and the sign's vehicle share certain properties: if the component has a certain number of units, for example, then the activation pattern that defines the vehicle will have an equal number of elements. This way of drawing the distinction between mapping devices and iconic signs can be applied to the brain. In this case, the population of neurons arranged topographically are the mapping device, the vehicle of the signs is the pattern of excitation that this population has at any one time, and the content is what is extracted from this pattern and delivered elsewhere to be consumed.

Let's start with a toy model of the brain in which many simplifications have been made to allow us to make a clear distinction between agents and signs. We will, first of all, ignore binocular vision and pretend that the process involves only one retina and one section of the optic array. Second, this single retinal array will be assumed to be mapped directly into the *primary visual cortex*, the part of the brain that serves as the main entry point for visual information. This cortical area is also known as the "striate cortex," "visual area number one," or "V1." In reality, there are two important relay stations between the retina and V1 (a subcortical organ and output devices in the retina itself) that prepare the signs produced for their eventual cortical consumption. The mapping device itself will be defined by its *architecture* and by the capacities to process information with which this architecture endows it.[3] Because these capacities are cognitive we will refer to V1 with the expression "mindless cognitive agent." Readers who feel uncomfortable with homuncular references can regard V1 simply as a neural mechanism for the extraction of intentional signs from the luminance and spectral properties of the retinal array. The choice of words in this case is immaterial because by hypothesis a mindless cognitive agent *must be just a mechanism*, as is required by its role of guarding against the threat of infinite regress.

Like all cortical areas, V1 has a horizontal and a vertical architecture. On the horizontal axis it has a *laminar organization*, consisting of six layers distinguished from each other by the type of neurons composing them and by the origin and destination of their connections. Layer 4 is considered to be the point of entry for retinal information.[4] On the vertical axis, V1 has a *columnar organization*, in which slabs of neurons arranged laterally next to each other traverse all six layers perpendicularly. We will represent the layers as flat arrays of neurons arranged topographically, and the columns as cylinders arranged like a regular mosaic covering the full area of the layers. In both layers and columns the composing neurons are characterized by their location and by their receptive fields. Each column can be thought as having two components: a thick column that we can refer to as a *location column*, and many thinner columns referred to as *orientation columns*.[5] The receptive fields of neurons in location columns are straightforward, connecting to a specific subpopulation of light receptors, the entire mosaic of location columns covering the whole retina. The receptive fields in the smaller orientation columns, on the other hand, have more structure. These neurons have as their preferred stimulus linear discontinuities in luminance oriented at a particular angle. The explanation for this preference is that, as we argued before, given the relative abundance of solid objects in this planet, such discontinuities tend to be caused by an object's edges (and other boundaries), which makes them natural signs of an important geometrical property. On the other hand, this early in the processing of the retinal array, we cannot assert that the intentional signs produced from these natural signs stand for edges, but rather for a simpler geometrical entity: *oriented line segments.* (We can mark this distinction by placing the suspect words inside quotation marks.) How does the structure of a receptive field explain the preferred stimuli of neurons in orientation columns? To answer this question we can divide the task these neurons must perform into two: detecting the presence of an "edge" and detecting its inclination. The first subtask requires receptive fields subdivided into a center and a surround, the center being preferentially stimulated by darkness while the surround is stimulated by lightness, or vice versa. The presence of a sudden transition from light to dark in these receptive fields causes a response, and conversely, a smooth distribution of luminance causes no response. The second subtask demands a bit more structure: the receptive fields must have an extended narrow central portion flanked by two antagonistic areas, which can vary in their inclination. Depending on the angle of inclination, neurons with these fields will have a preference for sudden changes in intensity at a given angle.[6]

Let's imagine a population of neurons composing an orientation column. They all have as preferred stimuli a luminance discontinuity at a given angle, so the full column responds to that angle. If we bundled together a full set of these orientation columns, that is, a set containing one column for every angle between 0 and 90 degrees, and placed each bundle inside a location column, we would cover the entire retina with bundles of orientation columns, each capable of detecting whether its patch of retina has a discontinuity in it, convert it into a line segment, and assign to it a particular angle. The extracted lines do not yet stand for an object's edges because the line segments may correspond to the boundaries of shadows casted on its surface, or of textural elements on that surface. Nevertheless, the whole made by the six layers and their mosaic of columns can be viewed as a device capable of consuming natural signs for boundaries in different orientations, and producing intentional signs for oriented line segments. Although the signs produced by any one bundle may be considered an index of the objective boundary that caused a discontinuity, what matters for the consumers of those signs is the entire distribution of line segments in the retina, which is an icon, because it is this icon that becomes useful for further steps in the process, such as finding lines that are both near each other and have similar orientations so they can be collected together to form a contour.

Despite being oversimplified this description of the function of V1 serves as a good illustration of what a mindless cognitive agent would be and how it should be distinguished from the signs it consumes and produces. The agent itself should be defined by its laminar and columnar architecture and by the (relatively humble) cognitive capabilities with which its architecture endows it. Layers and columns can be characterized without reference to the signs being processed at any one time by the receptive fields of their neurons and by their connectivity. The emergent properties of a column, for example, depend on the fact that its composing neurons share receptive fields and are more strongly connected to each other than they are with neurons outside. In addition, the components of V1 form a dynamic ensemble that may have its own preferred states, like a preferred interpretation of the retinal array's information.[7] As we said, the retinal input (or more exactly, thalamic input) goes mostly to layer 4 but as those long fibers make contact with cells in this layer, connections to other layers allow the information to propagate horizontally within the same layer and vertically to other layers. This is required because the number of synapses established by the thalamic fibers on layer 4 is rather limited and must be amplified by feedback from other layers so the analysis of the retinal array may be extended in time.[8] And much as the identity and individuality of the cognitive agent can be unambiguously defined, the signs that it consumes and produces can also be clearly specified. The vehicle is, as we said, the state that a component of an agent has at any one time. This implies that the vehicle of the signs will share some properties with the component that holds them. Layers have a retinotopic organization, so the pattern of excitation that constitutes the vehicle must share the same spatial arrangement. The content of the signs, in turn, is determined by how the output from V1 is consumed by other agents: they must be capable of treating this information as being about line segments with specific geometric properties, not about intensity discontinuities.[9]

We can make this toy model more realistic by removing, one at a time, the simplifying assumptions, a task we will attempt further down. But before we do that let us examine a model used in the field of machine vision to get a clearer picture of the nature of the overall task that agents in the visual cortex must perform. In the past, the project to endow machines with visual capacities was performed without making any assumptions about the world, such as the relative abundance of solid objects, and using only the contents of the retinal image together with knowledge about the kinds of objects present in a scene. The goal of such an analysis was to segment the image and determine, for instance, what is a figure and what is the background. But more recently, a new breed of models not only makes intensive use of the statistical structure of the world but also has a new goal: to recover from the retinal array *the actual geometry* of the shapes projected on it.[10] The process of recovery proceeds one step at a time, extracting line segments from an image and grouping these into one dimensional entities to represent boundaries of different types (the primal sketch); selecting and grouping those lines to create two-dimensional contours representing surfaces, while at the same time incorporating information about their distance and orientation from the observer (the $2^{1/2}$D sketch); and finally, assembling those surfaces into a solid shape using a simple stick figure to define the articulated segments and the spatial distribution of the surfaces. (the 3D model).[11] Each step demands that the iconic signs produced possess geometric properties specified with reference to different coordinates. The primal sketch is produced using the retinal "image" as its frame of reference, so it uses *retinocentric* coordinates; the $2^{1/2}$D sketch must go beyond this to capture the relation of projected surfaces to the body's location in space, so it uses *egocentric* coordinates; finally, the 3D model must be independent from any point of view, so it uses *allocentric* coordinates.[12]

The primal sketch begins with the identification of intensity discontinuities, using a mathematical function that mimics the operation of a center-surround receptive field, and that can be adapted to simulate a preference for discontinuities oriented at a given angle.[13] Changes in intensity lead to a variety of iconic signs, not just oriented line segments: there are segments that start or terminate within the receptive field (terminated segments), parallel pairs of segments (bars),segments that are doubly terminated and delimit irregular sets of points (blobs). These iconic signs have definite properties, such as length, position, width, and orientation, and can be recursively combined into larger iconic signs, using relations of proximity, similarity, and arrangement.[14] As the recursive process of selecting and grouping proceeds, new entities may begin to appear, with many segments that are similarly oriented and in close proximity to one another yielding *contours* standing for a wide variety of features of actual objects: occluding edges; internal edges caused by changes in surface orientation; shadows, creases, scratches, and textures. These features depend on the position of the observer relative to the object: an occluding edge forming part of the silhouette of an object from one point of view can be an internal edge from another point of view.[15] Thus, we cannot assign a referent to the icon of a contour unless we switch from retinocentric coordinates to egocentric coordinates.

This switch is performed in the next step, the $2^{1/2}$D sketch. This processing step must occur before the identification of an object, that is, when the visual system is dealing only with surfaces and surface layouts. Among the statistical regularities exploited at this stage is the fact that the points that belong to the silhouette of an object, viewed from a given perspective, tend to correspond to actual points in its surface, and that nearby points in its silhouette correspond to nearby points in its surface.[16] Other linear elements from the primal sketch also contain useful shape information. Blobs are formed when a surface has repetitive texture elements, and if these are regularly spaced the gradient of sizes they form contains information about distance from the viewer (texture elements getting smaller and closer spaced with increased depth) and about the angle of inclination of the surface relative to the viewer.[17] In short, this processing step involves the extraction of information about two-dimensional shape (shape as projected from a particular point of view) and the addition of information about surface depth and slant in three dimensions (forming the "half" of the $2^{1/2}$ dimensions).[18] The final step in the process, the 3D model, requires a switch from coordinates centered on the body to coordinates centered on external objects, a transformation that can be performed by identifying *axes* in those objects. Elongated objects, for example, have an easy-to-grasp axis running along their length; an object that is bilaterally symmetric has an axis defined by its mirror symmetry; and rotating objects can be assigned the axis around which they rotate. There are, of course, many shapes that allow for more than one axis, as well as irregular shapes, like a crumpled piece of paper, that have arbitrary axes.[19] More complex objects, like animal bodies, can be broken into articulated segments, each representing a body part bounded by joints, with a different axis assigned to each segment. Once the different axes have been determined, a simple three-dimensional model can be built by replacing each axis with a thin, cylindrical icon, to form a stick figure that captures the volumetric arrangement of surfaces in the object.[20] These voluminous iconic signs are far from sufficient to generate the fully rendered objects of phenomenal experience, but they suffice to perform unconscious tasks like object recognition, or matching an object's shape to that of the hand that is trying to grasp it.[21]

Let's summarize the first part of our argument. We can finally replace artificial neural networks as our main example of a mindless cognitive agent with something more realistic, while at the same time benefiting from the lessons learned from those devices regarding the dissection between agents and signs. In the cortex, an agent is defined by its vertical and horizontal architecture and the cognitive capacities that emerge from this architecture. The vehicle of a sign is typically a state of the component of an agent that holds it in place, so it is easy to confuse the two, as when we speak of a layer of V1 as a map implying that it is a representation (a self-interpreting one, perhaps). But this error can be avoided by a more careful analysis. The content of the sign, in turn, is defined by the interaction between producer and consumer agents, an interaction shaped by coevolution, so we will need to wait until we connect V1 to other visual agents to clarify its nature. The task the visual system must accomplish, recovering an object's geometry from its retinal projection, on the other hand, can be specified without going deeper into the brain. We can derive some insights from machine vision models that construct signs for solid objects recursively, building contours from lines, surfaces from contours, and objects from surfaces, each set of entities having its own emergent geometrical properties. Our next task will be to remove the simplifications in the toy model, and to try to determine what parts of the machine vision model can be assigned a neural realization.

The first simplifying assumption was modeling the retina as a device to obtain a section of the optic array, the way in which an ordinary camera projects a slice of structured light on its back plane. It is true that the eye resembles an optical device, with a lens and a set of muscles that can change its curvature allowing focusing at different distances. But that is where the analogy ends. In what follows it is important to think of the retina as capturing not pictures resembling objects but an array of intensities isomorphic with the optical phenomena in the section. The array itself consists of the activation pattern in a population of photoreceptors of two types: one type that works better with dim light (rods) and numbers around 120 million, while the other functions best with bright light (cones) and numbers around 6 million.[22] The second simplification was to assume that the retina sends to the primary visual cortex the raw array of intensities. In reality, it performs a preliminary analysis of its content using special output devices known as *retinal ganglia*. The receptive fields of retinal ganglia have the same center-surround structure we saw earlier but these are not used to detect boundaries but to encode *differences or contrasts* as such, the ganglia responding strongly to differences in luminance in the patch of retina to which they are connected, and weakly if the patch has a uniform luminance. These output devices can encode the achromatic component of light: if their center is stimulated but their surround is not, they encode "white"; if their surround is stimulated but their center is not, the result is "black"; and if both are stimulated the result can be labeled "gray." In addition to this achromatic component, light has a chromatic one, so there are retinal ganglia that can encode *opponent pairs*: "red" and "green," "yellow" and "blue."[23] The quotation marks are there to indicate that these are just names given to the outputs, since colors do not exist at this processing stage.

The third simplifying assumption was that the retina is directly connected to the cortex. But the intentional signs produced by retinal ganglia are consumed by a subcortical structure called the *thalamus*, and more specifically, by a component of it referred to as the *Lateral Geniculate Nucleus* (or *LGN* for short). Like V1, the LGN has six layers composed of neurons with a center-surround receptive field, which in this case are used to transform discontinuities in intensity into signs for line segments. This makes the LGN the first brain area where the most basic geometrical signs are produced. But the input to the LGN is more complex than this, because it also receives information about color, motion, and depth, so its different layers must be composed of neurons specializing to process these separate streams.[24] If the input comes from retinal ganglion cells with small receptive fields that are connected preferentially to the fovea, for example, it will go to those LGN layers that require high-spatial resolution to specify shape and color. But if the input comes from ganglion cells that have larger receptive fields sensitive to the direction of motion, it will be received by LGN layers in which movement and depth are processed. What this means for our toy model is that layer 4 of V1 gets its thalamic input already processed along these different dimensions so it must possess neurons with receptive fields that are structured accordingly.[25] The final simplification concerns the flow of information, which we assumed moved in a forward direction (from retina to V1) but that in reality also flows in the opposite direction. We could refer to the backward direction as "feedback," but this would invite confusion because the term "feedback" is used to refer to the transmission of error information from sensor to actuator through a single channel. For this reason a separate term has been introduced to refer to the backward connections: *reentrance*. Unlike feedback, reentrant connections are massive, reciprocal, fully parallel, and convey multiple kinds of information.[26] A good illustration are the reentrant links that project to V1 from extra-striate areas: as V1 performs the extraction of information useful to represent boundaries, it gets information from later stages of processing—about occlusion relations between surfaces, for example—that it can use to disambiguate a particular interpretation of its thalamic input.[27]

Even with all the simplifying assumptions removed we are still dealing with a model but hopefully not a toy. The first stage of visual processing can now be pictured as involving three separate cognitive agents consuming and producing signs about distinct properties (shape, color, motion). The agents process these signs in successive steps, each more sophisticated than the previous one, but they are also wired to receive useful information in the opposite direction. Let's follow the flow of information forward (keeping in mind that reentrance is ubiquitous at all stages) starting with the output from V1. As is well known the brain displays a striking specialization following a left-right axis, a specialization best displayed by the two cerebral hemispheres and their linguistic and visuospatial functions. But an even more striking example of specialized processing follows a *top-bottom axis*. Visual processing along the top (or *ventral*) stream focuses on information required for the identification of objects, such as information about their shape or color. Visual processing along the bottom (or *dorsal*) stream deals with information about the spatial relations required to interact with the object, such as its position and state of motion. Evidence for the existence of these two streams comes from brain lesions that, depending on whether they affect areas above or below the axis, impair only object recognition or visually guided activity, but not both, showing that these two functions can be dissociated.[28] Despite their functional separability, the two streams interact at several points, their interactions depending on the nature of the task being performed.[29]

The extra-striate visual areas that continue the cortical processing begun by V1 and that share its retinotopic architecture are labeled by increasing digits: V2, V3, V4, V5, and V6.[30] As we ascend through these processing centers, receptive fields get wider, mapped to larger areas of the retina, while their preferred stimuli become more complex. The three channels in

V1 (shape, color, motion) are mostly preserved in V2.[31] In the case of shape information, while the preferred stimulus of many V1 cells are line segments oriented at a particular angle, the preferred stimulus of many V2 cells are lines the end points of which are located within the receptive field, what the computer vision model called "terminated segments." This allows V2 neurons to produce signs for corners (lines terminating at one end) as well as curves (lines terminating at both ends).[32] From V2, the two processing pathways begin to diverge. The ventral stream proceeds to areas V3 and V4. V4 is involved in the analysis of color, while V3 performs further analysis of geometric properties, projecting forward to areas that specialize on specific classes of shapes. An example is the fusiform gyrus that contains neurons with receptive fields attuned to human faces.[33] The dorsal stream, in turn, moves forward to V5 and V6. Both V5 and V6 process motion information, but while V5 represents the central area of retinal image, magnifying the fovea, and specializes in object motion, V6 represents the entire retinal array including the periphery, and processes signs of self-motion.[34] V6, for example, projects to the medial superior temporal area in which receptive fields are attuned to planar, radial, and circular motion patterns, the kind of content useful to process the information contained in optic flow.[35] If the analysis of V1 performed earlier is correct, that is, if we can identify it as a mindless cognitive agent by its architecture, then cortical areas V2–V6 can also be considered agents of this kind since they share the same laminar and columnar structure. A full specification of these agents would require a detailed analysis of the function of their columns and layers, a task we will not undertake here.

But assuming this can be done and that we can feel confident that we are dealing with actual cognitive agents, how should we think about the way their separate activities are *coordinated*? If we imagine a subject currently examining an object with the goal of interacting with it, how are the object's identity and the activities that it can afford be represented if its different properties (shape, color, state of motion) are processed by agents located in different parts of the cortex?

The properties and dispositions of neurons involved in collective coordination are different than those we have discussed so far, and like the other characteristics, they must be accounted for both dynamically and causally. The dynamical account states that the state space of a neuron is structured by a cyclic singularity referred to as a *limit cycle or periodic attractor.* This singularity endows the neuron with a tendency to oscillate; a tendency to return to the same stable oscillation after a shock; and, more importantly for our present purposes, a tendency to *synchronize* with the periodic behavior of other neurons.[36] The causal part of the explanation describes the mechanism through which these dispositions are actualized. It models neurons as an instance of a class of oscillators known as *relaxation oscillators*, the periodic behavior of which is composed of three distinct phases: the accumulation phase, when the neuron slowly becomes electrically charged; the active phase, when the neuron suddenly discharges; and the refractory phase, during which the neuron relaxes and gets ready to start recharging again.[37] The active and refractory phases are resistant to perturbations, which means that an interaction between neurons that occurs during these phases does not affect their oscillations.[38] But if an interaction takes place during the accumulation phase a neuron's oscillations can be affected by those of other neurons and brought into synch.[39] This involves a causal process through which the different phases of a neurons' cycle start to match those of other neurons, up to the point at which the active phases of an entire population coincide and the neurons' fire simultaneously.[40]

Let's illustrate the effect of synchronization with an example of coordination *within* a cortical area engaged in the task of grouping together linear segments with similar orientations and in nearby locations. In V1, for example, the columns are linked together by long lateral excitatory connections allowing neurons in distant columns to oscillate in synchrony if they have overlapping receptive fields and similar preferred stimuli. Roughly, if separate populations of neurons oscillate in synch it is likely that they represent the contour of a single surface, while if they are desynchronized they will tend to represent contours belonging to different surfaces.[41] A similar synchronization of activity operates *between* cortical areas, coordinating activity in the retinotopic maps of all six agents (V1–V6). If neurons with overlapping receptive fields but belonging to different maps are active at the same time the probability that they were activated by the same object increases. And conversely, if two active subpopulations are firing in a desynchronized way, odds are that they were activated by a different object. Because each of the six cortical areas produces signs for different properties, their co-activation can bring these properties together so they can be *bound* to represent one and the same object.[42] In Chapter 1 we argued that cognitive agents form transient coalitions for particular tasks, but we did not specify any recruitment mechanism through which a coalition may form. Neuroscientists think they have found one in synchronized oscillations.[43]

The synchronization of distributed agent activities happens spontaneously most of the time during the performance of automatic tasks. But it can also be *affected voluntarily* by attention. As we saw, the processing of the retinal array may be thought as a progression of stages, each one creating a whole out of parts: in the case of geometrical shape, the process starts with directed line segments, joins them into contours, finally generating surfaces and objects. For this reason the process is labeled "hierarchical" despite the fact that the existence of massive reentrant connections makes this term highly inadequate. In this hierarchy we can distinguish two directions: bottom-up, when going from the retina to later stages in the progressive synthesis, and top-down to refer to the action of later stages on previous ones. Voluntary attention is a paradigmatic top-down effect, a mental act performed by the subject (the highest level in the hierarchy) that can cascade down the hierarchy affecting even the earliest stages of processing. There is convincing evidence, for example, that neurons in V1 that have receptive fields corresponding to the place in the visual field to which the subject is presently attending magnify the intensity of their response. And the strength of the effect increases the higher the location of the cortical area in the hierarchy.[44] The mechanism behind this form of downward causality is based on an effect called *gain modulation*. The effect of increasing or decreasing the gain or amplitude in a neural population is to change its sensitivity or its tendency to synchronize, leaving its preferred stimulus unchanged. Sensitivity is measured by firing rates, higher rates magnifying the impact of the selected neurons on other populations, while a greater tendency to synchronize can bias the competition among rival coalitions.[45] For example, the receptive fields of neurons participating in later processing stages cover larger areas of the retina with enough room to include two or more perceived objects. These neurons can, therefore, be a target for recruitment by two or more coalitions. In this case, the role of attention may be to pick the winner of the competition.[46] Combining all these factors, the overall effect of attention is to increase the coding quality of the signs that stand for the attended object; decrease the noise in the signal transmitting those signs, so that the attended object produces the same neural response with less variance; and modify the responses of populations higher in the hierarchy, since they are more likely to fire synchronously if their inputs arrive simultaneously.[47]

In addition to its contribution to the coordination of distributed processing, voluntary attention is required in our model for another reason: it provides the indexical component of the hybrid signs used by cognitive agents, signs that so far in this chapter have been treated as possessing only iconic content. The downward effects of attention keep the brain informed about the relative importance of the different areas in a retinotopic map, indicating to it what the subject considers to be the most significant portion of the visual field at any one moment. This other (mostly hypothetical) role can be made clearer by describing the indexical role played by acts of attention. One task that requires paying attention is tracking the same object as it moves in the visual field. The ability to track objects can be explained in several ways. One explanation assumes that in order to identify an object and then to re-identify it as it changes location, we need a *description* of its properties. The object is taken to be a particular member of a general category, a token of a type, so it is necessary to have concepts to designate the properties that tokens must have to be members of that type: "bounded," "three dimensional" "colored," or "moves as a whole."[48] A different explanation rejects the need for general concepts, arguing that an object may be singled out *as a token*, before it is identified as a member of a type, as when one attends to a part of the visual field and asks "What is that?"[49] In this second account, attention acts like the nonlinguistic equivalent of indexical terms like "this," "that," "here," and "there." Like these demonstrative words, attention demands the presence of its referent, and like them it is limited in its referential capacity to a few items at a time: laboratory data indicate that we can track a maximum of four or five objects simultaneously. One way of expressing this is to say that when we use attention to select what objects to track we are tagging them with *visual indices*.[50] But as we just saw, selecting and privileging one or more parts of the visual field has effects that cascade down the processing hierarchy, also tagging the relevant portions of retinotopic maps. This downward effect, we can speculate, creates the indexical content of these maps. When we introduced the idea of a hybrid sign we used as an example a modern GPS map, with its iconic geographical information and its indexical dot showing the current position of the user in the map. In the brain, the gain modulated area of a map would play the role of the indexical dot, not with the content "You are here" but rather "Your attention is here."

To recapitulate the second part of the argument, having characterized V1 as a cognitive agent using its laminar and columnar architecture, we extended this characterization to various other agents: V2–V6. We then sketched how these agents, acting as a team, could perform some of the steps in the synthesis of phenomenal objects outlined in the machine vision model described earlier. The fact that V1–V6 are spatially distributed and that each specializes on different properties requires us to think about the way they must continuously coordinate their activities without the need for a central coordinator.[51] Different coalitions between agents, or more exactly *between parts of agents*, must rapidly form and dissolve as the contents that the world projects into the retina change, as when subpopulations in different retinotopic maps form a coalition in order to stand for the same object. Explaining how this is achieved must be done dynamically and causally. The dynamic part consists in showing that neurons have a tendency to oscillate with a stable frequency, a tendency explained by their possession of a cyclic singularity (a periodic attractor), and by the fact that dynamic oscillators can couple to each other spontaneously to act like a single oscillator (entrainment). The causal part takes into account the different phases of a neuron's cycle (charge, fire, wait) and its different capacities to be affected by other neurons, nudging it to oscillate a bit faster or slower until a whole population synchronizes. Finally, we discussed how this mechanism can be affected voluntarily by attention from the very top (the subject) and moving all the way down to V1, acting as an additional source of synchronization for the distributed processing. We also speculated that attention supplies the agents in the processing hierarchy with indexical information about what the subject is selecting and valuing here and now, such as the object he is currently tracking or, more generally, the object he is presently interacting with.

The next step in the construction of our model will be to connect perception to action. This will require thinking about the content of the ventral and dorsal streams from the point of view of an embodied subject. The history of the names given to these two processing pathways testifies to the need for this. They were originally named the "what" and "where" streams, one concerned with identity, the other with location and motion, considered as properties of objects. Later on, however, the "where" stream was relabeled "how" in recognition of the fact that the information in the dorsal stream is not so much about the spatial properties of objects, such as their absolute location, but about the spatial relations between objects and visually guided actions by the body. In other words, agents along the dorsal stream produce signs consumable by other agents as informing them how to act. Some argue that even agents along the ventral stream must be concerned with motor properties because their signs must be usable to identify not only types of objects but also types of action.[52] Or to put this differently, an object must be identified not only by its properties but also by its dispositions, the signs produced helping to match an object's affordances to the body's own skills.[53] The dorsal stream, in turn, must process information not only about the spatial relation body-world but, once an actual engagement begins, also the information required to control an ongoing activity. So both streams must process sensory-motor information, the ventral stream addressing what an object is and what can be done with it, while the dorsal stream specifies where it is and how to act on it.[54]

In order to follow these two streams beyond areas V1–V6, we need to get a better view of the cortex as a whole. Areas V1–V6 are located in one of the four lobes that make up the cortex: the occipital lobe. But there are three more lobes—named *parietal*, *temporal*, and *frontal*—populated by their own cognitive agents. Part of what is produced in the occipital lobe travels along the dorsal stream to the parietal lobe, and from there to the motor areas of the frontal lobe, while the other part travels along the ventral stream and reaches the lower half of the temporal lobe. The topographically organized *somatotopic maps* we described in the previous chapter are housed in the parietal and frontal lobes. These physical maps, as we said, contain neurons arranged in such a way that those responding to touch in the index fingers are adjacent to those responding to the middle finger which in turn are next to those for the ring finger.[55] The skin of the finger tips has a higher resolution than the skin in other parts of the body, for the same reason that the retinal fovea does: receptors on the finger tips are more numerous and have smaller receptive fields. Other body parts also have sensory receptors in the skin that covers them, organized using somatotopic maps, and connected through the spinal cord to both thalamic and cortical areas.[56] The information from these proprioceptive receptors, as well as those located in muscles, is passed to the cortical areas involved in the planning and implementation of actions.

When we first discussed the role played by maps of the body, we said that the planning of actions involved two areas working together in a loop—one area using information about the affordances of objects, the other area containing a repertoire of goal-directed actions—and that an unconscious process of selecting the action that matches an affordance was performed in this loop. We can now name these cortical areas, one located in the parietal lobe, labeled the "anterior intraparietal area," or *AIP*, the other located in the premotor areas of the frontal lobe, and known as *F5*.[57] Planning an action may involve integrating signs from the ventral and dorsal streams: information about the distance and location of the target object is needed for reaching, while information about its size and shape is needed for grasping, for example.[58] We used as an illustration a coffee mug, which may alternatively be grasped by its handle, by the rim along its top, or by its cylindrical body, depending on the task: drinking from it, washing it, or storing it in the kitchen's cabinet.[59] Many objects afford actions that can be performed in various ways, so the signs standing for different options must all be produced by AIP. Then the set of potential actions is passed to F5 for selection, where the kind of information used may depend on the nature of the task of which the action is a part. Thus, a grasping action in the context of a task in which the target object is always visible uses only information from the dorsal stream, while the same action with a delay between the presentation of an object and its actual grasping needs signs from both dorsal and ventral streams.[60]

F5 stores information about action types, such as precision grip, finger prehension, whole hand prehension; about parameters for that action, such as grasp aperture; as well as about stages in the performance of the action: set, extension, flexion, hold, release.[61] Excitatory connections among populations of cells in F5 that represent the same action type and action stage lead to mutual co-activation, while discordant populations inhibit one another. This mechanism deselects some of the action types from the set sent by AIP and information about the selection is sent back to that area. As excitation travels through this loop, a larger number of neurons from populations in both AIP and F5 are recruited until most of the cells that belong to a single action type have become active.[62] F5 also projects to an area in the parietal lobe called the "secondary somatosensory cortex," or *SII* for short. SII may be said to represent tactile expectations allowing it to detect any discrepancy between the selected grasp and what takes place once contact with the object is achieved. If a mismatch is detected the loop between F5 and AIP may be reactivated to program a new action.[63] A large-scale simulation of action planning uses AIP and F5 to represent the dorsal stream, and adds two temporal lobe areas, known as the "inferior temporal gyrus" and the "superior temporal sulcus," or *IT* and *STS* for short, to represent the ventral stream.[64] The simulation focuses on action planning, so motor execution is highly simplified, represented by a single area of the primary motor cortex, F1, while the final output (a grasping action) is reduced to the motor action of the fifteen joints of the hand.[65] The results were very encouraging: they qualitatively reproduced measurements of the activity of neuronal populations during the execution of different tasks and confirmed the central role played by the loop AIP-F5 in the cooperative computation of action plans.

As before, this is a highly schematic description but one that captures some of the most important ideas. Making the model more realistic involves, among other things, adding the contributions of the agents producing the signs consumed in the AIP-F5 loop, and those of the agents that consume its products. Among the former is IT, the large area of the temporal lobe we just referred to. IT is not really a single cognitive agent but a team of agents all of which have very large receptive fields and specialize in the recognition of objects of different categories (faces, tools, scenes).[66] The agents in IT are located at the end of the ventral stream, so it is considered to be the place where the progressive geometrical construction of object signs ends. Unlike area V4, which supplies some of IT's inputs, the latter is not topographically organized but retains a distinction between neurons mapped to the fovea and those mapped to the visual periphery. The objects that constitute IT neurons' preferred stimuli can trigger a response even if viewed from different angles, so the iconic signs used by IT agents are less reliant on how objects are projected into the retina.[67] And complex objects are processed hierarchically: faces may first be analyzed into features (mouth, nose, eyes), then into configurations of features, and finally into faces that belong to a given individual. But, as with all processing "hierarchies," the massive reentrant connections going from IT to lower areas prevent us from thinking about its workings as proceeding in a strictly forward direction.[68] The consumers of the signs produced in the AIP-F5 loop, in turn, are located in the primary motor cortex, where muscles that are adjacent to one another are mapped into nearby neuronal populations.[69] The primary motor cortex has a direct route to the spinal cord via corticospinal fibers with connections that can be as long as 1 meter.[70] In the previous chapter we argued that the commands that travel through these long fibers select preferred configurations of joints, muscles, and tendons. Evidence for this comes from experiments involving direct stimulation of interneuronal regions in the spinal cord, proving the existence of a limited number of circuits that, when activated, produce balanced contractions in *groups* of muscles.[71] The relative autonomy of these circuits is shown by the fact that they retain their capabilities even if the corticospinal fibers are severed. On the other hand, involvement of cortical areas is necessary to stitch together several of these building blocks into a coherent action sequence.[72]

Let's illustrate the interactions that lead to the implementation of an action plan with a relatively simple component of a limb's movement, its *direction*. As in other cortical structures, motor neurons are organized into columns with similar preferred stimuli, which in this case means analogous directional tuning. The response of cells in a given column is a function of the difference between the actual and the intended direction of a movement: maximal activity results if the two directions match, minimal activity results if the two directions do not. Measuring the activity in many of these columns and combining it together yields what is referred to as a *population vector*.[73] The representational role played by this vector is vividly illustrated by a laboratory experiment. Rats are trained to press a lever to obtain a reward but the lever is connected to the food dispensing mechanism through a programmable robotic arm. After training, careful measurements of the rat's motor neurons are made and the population vector associated with lever pressing is calculated. Then, the link between the lever and the robotic arm is disconnected, while the signal from the former to the latter is replaced by the population vector. For a while, the animal continues to press the lever as it was conditioned to do, but after a while it stops pressing it, as if it realized that simply *intending to perform* the action can move the robotic arm and yield the reward.[74] With monkeys more complex actions (such as reaching and grasping) have been successfully subjected to this procedure, the monkeys literally controlling the robotic arm with their minds, raising the hope that population vectors may one day be used to help human beings paralyzed by spinal injuries.[75]

This is a striking demonstration that internal signs standing for the direction of a muscular action are produced and consumed in the primary motor cortex. But this cortical area is more than a map of muscles, with one column per muscle, and the preferred stimuli of its neurons goes beyond simple properties like direction. The first piece of evidence for this came from experiments using direct stimulation. Electrically activating a motor neuron caused a limb to follow not just a specific direction but to adopt the *final state of a specific posture*. Regardless of its initial position, the limb would move to its goal position, as if the latter was its preferred stimulus, movement direction being only one component.[76] Measuring the activity of motor neurons, while the animal engages in the full range of activities it does in the wild, confirmed this result: motor neurons were most active during movements that terminated near or at the final position characteristic of a posture. How are different body parts represented in these areas? The hand can participate in many postures so it may have to be represented several times in areas that overlap those for the mouth, for the activity of feeding, or overlap those for the arm for the action of reaching and grasping.[77] Moreover, the acquisition of new manual skills can modify how and where signs for the hand are stored, as the motor cortex map is changed to reflect the enhanced movement repertoire of the organism.

This has consequences for the way we imagine the layout of motor maps: different parts of the body cannot be discretely represented in separate areas, as in the case of the original body maps, because in order to represent different postures sharing some joints and muscles, a map must have fuzzy borders, overlapping areas, and gradients. And a similar point applies to the areas that represent objects, like the area IT mentioned earlier. When the retinal array is mapped into a layer of V1, for example, the mapping is between a pair of two-dimensional spaces. But an object represented in IT is characterized by many properties, each requiring one dimension to be represented, so the mapping is between a many-dimensional space and a two-dimensional layer. This is bound to produce many discontinuities: if we imagine each column as standing for a different property of an object, the full iconic sign would be formed within many distant columns synchronized by lateral connections.[78] This complication may require revising the idea that iconic signs require a strict isomorphism (a mapping one-to-one) and extending their definition to include more complex homeomorphisms, since the vehicles of the icons would have to share the discontinuous and overlapping architecture of the motor and object physical maps.

To finish this section let us examine the question of how retinotopic maps are used in conjunction with somatotopic and motor ones to plan and execute actions. We saw earlier that machine vision models of the piecemeal geometric construction of signs for solid objects required changes between different coordinate systems: retinocentric, egocentric, and allocentric. In a similar way, combining the content of visual, cutaneous, and muscular maps involves the performance of coordinate transformations. The location of contents in the retinal array, as well as those in retinotopic maps, can be fixed using eye-centered coordinates. But in order to link this two-dimensional space to the objective three-dimensional space in which the body must act, a sequence of transformations must be performed. First, a set of *head-centered coordinates* must be generated. This can be done by combining the visual information with proprioceptive information about the position of the eyes in their own sockets, that is, information about the direction of the gaze. Second, a set of *body-centered coordinates* is obtained by combining iconic signs using the head as a frame of reference with proprioceptive information about the position of the head as it rotates around the neck.[79] Finally, the iconic signs obtained from this transformation are combined with information from other sources depending on the action to be performed, to yield object-centered coordinates. Where does this information come from? One possible source are special neurons, the preferred stimuli for which are spatial locations viewed from a variety of angles, as well as the objects located at those places. The signs produced by these neurons may not be, strictly speaking, allocentric (the object in place as viewed from nowhere) but by integrating several points of view they do represent the object in a way that is less dependent on where the body is at any particular time. Neurons like these can be found in the hippocampus, and will be discussed in more detail in the following chapter.[80]

These coordinate transformations involve combining information from different sources. Are there specific neural mechanisms that explain how these combinations are performed? One hypothesis proposes that gain modulation, discussed earlier in connection with attention, could also be used more generally to combine any two maps, including maps for different sensory modalities and those using different coordinates. When gain or amplitude is not evenly distributed in a given population the overall pattern is referred to as a *gain field*, a field that can be used to combine contents: the direction of the gaze, for example, can be converted into a gain field which, when applied to a retinotopic map, can produce a new map the content of which is less dependent on retinal coordinates.[81] And similarly for the next step in the process in which a gain field generated from proprioceptive information about the position of the neck or from information about head rotation and linear acceleration produced by the inner ear's vestibular system are combined with the product of the previous step. More generally, the formula for this type of mechanism can be expressed like this: if the receptive fields of neurons tuned to X are gain modulated by Y the result is an iconic sign for X+Y.[82] Early processing steps, those performed by the LGN and V1, do not seem to use gain fields, and are, therefore, thought to operate in retinal coordinates. But two areas in the parietal lobe (areas 7a and LIP) do have gain fields, and are, therefore, suspected to be the place where the transformation from retinal to head coordinates takes place, and in coalition with other areas, may also be involved in the transformation to body-centered coordinates.[83] Finally, we must complement this forward moving process with the contributions from connections going in the opposite direction. Reentrant connections can organize the workings of a distributed mechanism in which agents producing and consuming iconic signs in different coordinate systems can coexist and be recruited as needed depending on the task.[84]

To summarize, we added a number of new mindless cognitive agents to those we had already discussed to sketch the relations between perception and action. Our discussion centered around a pair of cortical areas working as a loop (AIP and F5) in which, roughly, one area represents affordances and the other the matching effectivities. Because one and the same object may afford different actions and require different skillful responses, many passes through this loop may be needed to slowly converge on the right combination. We also gave a rough description of the areas that produce and consume the signs used by the AIP-F5 loop: the inferior temporal gyrus (IT), the possible end point of the ventral stream where signs for objects are created, and the primary motor cortex, where signs for planned actions are converted into signs for postures and other complex motions. Both of these areas include physical maps that are more complex than either the retinotopic maps used in the visual cortex or the somatotopic maps used to organize proprioceptive information. Because the vehicles of the icons used in these areas must match the architecture of the physical maps, we may have to extend our definition of an iconic sign to include mappings that are not strictly isomorphic. Finally, we gave an equally rough description of the operations required to combine the content of all these maps, and to perform transformations between retinal coordinates, body coordinates, and object coordinates.

Let's move on to consider the role that the biological value system we discussed in the previous chapter plays in this process. If we consider that the agents we have described must enter into different transient coalitions to meet the needs of different tasks, the question arises as to how, when two or more coalitions compete, their conflict is resolved. The alternatives must be rapidly evaluated and the appropriate coalition selected using values reflecting basic homeostatic needs, basic emotions caused by those needs, or more complex emotional responses. This biological value system is implemented using over forty chemical substances in different combinations. Originally, the hope existed that these substances could be classified by the function of the areas where they are typically found, so that a clear distinction could be made, for example, between chemicals in the brain and the hormones involved in the regulation of the internal environment. But more recent research has revealed that brain chemicals can be found elsewhere in the body, while gut and sex hormones are found in the brain. If we keep in mind that one and the same substance is capable of playing different roles we can classify these chemicals into three different categories. A *neurotransmitter* is defined as a substance released by the nerve ending of a neuron that affects nearby neurons.[85] A *neuromodulator*, on the other hand, is a substance released by a neuron that can affect many faraway neurons, by altering the strength with which information travels between them, or the amount of neurotransmitters that they can produce. Whereas a neurotransmitter is directed from the presynaptic neuron to the postsynaptic neuron, a neuromodulator is literally broadcasted to an entire population of neurons. Finally, there is a third category of substances, *neurohormones*, that are produced in special endocrine cells and released into the bloodstream.[86]

The cortical structures we have examined are not directly connected to the visceral sources of valuation. Rather, there are several relays, each involving its own distributed mechanisms, conveying both descriptive content about the state of the body as well as directive content about the emotional response to those states. One "relay station" is made of three appendages, the first of which is an organ known as the *basal ganglia*, or *BG*, the outputs of which project, via the thalamus, to each of the prefrontal cortex areas underlying the distributed mechanism of attention.[87] The neuromodulators that act as one of BG's inputs carry information about the saliency of object and action representations, the probability of receiving a reward after an action, and the degree of expectancy of such reinforcement.[88] BG has three functions: to participate in evaluation processes, to help in the planning of actions by selecting one among several alternatives, and to aid the process of habit acquisition through the use of rewards.[89] As was the case with IT, BG may be not just one agent but a team of agents. And similarly for the second component of the first "relay station," the *cerebellum*. This organ has long been identified with the finer control of limbs, gait, posture, and equilibrium, but more recent studies have shown its involvement in emotional modulation. In particular, the cerebellum has somatotopic maps which it uses to organize its motor inputs, as well as various neuromodulating links from areas associated with affective valuation, allowing it to correlate sensorimotor acts with mood states.[90] The main function of the third appendage, the *hippocampus*, is the creation of spatial maps of the environment of an organism. As a veridical spatial map is built, affective values are attached to both the locations and the objects represented in the map.[91] Like the cerebellum and the basal ganglia, the hippocampus is chemically connected to areas dedicated to the modulation of emotion, giving it the capability to control some affective aspects of exploratory behavior, such as the degree of curiosity or the attitude toward novel objects or places.[92]

The type of connectivity between the first "relay station" and the cortex is different from that of the thalamocortical system itself. Because of the ubiquity of reentrant connections the latter resembles a dense *mesh* in which a change in one place is felt rapidly everywhere else. The three appendages just described, on the other hand, are connected to the cortex through many long loops resembling a set of parallel *chains*. These chains start in the cortical areas involved in the planning of action, make multiple synapses within the appendages, and then loop back to the cortex via the thalamus. Information travels in these loops unidirectionally, with limited interactions between the content of the different loops, a connectivity well suited for the execution of visuomotor routines that must be functionally isolated from each other. On the other hand, these appendages are not directly connected to visceral sources of biological values, so our model needs a second "relay station" formed by the *brain stem*, *the hypothalamus*, and *the amygdala*. These organs, each composed of a team of agents, display yet another type of connectivity, one that resembles that of a *fan*, with its origin centered in those organs and its endings forming a divergent set of fibers reaching deep into most thalamocortical and subcortical areas.[93] This second relay station plays a dual role: to control chemical imbalances in the viscera and to control arousal in the brain. In the case of the hypothalamus, the control of arousal plays both a motivational and a reinforcement role. Direct stimulation of this structure, for example, can produce rewarding and aversive effects that are real enough to be used in instrumental conditioning.[94] But from the point of view of the neural basis of the biological value system, the amygdala is probably the most important component.[95]

Appraisals by the amygdala take place at two different speeds depending on the urgency of the situation. Perceived facial expressions of fear, for example, can be evaluated very rapidly using the output of *coarse* perceptual processing, that is, without having to wait for a complex icon of the perceived face to be produced.[96] Unlike this bottom-up and largely unconscious evaluation, there is a slower route that uses the products of *detailed* perceptual processing from both ventral and dorsal streams, together with inputs from structures involved in the planning of action, as well as from areas in the prefrontal cortex exerting top-down modulatory effects, to yield more contextualized evaluations.[97] These two routes place the amygdala at a central position in a circuit controlling motivational states, although this control requires the collaboration of several cerebral structures, some located in the same "relay station" (the hypothalamus), others in the previous one (the hippocampus). The entire circuit is capable of assessing the risks and opportunities afforded by the target objects of goal-directed behavior, of using memories of the outcomes of previous engagements with similar objects to rate the plausibility of success, and of ranking different internal needs by their relative importance.[98] Estimates of biological value along these separate dimensions are needed to account for even relatively simple forms of learning, like the conditioning of habits, because an animal may experience something as a reward or a punishment depending on the internal state it is in at the time, as well as on its previous experiences.[99]

The amygdala has been traditionally linked with certain feelings, such as fear. But as we saw in the previous chapter, emotions (or more exactly, emotional responses) are a compound of endocrinal, neural, behavioral, and psychological components. The orchestration of these heterogeneous parts into a recurring and patterned response could be accounted for, as we argued, if the ensemble forms a dynamical system that can be controlled parametrically. In other words, we argued that interoception is like proprioception, with its recurring configurations of joints, muscles, and tendons that can be selected by manipulating parameters, rather than by issuing detailed commands. But if this parallel is correct, then what plays the role that the visual and motor cortices play in the case of normal perception and action? The answer is two cortical areas referred to as the *insular* and *cingulate cortices*. Both are multifunctional centers receiving inputs from many different parts of the brain, but here we will focus on their interoceptive function, both being reciprocally connected with all the organs that make up the two "relay stations" we just discussed. The insular cortex has layers organized into somatotopic maps of visceral and homeostatic receptors, their iconic content representing the state of internal environment at any one time. This topographically organized content is thought to play an important role in the generation of feelings, or more generally, of the phenomenal component of the response.[100] The motor component, such as facial expressions and vocalizations, is controlled by the anterior cingulate cortex. For example, lesions to this cortical area can prevent spontaneous smiling, that is, smiling that is not voluntarily produced.[101] In addition, both the insular and cingulate cortices are involved in more general evaluative functions, such as the estimation of the risks of alternative responses and the comparison of the outcomes of bodily action with its original goal to perform error detection.[102]

To recapitulate this part of the argument. To our simple model of coupled sensory and motor cognitive agents we added a value system to guide the local decisions required in the planning of actions. This addition was made at an even rougher level of detail than the two previous components, since we did not discuss the architecture determining the kind of agency involved nor the nature of the signs used. Clearly, a more complete account of both agents and signs is needed. The reason for keeping the discussion so rough is that, unlike the case of the visual cortex, our knowledge of these other agents and their signs is rapidly changing and any speculation is bound to be obsolete in a few years. We could, for instance, argue that the isomorphism required for iconic signs could be modeled after that of some social insects which use chemicals with neural effects (pheromones) to communicate with one another indirectly through the mediation of their effective environment. Some ant species, for example, use a pheromone as an *alarm sign*: if the danger to the colony is momentary, the chemical substance fails to accumulate and dissipates; if the danger persists, the substance recruits other ants by exciting them, and as they add their own pheromones the sign persists.[103] In this case, the isomorphism is between the duration of the natural signs for danger and that of the intentional signs for danger. A simple mapping like this is unlikely to occur in the brain's value system because of the large number of substances involved, but some isomorphism between the degree of concentration of different chemical signs and the intensity of different responses by users of those signs is not implausible. Nevertheless, and given our limited knowledge of the details, it is probably better to leave this part of the argument deliberately vague.

We have now a rough sketch of the neural infrastructure required to join perception to action without the need for deliberate control. But as we have argued from the start, on top of this mindless infrastructure we postulate several levels of progressively more sophisticated agents. We will return to these other agents in the next chapter, but to prepare the ground for that discussion, the following section will deal with some issues raised by their neural implementation. To begin with, given that we need consciousness and intentionality to emerge gradually, we must give up any model that includes only two levels, such as the brain and the mind.[104] Let's analyze a concrete example to illustrate the problems caused by considering only two levels. One variant of this kind of model postulates a sharp contrast between conscious and unconscious mental processes, on the basis of results from laboratory experiments on two different phenomena: *subliminal perception* and *conscious confabulation*.[105] Subliminal perception can be induced in a subject by flashing words for periods of time too short to lead to full awareness and observing how the content of the words affects his subsequent conscious evaluations of perceived objects or events. If the words have hostile connotations, for example, they will bias the subject to judge the actions of people he observes or hears about after the flash as aggressive, without being aware of why he was inclined to judge them so.[106] Conscious confabulation can be studied using hypnotic suggestion. Subjects who have been hypnotized and told to perform a particular action when hearing a trigger word are first induced to act using the trigger and then asked to explain why they behaved the way they did. Because the subjects have no access to the real cause, they tend to fabricate a causal explanation that involves conscious choices as their way of making sense of what they just did.[107] A similar thing happens to patients who have suffered lesions or undergone surgical interventions that remove certain parts of their brains. Subjects who have lost their ability to form new memories, for example, will spontaneously fabricate stories to explain their actions when they cannot remember the real causes. So do patients whose two brain hemispheres have been separated so that the one half with linguistic abilities has no access to what its nonlinguistic counterpart has just experienced.[108]

We must be careful when generalizing from these phenomena because they are difficult to observe outside the strict conditions of the laboratory: subliminal perception, for example, does not take place in the world of advertising.[109] But a possible generalization is this: first, the conscious subject does not have access to many cognitive processes taking place in his mind, as shown by priming effects; and second, this lack of access, coupled to the tendency of the conscious mind to make sense of its decisions and actions, results in the fabrication of explanations after the fact. We can illustrate this with a situation outside a laboratory, such as seeing a predator and running away from it. The mechanism behind this behavior bypasses the cortex, using the fast track between amygdala and thalamus, and it should be described as the sequence: predator perceived–running initiated–feeling of fear experienced. But the conscious explanation of the same behavior given by subjects is "The sight of the predator caused me to feel afraid which then caused me to run."[110] This may not be as dramatic as the confabulations concocted by patients with damaged brains, but it points to a more general conclusion: that retrospective reports of what goes on in subjects minds should be treated carefully. The lesson from this conclusion will be taken seriously in the next chapter, but what matters at this point is not to muddle its content by using a two-level model in which the inaccessible processes behind the response to the predator are grouped together into a single entity, the so-called *cognitive unconscious*, while the reportable parts are attributed to the conscious subject.

The cognitive unconscious corresponds to our mindless cognitive agents. Subliminal stimuli, for example, have effects on behavior that imply that they are processed all the way up to the categorization stage.[111] This stage is represented in our model by the activity of IT belonging to the level of mindless mechanisms. And what is referred to as "consciousness" in this line of research corresponds to what we referred in the previous chapter as the "autobiographical self," a producer of narratives created to make sense of his past history and future projects. The lists of properties that characterize each level confirm this. In one list, for example, the cognitive unconscious is said to be fast and automatic, and to operate in parallel using domain-specific signs, while the conscious mind is slow and voluntary, using a sequential approach in his operation which invariably involves symbols.[112] A different but related way to characterize the two levels ascribes to the cognitive unconscious the ability to represent the world in a way that lacks detail and is bound to the here and now, while the conscious mind has a much more accurate picture and can use memories of the past and anticipations of the future to guide decision-making.[113] What is never explained in these models is how one level emerges from the other. We suggested in the previous chapter that the explanation will involve introducing intermediate levels between the two. We need simple agents with the minimum of consciousness required to experience feelings and sensations without integrating them into an object with enduring identity, a kind of agent we have referred to as a "protoselves." The original version of a protoself was created to deal with interoception but we will show in the next chapter that it can be adapted to deal with perception more generally. We will also need more complex agents that are already protagonists and owners of experiences, but which are confined to the present moment and lack access to language, what we referred to as a "core selves." Grouping these two intermediate levels with the unconscious infrastructure that accounts for subliminal effects seems wrong, as does grouping them with the confabulatory autobiographical self.

In order to understand what the neural substratum of these other forms of agency could be, we can take inspiration from other disciplines. In physics, for example, microscopic entities like atoms of gold are related to macroscopic ones, like a large chunk of gold we can hold in our hand, by several intermediate entities that include crystals and grains (crystal populations growing in the same direction). The latter two structures are referred to as "mesoscopic." The brain also possesses a *mesoscale*: between macroscale phenomena, like the alpha, gamma, and beta rhythms measured over the entire brain, and microscale phenomena, like the behavior of ion channels and action potentials in single neurons, there are multiple intermediate scales with their own dynamics.[114] Operating above the anatomically well-defined cortical areas at the basis of mindless agency, there are structures consisting of up to a million neurons, which consume the signs produced in many scattered areas and are much less constrained by anatomy in their operation. These structures are referred to as *transient assemblies*.[115] The neurons that enter into these fleeting collectives are recruited rapidly and set free equally fast, so they can enter into other assemblies. How extensive the recruitment is at any one moment depends on parameters like degree of synchronization, input strength, and degree of concentration of neuromodulators.[116] There are several properties of transient assemblies that are noteworthy in the present context. First, their content is a result of *monitoring* the activity of other brain areas; that is, they are the product of the brain monitoring itself.[117] Second, these transient assemblies are *combinatorial*: much as single neurons can be recruited to form an assembly, entire assemblies can be recruited to become a component of a larger assembly.[118] And third, attention plays an important role in guiding their combinations and recombinations.[119] Of these three characteristics of transient assemblies the most important for us is their combinatorial nature because we need protoselves to enter into part-to-whole relations to form core selves, and we need the latter to be capable of becoming components of autobiographical selves.

To conclude this chapter we need to take a more abstract look at the brain as a whole and defend our representationalist approach against possible objections. In particular, it is well established that the brain exhibits spontaneous activity *even in the absence of perceptual inputs*. This capacity is normally explained by modeling the brain as a dynamical system and showing that its state space has structure.[120] But if the brain has its own preferred states, forming a kind of dynamic repertoire of responses to sensory inputs, does this mean that the external world supplies it only with content-free triggers for these endogenous responses? And if so, is there any need for the brain to internally represent anything at all? We can accept the premise to this argument, that the brain as a whole is dynamically stabilized and that it may possess its own preferred states, but reject the anti-representationalist conclusion. So let's begin by clarifying the premise and then offer an argument against that conclusion. How should the brain be modeled to reveal its dynamics? When neuroscientists confront this question they look first at the brain's *patterns of connectivity*. These patterns can be modeled mathematically if we represent brain structures at different scales (neurons, columns, cortical areas) as abstract *nodes*, and the connections between them as *edges* linking those nodes. This detaches the study from any particular scale, and indeed, from any particular realization, since the results of the analysis apply to all kinds of networks (neural, ecological, social).

Different patterns of connectivity yielding networks with very different emergent properties can be created by following a well-defined *construction procedure*: start with a fully disconnected set of nodes then connect them with edges following a particular rule. We can, for example, start with a set of nodes placed in a particular spatial arrangement, adding one edge at a time between two nodes picked randomly, until all nodes are connected. The construction rule in this case is to connect nodes in such a way that all of them have the same probability of ending up connected. A different construction procedure uses the rule that the probability that two nodes get connected depends on their proximity to each other, so that neighboring nodes always end up connected. The first procedure yields a *random network* with the emergent property that *path lengths*, the average number of nodes that it takes to get from one node to another, are short: with so many equiprobable connections there is always a short path between two points. The second procedure produces a *regular network*, with the emergent property of a high *degree of clustering*: with so many connections between neighbors chances are that if two nodes are linked to a third they are probably connected to each other and form a cluster. These two types of networks form two extremes of a continuum, with most designs occupying the middle range. The exploration of this middle part was at first guided by the search for designs that had both short path lengths and a high clustering degree, that is, for networks displaying the emergent properties of both random and regular designs. Networks with this combination of properties are referred to as *small-world networks*, the simplest one of which can be constructed by starting with a regular network and adding to its dense mesh of short-distance connections a few, randomly placed, long-distance ones: the many local links yield clustering tendencies while the few global links reduce the average path length after a critical threshold is reached.[121]

The relation between this kind of connectivity pattern and the dynamics of the brain can be glimpsed from the fact that if we take a small-world network and replace the abstract nodes by concrete oscillators we get an emergent dynamical effect: the oscillators will tend to synchronize their pulsations with each other, using the few long-distance connections to transmit and spread their influence on one another.[122] As it happens, the kind of small-world networks that exist in the brain have a more complex structure than this, but one that can also be generated using a well-defined construction procedure. The main difference is that, in the final product, the short-distance connections generate specialized clusters, or *modules*, while the long-distance connections are effected by special nodes referred to as *hubs*.[123] At the scale that we have been exploring in this chapter, the areas of the visual cortex we called V1, V2, and V3 exemplify specialized modules, while V4, which is multiply connected to areas that are not connected to one another, exemplifies a hub.[124] This way the anatomical or *structural* connectivity of the cortex can help explain the segregation of areas with distinct functions and their integration using long-distance links. On the other hand, the structural connectivity is relatively static at time scales of seconds or minutes, even if it retains a certain plasticity at the scale of hours or days. This matters because the recruitment of neurons, the formation of coalitions, and the appearance of synchronized patterns of coordinated activity happens at time scales of hundreds of milliseconds.[125] Synchronization and modulation, both of which were briefly discussed earlier are two of the ways in which *functional* connectivity can emerge and define the brain's dynamical behavior. Although we lack detailed state space analyses of these dynamics, we can make an educated guess about its nature based on the behavior to be modeled. A dynamical system with multiple stable states and fast transitions among them suggests a distribution of singularities similar to the one we discussed in the previous chapter for the neural control of configurations of joints, muscles, and tendons: a state space with many attractors and basins that can be changed from deep to shallow by manipulating a parameter so that the singularities can capture trajectories and rapidly release them as the parameter changes. This state is referred to as a *metastable* state.[126]

Such metastability is to be expected when a brain must constantly confront ever-changing sensory inputs and respond with equally varied motor outputs. But as we just said, the brain adopts a metastable state in the absence of sensory inputs. This endogenous activity is explained by its small-world anatomical connectivity, by the electrical properties of the neurons, and by the spread of synchronization. Entire populations of neurons can, for example, synchronize their phase to increase their responsiveness to stimulation, and in this state they can lead to the emergence of recurrent sequential firing patterns. The brain's own repertoire of preferred states may be based on these coordinated populations and spike patterns.[127] And this brings us to the question that began this section: if the brain is a dynamical system with its own preferred states, and if it continues to be so even when the world is not impinging on it, does this imply that the world's contribution is merely to modulate the states in the brain's own functional repertoire? This is the position taken by the enactive approach, in which the brain is conceived as a *closed system*. This does not refer to an absence of interactions with the environment but rather to the fact that all neural activity always leads to more neural activity (operational closure).[128] In other words, this definition of closure does not rule out external interactions but it does reduce them to mere content-free *perturbations or shocks*, exogenous determinations for the occurrence of endogenous changes. The brain itself, the argument goes, cannot tell whether a change was caused by its own internal dynamics or by an external event, a distinction that can only be made by someone who can see the boundaries of the body and decree that the event occurred inside or outside. From these premises enactivists go on to conclude that the brain has neither inputs nor outputs.[129]

Rejecting this conclusion does not commit us to assert that the brain can be reduced to a device to map sensory inputs into motor outputs. Avoiding this error requires making a sharp distinction between what happens at the level of sensory-motor processing and what takes place at the phenomenal level. It must be crystal clear that *perceptual experience is not an input from the world to the mind,* and that *deliberate action is not an output from the mind to the world.*[130] Far from being an input from the world, perception is more like an intermediate output, and the volition behind an action is not an output to the world but an intermediate input to the motor areas of the brain.[131] If this was the enactivists' claim, there would be no disagreement, but it is not. As we discussed in the previous chapter, their claim is that the components of a whole do not exist independently because their very identity is constituted by the role they play in the whole. We can clarify this claim by using a well-known classification of the relations between parts and the resulting wholes. The first category in this taxonomy is that of a *decomposable* whole, defined as a whole in which each of the components operates in relative independence, interacting with others through inputs and outputs, but maintaining a fixed function that is not changed by its role in the whole. This relative isolation makes the components easy to localize when the whole is submitted to analysis. A second category are wholes referred to as *nearly decomposable.* In these wholes, interactions within components are more important in the determination of their identity than interactions between components.[132] The properties that define each component emerge from the interactions among its subcomponents, not from its interactions with other components or with the whole. On the other hand, these properties serve as the basis for dispositions, and which of these becomes actual is determined by the role played by a component.

For this reason, a function may be distributed among several components, making it harder to localize. There is, finally, a third category of fully *undecomposable* wholes, in which the functions of the components are impossible to localize. These are the kind of wholes favored by enactivists.[133]

The simplest way to generate wholes like these is through the use of intrinsic relations, relations that constitute the very identity of what they relate. If the relation between parts and wholes is conceived as intrinsic, then the parts and the whole come into existence together, making the latter undecomposable.[134] When we use intrinsic relations to think about the relation between the brain, the senses, and the muscles, then sensory inputs and motor outputs cease to exist on their own. In addition, the claim that the brain has neither inputs nor outputs is defended by asserting that it engages in the "construction of meaning" not the processing of information. This other claim is defended by first arguing that the whole formed by an embodied subject, his brain, and his lived world is undecomposable. Then the environment, considered as a physical domain of interactions, is postulated to become a lived world when a *surplus of meaning* is added from an organism's own point of view.[135] But as we argued in the previous chapter, this use of the word "meaning" involves a conceptual confusion between signification and significance, leading to the idea that the content of the visual field can be identified with the way in which that content is evaluated. And if both value and content exist only within the undecomposable whole formed by an organism and its world, then the external environment cannot be a source of information but only of perturbations that have no content. Ironically, this way of conceiving the contribution of the environment comes close to reproducing the empiricist conception of it as a source of mere irritations of the sensory surfaces, and of the brain as a logical inference machine required to enrich the content of those impoverished stimulations. All that the enactivists have done is to replace the term "stimulation" with "perturbation" and replace logical operations with the (entirely speculative) operations behind the "construction of meaning." In other words, in both cases the thesis of the *poverty of stimulation* is implicitly assumed.[136]

The distinction between sensory input and motor output, on the one hand, and perception and action, on the other, deserves a more extensive treatment than this. But before we can do that we must confront the controversies regarding the content of the visual field because the philosophical community is far from having reached consensus on these matters. There are some who deny that the visual field has any content at all, or that its content is constituted by its intrinsic relations to something else. We will, of course, reject these proposals, but we must replace them with something else. We will distinguish three increasingly more sophisticated kinds of perception: the perception of properties, the perception of objects possessing those properties, and the perception of situations involving several interacting objects. After a detailed examination of these three perceptual modes, we will tackle the question of what kinds of cognitive agents are involved in each and how their agency is required to transform sensory inputs and motor outputs into a lived experience.

4 THE CONTRIBUTIONS OF THE MIND

The visual field has properties of its own. But what is the nature of those properties? Philosophically, properties can be of two different kinds: *intrinsic* and *relational*.[1]

Let's illustrate the distinction with something simpler than a visual property. As a homeostatic bodily state, thirst has many components only one of which is subjective, the sensation of thirst, a sensation that has a distinctive quality open to subjective inspection and comparison: most people can tell the difference between feeling hungry and feeling thirsty. The singular quality that makes the sensation of thirst recognizable by a subject would be an example of an intrinsic property. The alternative conception asserts that being thirsty is fully constituted by relations between states: the state caused by not having had water for a while and the state that causes the desire to drink.[2] All that matters is the functional relation between inputs (lack of water intake) and outputs (tendency to reach for a glass of water). This implies that there is no difference *for the subject* between his thirst and somebody else's thirst. Or to put this differently, that self-attributions of thirst are performed using the same inferential mechanisms as attributions of that state to other people. In the case of visual properties, a similar argument is used: the identity of anything that exists between sensory inputs and motor outputs, other than brain states, is fully constituted by the relation between the dispositions of objects in the world (such as their power to produce color sensations), those of the receptors in our eyes (such as their capacity to be stimulated), and those of our visually guided behaviors.[3]

There are, of course, many different ways to conceive relational properties, but most of them assume that the relations in question constitute the very identity of what they relate. Yet, as we have already argued, outside the realm of arbitrary social conventions, the concept of an intrinsic relation leads to a holistic view of perception that serves more to obfuscate than to enlighten.[4] We could, therefore, simply dismiss the very concept of a relational property just as we dismissed the concept of an intrinsic relation. But going over the differences between the two alternative views can be very instructive and would strengthen our confidence in our choice. So let's first sketch the approach we will take to defend the idea of intrinsic phenomenal properties, using as a foil an influential relational approach in which *verbal reports* of experience play the constitutive role. The importance of reports in the context of laboratory experiments should not be underestimated: in many cases, an experimental psychologist has no option but to take a subject's reports as the main evidence for the occurrence of a conscious experience. But what is the nature of these reports? Are they descriptions of the visual field, in which case the subject would be reporting the existence of intrinsic properties, or are they the result of retrospective judgments informed by the *beliefs* of the subject? If the latter is correct, then a subject is not describing intrinsic properties of his visual field but literally bringing them into existence by holding the belief that he in fact experienced them. Clearly, any defense of intrinsic properties must confront the premises that lead to this conclusion. The main premise can be stated like this:

If I am visually conscious of X, I must have the belief that I am conscious of X and possess all the required concepts, including the concept of X.

What makes us think that we cannot be conscious of something unless we believe that we are conscious of it, or that something cannot seem to us to be a certain way unless we possess the belief that it seems that way to us?[5] To answer this question we can start with a very rough contrast between two kinds of visual awareness: the *awareness of things* and the *awareness of facts* about those things. Breaking down perception like this can only be a first approximation because the former type must include not only objects and events but also properties (which are not things) and because there are ways to perceive facts (or rather, situations) that do not demand the use of concepts. But we can use it a point of departure, and agree that being visually aware of X does not require concepts, but being aware of the fact that X is Y does require the concepts of X and Y.[6] Less formally, what this formula states is that we can be visually aware of the presence of a colored object in front of us even if we do not have the concepts required to identify the object or its color, and cannot, therefore, form any verbally expressible beliefs about that object. On the other hand, we cannot be aware of the fact that this red object is an automobile without possessing the required concepts, as well as the belief that the object is a red automobile. In these terms, asserting that visual perception involves beliefs in a constitutive way is simply to assert that its only function is the perception of facts.

The argument in defense of this relational account continues by imagining that we are in a room covered with wallpaper displaying a well-defined repetitive pattern. We can describe this experience in two different ways: we can say that we are visually aware of a thing (a wall) that is textured with a certain pattern with definite properties, or that we are visually aware of the fact that there is a wall covered with that pattern. Assuming that both alternatives are equally plausible, we are then invited to break the tie by explaining a well-known phenomenon, the *blind spot*. The choice of perceptual phenomenon is inspired because the gap without any cones or rods where the optic nerve leaves the retina is quite large, being larger than the fovea, hence explaining why we do not experience a hole in our visual field is important. Those who believe that we are visually aware of things explain it this way: the brain has access to information about the wall's perceived properties, and it can use this information about the patterned wall *to fill in* the blind spot. For those who believe that all we are aware of is facts, this option is not available since there is no such information to begin with, and they must, therefore, assert that the blind spot is never filled in but it is rather *ignored*.[7] In the second explanation, the situation would be similar to that of viewing a partially occluded object, like a dog under the bed showing only its tail, without judging that the rest of the dog has disappeared. We simply form the belief that the dog is complete without having to provide the missing part by interpolation. Choosing between these explanations, however, cannot break the tie because they also seem equally plausible. So our only option at this point is to look into how the brain deals with the blind spot to see if the available evidence supports only one account. To explain how the brain performs the filling in operation, all we need to assume is that the retinal output is mapped onto the primary visual cortex (V1) in a way that preserves relations of contiguity, so neurons in the blind spot area can use the content of the receptive fields of neurons just outside that area to interpolate the missing parts.[8] The other explanation does not have any neural basis and seems to be based on *a priori* neurophysiology: there must be a mechanism allowing the brain to form the belief that, given the fact that the whole wall is papered, more of the same wallpaper must exist in the blind spot area, so the brain can just ignore it.[9] The absence of a neural mechanism does not disqualify the idea that the blind spot is ignored, rather than filled in, because neuroscientists may one day discover a mechanism, but it does show that, given what we know about the brain, one of the options is better supported than the other.

This way of presenting the alternative views shows that the choice between intrinsic or relational properties is closely related to the choice between awareness of things and awareness of facts, which is, in turn, related to the question of whether the content of experience is or is not conceptually structured. It follows that a defense of intrinsic properties must account for perception in a way that does not require concepts. To do this, we must first go beyond the distinction between things and facts, and give separate accounts of three increasingly more complex forms of perception: *perceiving properties*, *objects*, and *situations*. The simplest form of perception can be illustrated with our ability to see disembodied colors, that is, colors that do not belong to an object. This simple form of vision tends to occur more often in laboratories in which stimuli are deliberately simplified (e.g., using colored lights in a dark room) but as we will see it also takes place in ordinary environments. We share this capacity with insects. We are also able to perceive properties as belonging to objects, and to visually separate those objects from their backgrounds. We share this capacity with other mammals. Because neither insects nor nonhuman mammals have concepts, it is not hard to imagine that a nonconceptual account of these two forms of perception can be given. But we can also perceive situations in which several different objects interact, some animate some inanimate, and we can understand those situations. We will argue later that in the case of simple situations in which the events are unfolding in front of our eyes, we can make sense of what is taking place without concepts, using only the nonlinguistic equivalent of indexicals, like "here" and "now." We share this capacity with other primates. Finally, we can perceive and understand complex situations that require that we describe them to ourselves using language and that we form new beliefs about the objects involved. It is only in this case, which is uniquely human, that we may legitimately speak of the perception of facts.

What then is the perception of properties? We may begin with an analogy between perceiving properties and *measuring properties*. An instrument like a speedometer or a thermometer represents objective properties (speed, temperature) by its possession of a range of internal states that correlate with different degrees of intensity of those properties.[10] Thus, the column of mercury inside an analog thermometer can be in different states of expansion, moving up or down the glass tube accordingly. A given height of the column can stand for a temperature degree because the set of states of expansion of the mercury is isomorphically mapped onto the range of degrees of temperature the instrument can measure. Similarly, the needle of the speedometer in the dashboard of a vehicle can be in different states, changing position as the number of rotations of the car's tires changes in a given unit of time. A particular position of the needle can stand for a speed because the range of speeds at which the car is capable of moving is mapped onto the range of positions the needle can adopt.[11] In both cases an isomorphism between extrinsic relations among states and extrinsic relations among degrees of intensity generates the iconic component of the sign. On the other hand, when the instruments are actually used, they will interact with a particular body or a particular vehicle, which means that at any given time they are not just representing temperature or speed, but the temperature and speed of *this body or this vehicle now.* These readings are the indexical component of the hybrid sign.[12]

There are several advantages of this account of the perception of properties. The first is that the model is not a traditional causal account, that is, one in which objects in the world are assumed to *directly cause* the content of the visual field. It is rather a representational account in which indices do not need to refer to any of the *intermediate causal links* in the chain from external intensities or quantities to internal states: the height of the mercury column stands for the temperature of a body, not the degree of expansion of the metal; and the position of the needle stands for the vehicle speed, not the number of rotations of the tires per unit of time.[13] This raises the question of how the right referent is selected from what can be a very long causal chain since, after all, an index can carry information about every step in the chain. In the case of measuring instruments the answer is that a human designer selected the referent by giving the instruments a function: to measure temperature or speed, not expansion rates or number of revolutions per minute. In the case of sensory organs we have an equivalent explanation: evolution "designed" the visual system to provide us with information about the world, not about the happenings in the retina or the brain, because only the former plays a role in guiding successful action. In both cases, to know what a given index refers to we need to examine the *history of its utilization.*[14] The iconic part of the signs also needs to operate at a distance from its causes. In the case of color, it requires that there should be a mapping between a range of light wavelengths reflected from surfaces and a range of representational states: the color space. But this need not be a one-to-one mapping. There are many combinations of reflected wavelengths that are represented by the exact same color experience, a phenomenon known as *metamerism.* Many-to-one mappings can also exist in the case of measuring instruments: if we designed a speedometer using a mechanism that measured not the number of tire rotations per minute but rather the number of axle rotations, then for differently sized tires the instrument will give different readings. There will be many different "metameric speeds" that will cause the speedometer's needle to be in the exact same position.[15]

The solution to this is also a matter of how the signs are utilized and not about their causal relations: we may, for instance, *calibrate* the instrument to match a given tire size.[16]

A second advantage of this approach is that it avoids some of the problems with traditional causal models, such as the perception of *absences*. If we think of shadows as the absence of light, for example, and if light is conceived as the main causal agent stimulating and informing our retinas, then strictly speaking, a shadow should not be able to interact with our retinas. But if the vehicles of natural signs standing for shadows cannot interact with us, then how can their referent have any *representational* effect on us? We could argue that perceived shadows belong to the category of awareness of facts (being aware that there is absence of light) not to the awareness of things.[17] But there is an alternative answer: the instruments we used as an analogy can represent zero temperature or zero speed not as absences but as extreme values in a continuum. Similarly, the result of mapping a range of intensities onto a range of brain states should allow for readings of *zero intensity* referring to presences, not absences. Some philosophers approach this question arguing that internal signs are analog data structures equipped with a *magnitude parameter*, allowing these signs to represent different intensities (color saturation, brightness) or different quantities (distances, angles).[18] This is equivalent to our own version since we are also proposing analog icons—the result of mapping a continuous range of values into a continuous set of states—and our indexical signs are the same as the value that the magnitude parameter can have at any one time.

These remarks do not mean to suggest that perception equals measurement, only that the perception of isolated properties does. As we said earlier, occasions for the exercise of this simple form of perception are rare outside of laboratories. It is nevertheless a real capacity that works alone sometimes and in conjunction with more sophisticated forms of perception most of the time. On the other hand, while the perception of properties is easy to conceive as working without the need for concepts, the perception of properties *as belonging to objects* is not.[19] So far we have dealt with the perception of objects exclusively in terms of the progressive construction of geometric icons that stand for those objects. Because of the nature of the construction procedure, the properties of the final, voluminous icons can be unproblematically ascribed to the objects for which they stand: edges, for example, appear at first as mere line segments but as the construction proceeds they are first separated from other boundaries (shadows, textures) and then joined together into an icon for the contour of a surface. At that point, the resulting signs are not of disembodied geometrical properties but of properties belonging to surfaces. But what about other properties? In the more general case, we cannot rely on the nature of the construction procedure and must address the various ways in which the brain achieves a *separation of the perspectival from the factual.*[20] We are using the term "factual" to refer to the properties that an object has as a matter of fact, not to the idea that the possession of those properties is represented by the subject as a fact, or believed by him to be a fact. Because the content of perception mixes up how objects appear to be and how they really are, and because successful action depends mostly on the latter, our brain must have a way to separate these two components.

The outcome of this separation can be illustrated with a familiar perceptual phenomenon: *constancy effects.*[21] Many properties of an experienced object—its size, shape, speed, color, brightness—appear to remain unchanged even as its appearance undergoes a drastic change. The perspectival properties of the object change, but our experience matches the fact that the object's properties stay the same. Take for instance *size constancy*: when at the end of a conversation our interlocutor walks away from us, his perceived size shrinks as his distance from us increases, and yet we do not perceive him as getting physically smaller in size.[22] Or take *shape constancy*: when we see a round plate tilted away from us, its retinal projection and its final perceived shape are both elliptical and yet we perceive the object as keeping its objective circular shape. Both effects can be explained by pointing to the fact that certain extrinsic relations between the properties of a perceived object tend to stay constant, such as the ratio of apparent size to apparent distance, or that of apparent shape to apparent slant.[23] All that this explanation requires is the possession of an ability to detect not just properties but simple extrinsic relations between them: ratios, gradients, and rates of change.[24] Using these higher-order properties as an input, the brain can perform a separation of the perspectival from the factual, yielding an object perceived as more than just a mere bundle of properties. On the other hand, the second set of terms in the earlier ratios, apparent distance and apparent slant, would seem to require subjective judgments of facts, or at least unconscious inferences about facts, either one of which would involve concepts. So to conclude that constancy effects are nonconceptual, we must show how distance and slant can be estimated using natural signs already present in a given section of the optic array.

Signs indicating the approximate distance of an object from the subject are conveyed by various optical and physiological effects: the accommodation of the eyes' lenses to focus on the object; binocular vision; occlusion; motion parallax; the presence of texture gradients on the ground and of parallel lines appearing to converge at the horizon; and even atmospheric effects, like the blurring or tinting of objects located far away. Each of these effects indicates depth, but they vary in their accuracy and range. For example, for short distances fairly good estimates can be made using lens accommodation, while motion parallax—distant objects appearing to move slower than nearby ones to a laterally moving subject—is a better index when greater distances are involved, but only if the subject is not moving too slowly.[25] In general, the usefulness of each of the indices of depth increases if they are used in combination (e.g., motion parallax combined with occlusion) and if each combination fits a particular task and the conditions under which it is performed.[26] In addition, there are quantities available in the optic array that can be used as indices of both size and distance. As we saw in the Chapter 1, the optic array at any one point in space can be conceived as if composed of many *solid angles*. A solid angle can be visualized as an irregular pyramid made up of light, the base of which is the outer contour of an object as viewed from a given point of view, with its apex located at that point of view. The magnitude of these solid angles is preserved in the section of the array sliced by the retina. It can be shown that the ratio of the angle subtended by an object to the mean of the angles subtended by its surroundings remains roughly constant with viewing distance, so this ratio can be used to replace the one between apparent size and distance. If, in addition, the object is on the ground and the latter is regularly textured (made of pebbles, grass, mosaic tiles), the texture gradient provides a local metric already scaled for distance which can be used to calculate the object's true size.[27] None of this involves the possession of concepts or beliefs.[28]

So far we have given plausible arguments in favor of the idea that perceiving properties and objects is not a conceptual matter. But what about situations? Can nonhuman animals perceive relations between objects and recognize that some relations belong to certain classes of situations demanding different responses? Other primates seem to be able to do this, at least for situations involving them as one of the participating objects. Vervet monkeys, for example, have three distinct alarm calls that they emit to direct others' attention to the presence of three kinds of predators: leopards, eagles, and snakes. The vocalizations are a means to warn other monkeys of the dangerous situation and to inform them about the kinds of action that are appropriate to avoid it: climb up a tree if it is a leopard; run into the bushes if it is an eagle; or stand bipedally and gaze steadily at the ground to locate and attack the snake.[29] It can be argued that what the monkeys are doing is similar to what we do when we direct someone else's attention to an ongoing situation by pointing to it with our finger, or when we use sentences like "That is the situation I wanted to avoid." In both cases, directing one's attention to an ongoing situation and having a practical grasp of the actions required to respond to it are enough to understand what we perceive. We will return later to the question of whether or not the referent of a pointing gesture, or of the word "that," can be fixed without the use of concepts.

But assuming that it can, can we also assume that animals can judge the relations among the objects involved in a situation without using concepts? In this case we need to distinguish two different kinds of judgments, some being exact and quantitative, others inexact and qualitative. The two kinds may be defined by the nature of the signs employed, or more exactly, by the nature of the vehicles of those signs. The vehicles of concepts (and of symbols more generally) are *discrete*, and this enables them to be used to make precise judgments. The vehicles of icons and indices, on the other hand, can be *continuous* (or analog), making them useful only for qualitative assessments.[30] Using this distinction we could argue that an animal can qualitatively judge the relations between objects in a situation without using any concepts. Imagine a rabbit being chased by a hungry fox, scanning its surroundings looking for a place to hide. This is not the case of object perception, like spotting a fox and understanding that it affords danger, but a more complex situation in which various affordances (the fox's, the rabbit's, and the terrain's) and their changing relations must be understood. If the rabbit sees a hole in a nearby hill it will see it as affording shelter only if it judges that the hole is large enough for it to fit in it but not so large that the fox can also fit. The qualitative evaluation of relative sizes in this example, and the understanding that the hole provides protection in a dangerous situation, can be done using a combination of retinotopic, somatotopic, and motor maps: peripersonal maps can inform the rabbit's brain about the extension of the boundaries of its body; maps of the rabbit's retinas can inform its brain that the contour of the hole defines an opening affording passage; and motor maps can allow it to rapidly simulate and judge whether it, but not the fox, can fit through it.

What we have done so far is to give a rough sketch of the way in which we will frame our account of perception: we showed that it was plausible to view the perception of properties as performing a measurement function, to view the perception of objects as performing the function of separating the perspectival from the factual, and the perception of situations as having the function of allowing qualitative judgments about the relations between objects. This had the advantage that we could ignore causal mechanisms and deal with functions at a more abstract level. Because we will adopt this *functionalist* stance whenever we lack knowledge of causal mechanisms, we should add a few general remarks about it. There are several variants of functionalist philosophy, but the most influential one relies on a computer metaphor to argue for the independence of function from mechanism.[31] The hardware of a modern computer is, basically, a complex system of logical gates controlling the flow of electrons, and realized as transistors etched on a piece of silicon crystal. However, a device that performs the same function can be created with valves controlling the flow of water in different channels, and the software we would normally run on an electronic machine could also be run on the hydraulic version. This implies that one and the same software application (a word processor, a web browser) can have *multiple realizations*, as the hardware that supports it changes. All of this is, of course, true and important. But like the other mechanism-independent approaches we have discussed, it can also be misleading. Defenders of functionalism first make the apparently harmless claim that there is a parallel between *mental states* and the states that a computer has at the level of its software, and another parallel between *brain states* and the states that a computer has at the level of its hardware.[32] But then they go on to argue that given that there are an *unlimited number* of hardware realizations, and given that the human brain exemplifies only one of these numerous variants, there is nothing about neural realizations that should constrain how we explain mental phenomena.[33] The problem with this conclusion is that finding alternative mechanisms for a given mental function is quite hard, and that this degree of difficulty suggests that realizations are not unlimited in number.[34]

To avoid this problem the next step in our argument must address the question of brain mechanisms, starting with the perception of color. Expressed as a formula, our definition of property perception is as follows: a phenomenal property X stands for an objective property Y if X possesses *the function of indicating* the presence of Y. When this function is acquired through evolution, we must show that the objective correlation between intensities or quantities of Y and states of X gives a species behavioral advantages that lead to greater reproductive success. On the other hand, because reproductive success is achieved by the animal as a whole, natural selection may not have uniform effects on all the animal's parts. Take, for instance, the case of anatomical features that have been selected not because they have an adaptive function but because they are contingently linked to a feature that does: the jaw is adaptive, allowing animals to bite larger morsels, but the chin is not, its presence in some animals being an accident of its anatomical connection to the jaw. And a similar point applies in the case of color. The number of distinct physical properties that can play a role in the production of phenomenal color is extremely large, and their phenomenal effects depend on whether light is reflected by objects, emitted by them, or transmitted by them.[35] Statistically speaking solid objects bounded by opaque surfaces are much more abundant than glowing and translucent ones, so we can expect reflecting surfaces to have played a greater evolutionary role: the capacity to distinguish edible red berries from inedible green berries would be the equivalent of the jaw; the capacity to tell rubies from emeralds, the equivalent of the chin.[36]

The function of color may not be as specialized as this—to indicate the presence of ripe fruit, important as this may be—but more generally to participate in the detection of the boundaries of solid objects. As we saw, boundaries can be detected by using differences in luminance, but spectral differences can greatly amplify this capacity, allowing an animal to see, for example, a predator hidden in the bushes: if the predator's body and its plant cover reflect light with different spectral composition, they will be clearly distinguished even if the continuity of its body's contour is broken by the branches and leaves under which it is hiding.[37] The surfaces to be detected (the skin of the hiding predator) are characterized by both properties and dispositions: the properties include having an actual chemical composition and physical structure, the dispositions include the tendency to absorb some wavelengths of the incident light while reflecting others, a tendency that may not be actualized if the surface is in a dark room or is surrounded by a moonless night. This tendency is referred to as a surface's *reflectance.* The light that reaches the retina is a combination of the effects of reflected light and the light used for illumination. For this reason it does not correlate well with phenomenal colors. But reflectances do, making them our best choice for the referent of colors.[38] On the other hand, we must avoid *identifying* colors and reflectances, making colors an objective property of surfaces. This would be like identifying smoke and fire, or symptoms and disease.[39] We must also resist the temptation of concluding that since colors are not properties of material surfaces, they must be mere illusions.[40] This would be like asserting that the perceived properties of dark clouds that indicate a storm is coming or the perceived properties of footprints indicating the presence of an animal are figments of our imagination.

To tackle the question of the mechanisms behind color perception we need to go back to some of the ideas explored in the previous chapter concerning the photoreceptors acting as input devices for the retina, and the retinal ganglia that function as its output devices. Despite the fact that these components operate very early in the processing of incoming light, they have a marked effect on the shape of the resulting color space. To begin with, the spectral composition of sunlight forms a continuum, containing an infinity of wavelengths. We can reduce this infinite space by sticking to the visible part of the spectrum (roughly, wavelengths between 400 and

700 nanometers) and by sampling it at intervals of 10 nanometers. If we assign one dimension to each of the resulting wavelengths, we obtain a space with thirty dimensions, a space still enormous but not infinite.[41] The first step in the mapping of this wavelength space into phenomenal color space takes place at the level of photoreceptors (cones) that can detect different wavelengths. This step involves an enormous reduction of dimensionality, from thirty dimensions to the three-dimensional space formed by three different cone types, partly explaining why the mapping must be many-to-one. But we are still far from anything that resembles phenomenal color space because each of the three cone types responds to a *wide range of wavelengths*, displaying a considerable degree of overlap. If we plot these responses as curves to show the overlaps we can verify that the three types of responses have a maximum (the wavelength a cone type is most sensitive to) and that these singularities do not overlap. It would be tempting, therefore, to try to identify the three singularities with the three primary colors, but it does not work that way: the peak of activity of the cone type that will eventually map into the color red occurs at 560 nanometers, but that wavelength of light is perceived not as red but as a greenish yellow.[42] For that reason, cone types are not referred to by using color names, but labeled S, M, and L cones according to the relative sizes of the wavelengths in their range: small, medium, or large.

The next step in the process depends on the fact that the retina does not output the raw signs produced by its population of receptors directly but uses retinal ganglia to structure this output. As we saw, the center-surround structure of the receptive fields of the neurons in these ganglia allows them to detect extrinsic relations of *contrast:* either "black" versus "white" for the achromatic component of light, or "red" versus "green," and "blue" versus "yellow," for the chromatic one. For example, a retinal ganglion may be excited by the output of L cones but inhibited by the output of M cones, so its output represents the contrast between "red" and "green."[43] What mechanism explains the production of signs standing for contrasts? First, a retinal ganglion compares the excitatory input from one type of cone with the inhibitory input from another type, a comparison that may be seen as a subtraction operation that calculates *the difference* between the two. Then, the ganglion compares this output to its own spontaneous activity, its base rate, to determine whether the latter is increased or decreased. For the information that will eventually become phenomenal red and green, this transformation would work like this: first, the outputs from M and L cones are received by a ganglion with a center sensitive to one, and a surround inhibited by the other; second, M is subtracted from L and the result is checked against the ganglion's base rate; finally the ganglion's output is labeled "red" or "green" depending on whether its activity is above or below its base rate. Similarly a "yellow-blue" ganglion would add M and L and subtract S, and then compare the result relative to its base rate: if it is above then its output is labeled "yellow" and if it is below it is labeled "blue."[44]

Although at this stage the information labeled "blue" or "red" is still far from subjectively experienced blue and red, some of the defining traits of the *structure of color space* have already begun to emerge. There are many ways of depicting this three-dimensional space but all have in common that the achromatic component defines one dimension (brightness) while the chromatic component defines the other two dimensions (hues), forming a plane that is partly structured by opponent hues (e.g., the familiar color wheel). These two characteristics of phenomenal color space—the segregation of brightness and hue into different dimensions, and the role of opponency in organizing the plane of hues—are already present in the output of the retina. And because many thalamic and cortical neurons share the center-surround structure of the receptive fields of retinal ganglia, the antagonistic hue arrangement and the separation of chromatic from achromatic information are preserved in later stages.[45] We suggested earlier that the perception of properties can be compared to a measuring operation, the output of which is a hybrid of an index and an icon: the iconic part is the result of mapping a range of values for a measurable property into a range of values for a measured property, while the indexical part is the measured value of a property at any given time. The analogy holds in the case of color because despite the fact that the range of wavelengths available in ambient light is not isomorphic with our color space (the mapping is many-to-one) the range of surface's reflectances approximates a one-to-one mapping.[46] In other words, despite the much higher dimensionality of the space of possible wavelengths it can be shown, using formal methods of dimension reduction, that the three dimensions of phenomenal color space—hue, saturation, and brightness—do capture *fundamental indicators* of the reflectances of solid surfaces.[47] On the other hand, we should keep in mind that while a point in color space is a reliable index of the dispositions of opaque, reflecting surfaces, it does not have the evolutionary function of indicating the dispositions of transparent or glowing objects.

To finish this section we need to consider some objections to our argument. If the referent of a color index is determined by its evolutionary role, does this not imply that colors are relational?[48] This role, the objection goes, would constitute the identity of both perceived colors and the perceiver of colors. But this *confuses the role with the role player*.[49] A social convention may constitute the nature of a role (e.g., the role of brother or sister), but it does not determine the identity of the incumbents to that role. In biological evolution, the arbitrary determination of the identity of a role may occur in the case of frozen genetic accidents (as may be the case with the genetic code) but even when roles are relational in this sense, role players must have certain intrinsic properties in order to play them. In the case of color this implies that while the qualitative character of an experience of red may be required for it to perform its function, the quality is not the same as the function. What about the referent of a color icon? The entire range of visible wavelengths must be mapped onto phenomenal color space for the signs to do their job, but does this not imply that red is what it is because of its relation to all other colors within that space? Is not the relation of being antagonistic to green, or being a component of orange, what constitutes red as a property? If this were the case it would imply that in order to see red we must be able to see all the other colors. But let's imagine that industrial pollution has contaminated the upper atmosphere with particles that reflect away all the wavelengths except for those that enter into the production of red so that the only color we perceive is red. We would still have all the anatomical equipment endowing us with the disposition to see the entire color space but the world would allow us to actualize only a portion of it. So, if many of the relations that red has with other colors had been eliminated in this restricted color space, could we not still experience red? We see no reason to believe that we could not, so the objection fails.

There are two more potential problems unrelated to the question of intrinsic relations. The first one is posed by *perceptual variation*. There are multiple sources of variation: genetic differences can alter the chemical composition of substances used by the eyes' photoreceptors, altering the range of detectable wavelengths; the light used for illumination, sunlight versus neon light, for example, can completely alter the chromatic appearance of a surface; the spectral composition of surfaces in the background surrounding a target surface can create contrast effects that affect how its color is perceived. The ubiquity of perceptual variation suggests that either *none of the variants is veridical or all of them are.* Does this undermine our claim about the intrinsic nature of color?[50] It could, but only if we *identified* colors and reflectances. But if we reject this identification, if colors are viewed as indices of reflectances, then there is no problem in accepting perceptual variation across species, within a single species, and between different viewing conditions for the same organism. Indices have a function, such as facilitating boundary detection, or even telling edible from inedible fruit, but this function can be performed even if the indices present in different visual fields are not of the exact same color. The second challenge derives from the problem of *determinacy*. If we conceived the visual field as a flat plane made out of patches with the property of being colored, then all the patches would be required to be of a determinate color. But the visual field is not at all like that. In particular, the degree to which a color appears to have a determinate quality varies with its distance from the fovea, most medium-sized objects having a clearly defined quality only at the center of the visual field, not at the periphery. Away from the center, colors tend to disappear, with reds and greens disappearing earlier than blues and yellows.[51] This implies that a color that is not present to us when it is on the corner of our eye can become present if we rotate our head and foveate it. Does granting the existence of this determinacy gradient require us to surrender to a relational approach? No. These cases are no more problematic for us than the fact that objects at the periphery of the field have indistinct shapes, or that objects that are closer than the point we are focusing on appear blurry to us. As we argued in Chapter 2, we can account for these cases using the mastery of sensory-motor dependencies which, in turn, can be explained using retinal, somatic, and motor maps in combination.[52]

To recapitulate, the simplest form of perception, the perception of isolated properties, can indeed be compared to an act of measuring, but we must go beyond an analogy with speedometers or thermometers and give at least a rough sketch of the mechanisms involved.[53] The latter will involve contributions from the world (reflectances), from the body (sensory-motor dependencies), and from the brain (detecting spectral ranges; producing and consuming signs representing contrasts between these ranges). The contributions from the mind, the transformation of a measured property into a lived property, is the most controversial and speculative of all, so we will return to it later. We acknowledged that perceiving properties not belonging to objects is rare in ecologically valid situations, but this capacity can be shown to exist in the laboratory and does play a role in normal perception, as when we see colored objects that are so far away or moving so fast that their identities are too vague to be discerned.[54] The fact that our account is not causal (reflectances cause colors) but rather representational—reflectances are one of many causal factors involved, but they are singled out as what the signs stand for by the evolutionary function of color vision—allows us to deal with the ubiquity of variation in color perception. Finally, we continued our rejection of constitutive relations, which are a poor substitute for the synthetic mechanisms that yield percepts of different kinds.

Let's move on to the perception of objects. As we argued earlier, the basic function of object perception is to separate the perspectival component of the content of the visual field from its factual component. We gave as examples of the outcome of this separation the phenomena of size and shape constancy. There is a chromatic version of these phenomena, referred to as *color constancy*, which we can use to get this section started. When looking at a uniformly colored object, only half of which is under the light, we do not experience it as having two colors, a lighter hue in its illuminated portion and a darker one in the shadowed portion, but as possessing a single color. How is this effect explained? The perspectival part in this case depends on the fact that the light reaching the retina contains information about the surfaces reflecting it as well as about the light's own properties prior to being reflected, so the constancy effect involves separating the contributions of reflectance and illumination.[55] When viewing conditions are such that observers can perceive the entire object at once their brains can perform this separation, and the resulting phenomenal effect—seeing a single hue instead of two—matches the object's reflectance better. But if we place a screen with a small aperture between viewer and object, so that only a small portion of the latter is visible, the effect disappears, and the observer experiences two different colors. This shows that color constancy effects arise as part of the perception of objects, not the perception of properties.[56]

The mechanism behind color constancy effects is still somewhat speculative. Illumination tends to affect many surfaces at once, so subtracting its contribution must involve comparing the L, M, and S wavelengths of the target surface with those of the other surfaces surrounding it. This comparison is most likely carried out in the ventral stream, the channel carrying information useful to determine the identity of objects. In the previous chapter we discussed five areas belonging to this stream, V1, V2, V3, and V4, in the occipital cortex, and IT in the temporal cortex, and said that while V4 specializes on color the different modules making up IT may be the place where objects (or rather, 3D stick figure approximations to them) are synthesized. Since constancy effects emerge in the perception of objects, it is possible that interactions between V4 and IT play an important role. Evidence for this comes from various sources. First, receptive fields get larger as we move up the stream, those of V4 neurons being 40 percent larger on average than the ones in V1, while those in the posterior part of IT are four times larger.[57] The larger the receptive field the more extensive the retinal area covered, facilitating comparisons between adjacent surfaces to detect the effects of illumination. In addition, while the preferred stimulus of V1 neurons is a range of wavelengths, there are neurons in V4 that do not prefer wavelengths but rather colors themselves: they will not respond to wavelengths alone even if these match the ones that would be reflected by a surface of the preferred color.[58] We must be careful here because strictly speaking phenomenal color does not exist at the level of mindless cognitive agents, so we should rather say that the preferred stimulus for V4 neurons are signs for reflectances. Area V4 outputs to IT, but there are reentrant connections from IT to V4, so it is possible that the signs at the basis of constancy effects are created in this loop, using information about surface reflectances combined with volumetric information.

Perceived constancies of size, shape, color, and other properties are part of what makes objects appear to us as entities that endure in time. But the persistence of their capacities to affect things other than appearances, such as their capacity to harm our bodies, may be more important as evidence of their separate existence. Hence, in addition to the stabilization of visual content through constancy effects, we must consider the way in which we evaluate that content by the opportunities and risks that perceived objects afford us: objects demand us to value them and these values may be said to be perceivable just as colors are.[59] As we have seen, these evaluations can be made at both conscious and unconscious levels, the latter using either homeostatic values or the valences of different emotional responses as reference. The separation of the perspectival from the factual in this case involves distinguishing the perceived affordances of an object from its real affordances. Although the opportunities and risks that an object affords us depend in part on our abilities, this does not imply that affordances change if the mind changes.[60] The objectivity of affordances implies that we can misjudge them: a real cliff affords us danger but a *visual cliff*, consisting of a piece of transparent acrylic held high by two supports, does not, and yet animals (and human infants) respond to the latter just as they do to the former.[61]

In the previous chapter we discussed what is known about the way in which affordances are represented in the brain: it involved an area of the parietal cortex (AIP) coupled in a loop with an area from the premotor cortex (F5). The preferred stimulus of neurons in AIP are the properties of objects that are relevant for a given action, while those of F5 are goal-directed actions. When there are several possible actions (like several different ways of grasping an object), AIP creates signs for the different properties (those of the object's handle, its rim, and other graspable areas) and passes them to F5 for selection. This process may take several passes through the loop, and make use of other cortical areas to detect mismatches between what we unconsciously expect to happen and what actually happens after the action is carried out. We can speculate that it is in this circuit that the separation of the perspectival (judged affordances) and the factual (real affordances) takes place, at least for the kinds of actions that can be performed involuntarily. In the case of the voluntary control of actions we must also take into account the role played by learning during an organism's lifetime. Through what mechanism does learning affect the separation of the perspectival from the factual? One possible answer is suggested by computer simulations of the AIP-F5 loop, in which F5 is modeled as composed of two separate modules. The second module adds a special kind of neuron referred to as a *mirror neuron*, the preferred stimuli of which are either deliberate actions performed by an animal or the same deliberate actions *observed in other conspecifics*.[62] Mirror neurons can serve a variety of purposes. An animal can learn about affordances by watching others misjudge the capacities of an object to affect them, and use signs standing for these mismatches as a means to hone its own judgments as to what kind of skilled action is required by a given object. Mirror neurons also provide a means to mentally simulate actions and their consequences, allowing an animal to explore the difference between an apparent and a real risk without endangering itself.[63]

To conclude this section, let's discuss another way in which the perspectival and the factual must be told apart: the separation of the perceived volume of space occupied by an object, as well as the perceived distance separating two or more objects, from the real volumes and distances.[64] The space occupied by a solid object is also a property that persists through time, but the endurance of this property indicates both the *causal continuity* of the object (its causal link with its own past) as well as the continuity of the space it inhabits. If the object moves, changing its spatial relations to other objects, that same causal continuity reveals the objective connectedness of the place from which it departed and the one at which it arrived. Moving shadows, which do not causally interact with one another, do not provide an observer with information about the connectivity of space.[65] The relation between an object's causal persistence and the endurance of the space it inhabits suggests that the operation of separating the perspectival from the factual is related to the coordinate system used to locate objects relative to one self and to each other. The perspectival component of the visual field can be characterized using egocentric coordinates, as when we use the axes defined by subjective left and right, front and back, and up and down. Separating appearances from reality in this case involves transforming egocentric coordinates into allocentric ones to yield iconic signs representing the extrinsic spatial relations that objects bear to one another regardless of the location from which they are perceived.[66]

Let's focus on the question of distances separating two or more objects, the perceived magnitude of which can change dramatically with point of view. It will be easier to explain the switch from a subjective to an objective representation of space if we take into account that, when we explore an environment, we learn what objects in it afford us an obstacle, which ones afford us passage, and which ones afford us guidance. In other words, spatial relations are not only represented they are also valued. In the case of egocentric coordinates exploration yields iconic signs for both *routes* and *landmarks*. Signs for both of these can be produced using information about the movements needed to reach a particular location and the way salient objects appear from different points of view. Routes are usually linked to specific goals, such as finding food or water, and the information they provide is used in relation to the body's current location: an organism must aim at reducing the distance between its position and that of its target, aligning its body coordinates with another axis, such as the line formed by two known landmarks. A complex route may involve several repetitions of these operations, particularly if the final destination is not visible from the starting point, so the iconic sign for a route may also involve keeping track of the number of turns made and attending to the changing spatial relations between landmarks after each turn. Nevertheless, the spaces covered will tend to be relatively small, capable of being experienced as directly present, or at least, as spaces that can be broken down into segments that can be experienced as directly present.[67]

But what about larger spaces, such as those covered by migratory animals? In this case, the iconic signs must represent *places and the way they are connected* using allocentric coordinates. Rats trained to learn about mazes may use one or the other coordinate system depending on the task: for a task involving only a small portion of a maze, spatial relations can be represented using routes, but navigating a larger maze needs a more abstract kind of icon, particularly if the task demands reaching a target location from a variety of starting positions. The need to switch to a more objective frame of reference arises outside of the laboratory in the case of animals that, for example, hunt in packs and that have the ability to break into two or more groups to converge on a single location.[68] Unlike icons using egocentric coordinates, which as we just said tend be relative to specific goals, those using allocentric coordinates are compatible with many goals. And while routes must be updated continuously, because icons for landmarks will tend to differ for different orientations of the body, places in an allocentric map need to be represented only once, further exposures consolidating but not updating it.[69] On the other hand, it is possible that animals may never use an allocentric frame of reference by itself, but always together with an egocentric one, since only the latter can directly guide perception and action.[70]

The transformation of iconic signs for routes and landmarks into signs for places and connections is performed in the hippocampus.[71] This organ can be modeled as composed of three separate modules. The first module receives spatial information in egocentric coordinates, combining simple patterns into complex ones and performing calculations about the angles sustained by different pattern elements. The second module takes these patterns and angles and produces iconic signs for places and connections in allocentric coordinates. The third module adds values, such as information indicating the presence of something new in a place or the absence of something old.[72] The last two modules contain a special kind of neuron named a *place cell*, the preferred stimulus of which is one (or more) actual location(s) in the environment. These neurons do not have receptive fields, which are defined in either retinocentric or egocentric coordinates, but rather *place fields*, defined in allocentric terms. It can be shown, for example, that place cells are activated not by objects at a given location viewed from a certain angle, as would be required if they were represented egocentrically, but by objects occupying a place viewed from a variety of angles.[73] The evidence also shows that what causes these cells to fire is the place itself not the amount of time an animal spends on a location or the nature of the activity performed there.[74] We may conclude from these remarks that the separation of the perspectival from the factual components of the visual field also involves different ways of representing space.

To recapitulate this part of the argument. The perception of objects is more complex than that of isolated properties, since it must not only measure intensities and quantities but also perform at least three separate operations: represent objects as having properties that endure in time; represent an object's affordances in relation to our bodily capacities; and finally, represent the space taken up by an object, and the space between objects. Our perceptual experience supplies us with information about persistences, affordances, and distributions in space, but it combines the contributions of factors that depend on a particular point of view from those that do not. In addition to the various neural mechanisms we just discussed, there are several others that deserve our attention. There are, for example, mechanisms that separate the perceptual effects of our own movements from those caused by an object's own motions. We can illustrate this with the phenomenon of *perceptual stability*: when we move our eyes or our heads from side to side, objects sweep rapidly across our visual field, and yet we do not perceive them as moving but as staying in place as we move.[75] Because we internally represent what occurs at the retina as well as where our eyes and our heads are pointing at any one time, we can subtract self-motion from object motion using a set of vector transformations.[76] Finally, given that all of these operations are performed in separate brain areas, an important contribution to object perception is the mechanism that binds the signs produced in a distributed way so they can stand for the properties of a single object. As we argued in the previous chapter, this binding operation is performed by the synchronization of the oscillatory activity of different areas, a mechanism that has long been taken seriously by nonfunctionalist philosophers.[77]

We are now ready to move on to the perception of situations, and our first task will be to clarify the difference between situations understood with the aid of concepts and those that can be made sense of nonconceptually. Let's begin with the case of human beings trying to understand a situation *using propositions*, and then make the case that despite the fact that they are using language, only one use of symbols requires us to postulate a mastery of concepts, the other requiring only the capacities of an embodied and attentive subject. We may refer to these two alternatives as the *descriptive* way and the *demonstrative* way of understanding situations.[78] Demonstrative sentences are characterized by the use of indexical words. All words, even those used in descriptions, depend to some extent on context to make contact with their referent, but indexicals are the only ones that depend on the current situation *systematically*: the word "here" has an entirely different referent if uttered at different places, and the word "now" has a different referent if uttered at different times.[79] But how can the referent of a demonstrative proposition be fixed without concepts? Is not the referent of "here" given by the phrase "the place where I am right now"? It is tempting to answer that the referent of indexicals can be established using human anatomy, and this may be true in the case of "in front of me" and "behind me."[80] But the referent of "above me" and "below me" is not defined by the direction feet-to-head because we can still use these indexicals when we are lying down on the ground. Thus, the dependence of indexical terms on the axes of the human body is less general than their dependence on the *possibilities for action* that are open to a person in a given direction. If this is correct then the referent of "here" would not be fixed by a phrase like "the place where I am right now" but by a practical grasp of what I can do from here.[81] In addition, the objects involved in a situation can be selected using only voluntary attention to track them and keep them in view, an operation that can be performed without using any concepts.[82]

Attention is a more basic form of intentional behavior than that mediated by concepts and beliefs, and the demonstrative thoughts they lead to are different than the equivalent descriptive thoughts: "That animal there" is not the same as "The animal that is hiding in the bushes." A possible objection to this is that even if we agree that these two factual statements are different, the use of the term "animal" suggests the need for a *sortal concept*, that is, a concept for a kind of thing.[83] If this were correct then facts represented demonstratively would be no different than those represented descriptively. But we do not have to accept this objection. We can surely ask a question like "What is that?" pointing to an object the identity of which (the sort of thing it is) is completely unknown to us.[84] But more to the point, vervet monkeys can identify different kinds of predators, attend to them, and make their conspecifics attend to them, without possessing any sortal concepts. So how is this achieved? We saw in Chapter 1 that simple neural nets can extract a prototype from a population of examples by mapping relations of similarity in the objects used for training into relations of proximity in some space.[85] The latter can be a physical space if the neural net we are considering is a self-organizing map. As we argued when we first introduced these ideas, the prototype extracted by this mapping operation does not stand for an essence or abstract universal. It is simply a construct capturing statistical regularities in the objects actually used for training. And a similar point applies to vervet monkeys: they learn to recognize different predator types using regularities in the appearance of the actual predators they have encountered in their lives, not by mentally grasping an essence of the kind that sortal concepts are supposed to stand for.

Unfortunately, there is very little evidence that a mapping of similarities into proximities is actually performed by the brain.[86] But there are other ways of extracting prototypes that are more anatomically plausible, and they share some features with neural nets. Specifically, as a neural net is trained the strength of the connections between layers is progressively changed until a pattern of strengths emerges determining how the space of possible activation patterns for its hidden layer is partitioned. After training, the neural net will treat as equivalent any object that causes an activation pattern belonging to one, rather than another, partition. This insight has been implemented in the form of a large computer simulation, involving 10,000 units—each representing one neural population sharing inputs, outputs, and receptive fields—linked by over a million connections. The simulation is anatomically realistic with most visual areas in both the ventral and dorsal streams included in the model.[87] The basic idea is to interconnect different retinotopic maps, each specializing on a different property (shape, color, motion), in such a way that statistical patterns in the activity of one map become correlated with the activity in other maps. Given this connectivity, many exposures to tokens of a given type (sharing geometric, chromatic, and dynamic properties) will shape the synaptic strengths so they end up defining partitions that stand for the type to which the tokens belong.[88] Assuming that simulations like these are on the right track, we may speculate that the statistical constructs extracted can replace sortal concepts in the demonstrative understanding of situations, at least for the kind of simple and stereotyped situations that vervet monkeys understand.

Can the distinction between conceptual and nonconceptual ways of making sense of situations still apply to situations that demand keeping track not only of objects but also of their changing extrinsic relations as a situation unfolds? What of situations that require not only adjusting our skills to an object's affordances but also changing those very affordances following a series of causal interventions? In Chapter 2 we discussed an example of this kind of situation: an expert cook preparing a meal who makes an intelligent use of his surrounding space, so he can offload cognitive effort into it. This, we argued, eliminated the need for the cook to possess a complete *internal description* of the kitchen's working surfaces, and of the tools and ingredients.[89] Thanks to the cognitive scaffolding surrounding the cook, he can have a first-person understanding of his situation using words like "here" and "there" as spatial indexicals to locate knifes, bowls, and other objects, and using words like "before" and "after" as temporal indexicals to guide the order in which ingredients must be mixed or operations applied. In addition, the cook must be assumed to be making use of *causal indexicals*, expressed with words like "too hot to handle" or "too heavy to lift."[90] A causal indexical works like the word "I" which refers to a different person depending on who utters it. The similarity becomes more obvious if we paraphrase the former indexicals as "too hot for me to handle now" and "too heavy for me to lift now." In other words, what a causal indexical refers to is determined on the basis of a user's current capabilities and the immediate consequences of his current activity. We may conclude that, just as in the case of the word "here," the referent of which can be fixed by a practical understanding of what I can do from here, causal indexicals can operate without requiring concepts and are, therefore, usable by intelligent animals.[91]

One final contrast between the two ways of perceiving situations can be made if we ask the question: In what conditions is my understanding of a situation correct? For descriptive propositions the answer is given by the *truth conditions* for the proposition. In the case of visual perception what makes it veridical (as opposed to hallucinatory) are *satisfaction conditions*: the perceived situation must actually exist and it must involve the relations between objects and their properties that the subject is ascribing to it.[92] But agreeing with this does not force us to accept that satisfaction conditions must be *explicitly* represented in the perceiver's mind. Part of what distinguishes a hallucination from a veridical perception is that what we perceive is caused (however indirectly) by real objects around us, so the existence of this causal relation is one of its satisfaction conditions. But does having a veridical perception require that the perceiver *explicitly believes* that?[93] There are many ways to check whether our demonstrative understanding of a situation is correct. The satisfaction conditions for the thought "The sharp knife is to my left" are exhausted by our ability to locate the object relative to oneself.[94] This assumes that our perception of objects (knives) and properties (sharpness) can be performed nonconceptually, but we have already shown how this can be achieved. On the other hand, merely locating an object using egocentric coordinates may not be enough. To visually verify the thought "This knife is not adequate for this action," the cook must not only select the object by focusing attention on it but also pick out the signs that indicate that the blade is good for chopping but not for peeling. And more generally, highlighting any object with our attention allows us *to notice* the properties that determine whether we need to experience the object from all sides, manipulate it in a specific way, or act on it to see how it responds, in order to check whether we were right about it.[95]

To recapitulate, we can make sense of perceived situations in two different ways, only one of which demands the possession of concepts. We described the two alternatives as if both required the use of language, but the words required to understand situations demonstratively can be replaced by using attention and a practical grasp of opportunities for action. This replacement can be done only for situations in which all interacting entities are immediately present and available for visual inspection. Other, more complex cases do require the use of descriptions and of the concepts used in these descriptions. Despite their differences the two ways of understanding situations are related, because the belief-independent content of demonstrative thoughts must not only be connected to behavioral dispositions, as in the case of vervet monkeys, but must also serve as an input to the processes that produce descriptive thoughts.[96] In both cases, the thoughts involved can be used to fix a referent: we can single out an object by attending to it or by using a linguistic description of it. This referential function, however, must be distinguished from the function of verifying that the object does in fact have the properties we used to select it.[97] For descriptive thoughts this can be done in the traditional way using the truth conditions of propositions. But for demonstrative thoughts it suffices that we use our attention to select and gather perceptual information that bears on their satisfaction conditions, but that obviates the need to represent them conceptually. It follows, to return to the issue that opened this chapter, that only in the case of the descriptive perception of situations it is correct to say that being visually conscious of X implies having the belief of being conscious of X. Beliefs and the conceptual mastery these imply are not required for the perception of properties, of objects, and of situations understood demonstratively. Finally, we must add that the question of the neural mechanisms behind the perception of situations was not addressed, but we will return to it later.

Our argument so far applies only to what philosophers refer to as the easy problems of consciousness, that is, the problems that can be tackled by cognitive psychology and the neurosciences. When giving mechanisms for color and object perception, for instance, we did not bother to show how we can go from the level of neural processing by mindless agents to the level of phenomenal experience. Bridging this gap constitutes the *hard problem* of consciousness.[98] In what follows we will attempt to build the required bridge. As we argued in the previous chapter, this will involve giving up two-level models in which consciousness emerges in one magical step from neural activity, and adopt multiple intermediate levels. We can begin by considering multilevel solutions to the hard problem framed as re-representation problems. The core of these solutions is the idea that the brain represents its own activity and that this self-representation can itself be re-represented all the way up to conscious experience. There are several variations on this theme, the variants differing on how they conceive the representations involved as well as their relations. On the one hand, we can think of the relations between the mental state performing the re-representation and the mental state serving as its target as extrinsic, so that both states are logically independent, and consider two different ways in which the representations should be conceived, either as *higher-order thoughts* or as *higher-order percepts*.[99] On the other hand, we can think of the relations as intrinsic and constitutive of the terms they relate, in which case the mental state that does the monitoring and the state being monitored become one and the same. This is the self-representational model of consciousness.[100]

We fully accept the idea that the brain monitoring its own activity is the key to the solution to the hard problem. But there are two problems with the solutions just mentioned. The first is that there are no self-interpreting signs: signs involve an extrinsic triadic relation between a sign, its referent, and a cognitive agent, so the different levels bridging the gap must be levels of agency, not of signs. Besides, even if we accepted the existence of signs that interpret themselves, how could we account for their ability to monitor the activity of other signs? Once we start attributing monitoring powers to signs, we are basically attributing agency to them: we treat them as agents but refrain from using that term for fear of conjuring up homunculi. But, to say it again, homunculi are only problematic when they are exact replicas of the full subject, since that leads to an infinite regress. The second problem is that the agents populating the upper levels cannot be said to produce further signs but must be conceived as pure consumers. Why? Because much as we need a bottommost layer of mindless agents to stop a downward regress, we also need the uppermost layers to block an *upward regress*: if agents endowed with greater degrees of consciousness were to produce their own signs, those signs would need yet another agent to consume them, since in our account, the content of a sign is fixed by its consumer. Preventing the upper layers of agents to produce any further signs *identifies* phenomenal experience with the consumption of signs, a consumption performed in parallel by collectivities of agents. If this is correct it follows that phenomenal experience is not a *representation of the world*, although it does require the consumption of a myriad of such representations produced at lower levels. This eliminates the idea that the visual field is like a veil separating us from reality, as well as the idea that the transparency of this veil must be accounted for. The question of why we tend to see objects and not appearances is then answered by the way we deploy our attention. Without any training we usually attend to the factual content because that is what is required to successfully act in the world, but we can train our attention (as many visual artists do) to notice the perspectival content instead. And when we do that, we do engage our upper-level agents in the production of new signs, signs standing for the appearance we are currently noticing.

Beyond qualifying the kind of sign consumption performed by conscious agents as "voluptuous," however, we left this proposed solution rather vague.[101] In what follows we will attempt to give a more detailed account. The transformation of signs into lived feelings is better understood in the case of interoception, where it plays the role of accounting for the subjective component of homeostatic or emotional responses. For this reason we borrowed the terms used in that field to label the two proposed intermediate levels between mindless agents and the full subject: *protoselves*, in charge of consuming signs standing for properties like the concentration of glucose in the blood, as feelings of hunger; and *core selves*, in charge of consuming signs for objects and the opportunities and risks they afford as, among other things, lived feelings of anticipation or dread. Thus, two of our three nonconceptual forms of perception are related to a form of consumption that mediates the transformation into phenomenal experience. The third perceptual kind, the perception of situations, involves *autobiographical selves*, who may be said to consume signs for relations among objects as, among other things, lived feelings of involvement. We will have to make several modifications to the three kinds of agents originally proposed to adapt them for visual perception. First of all, we need to rethink the postulated neural basis for the agents in question. The original protoself, for example, was assumed to emerge in three specific areas of the brain stem that integrate interoceptive content.[102] In our own more speculative version, protoselves emerge in transient neural assemblies, not anatomically localized areas, that continuously monitor the activity in those brain stem areas. This change is required if we want to use protoselves as parts of more complex wholes.

Our protoselves must also be allowed to consume signs that are not visceral. In the case of vision, the task of visual protoselves would be, for example, to consume signs standing for reflectances as lived colors. Some protoselves may remain free, not subordinated to a more complex agent, in which case they will contribute to those parts of the visual field that do not represent objects: a traffic light located in the periphery of our visual field or a distant object perceived as a colored fuzzy blob. Other protoselves would become the working components of a core self and would contribute their felt properties to a larger project: constructing an object lived as possessing those properties. Here too, we need not speak of a single core self, but of multiple ones, with some dedicated to a single object in the visual field. We can only guess at this point how interactions among protoselves can yield the emergent properties and dispositions of a core self. We saw before that the transient assemblies that form the proposed neural basis for these agents lend themselves to a part-to-whole combinatorics, which is encouraging but hardly definitive. But we can speculate that the control of attention will play an important role. Some objects in the visual field, those not being attended to, may indeed be lived as bundles of properties, requiring only a team of protoselves, while those which are being closely inspected will need a greater degree of integration that only a core self can provide. We must also imagine that these two kinds of cognitive agents evolved, and continue to evolve, along separate but related paths. The perception of properties may not have been originally evolved to represent how external objects are characterized, but to monitor the state of an animal's visceral and sensory surfaces.[103] Only the properties of those surfaces were the original referent. But then, following a separate evolutionary history, a different kind of monitoring activity emerged to answer questions like "What is happening out there?" and not just "What is happening to me as an embodied self?"[104] This is precisely the role that a core self is assumed to play. That the two kinds of content exist side by side can be shown by experiments in which they become dissociated. Special goggles can be designed to invert the section of optic array that reaches the retina. When subjects first wear these goggles they report that both geometrical properties and the objects possessing those properties are experienced as being upside down. But with practice subjects can learn to behave adaptively in a world of objects, to ride a bicycle around them, for instance, even as they continue to live in a world of inverted properties.[105]

This brings us to the consumption of perceived situations. In line with our speculative model, an autobiographical self should be composed of core selves. The latter, as we said, live in the present but the wholes they compose must have the emergent ability to recall long-term memories and to form expectations about future plans. We need not think of all core selves as components of more complex agents, since some may remain independent consuming signs for objects that are not part of a currently perceived situation. For this reason, those objects may not become part of a remembered episode, or be taken into account when thinking about future projects. The core selves that are part of a larger whole, on the other hand, would contribute their integrated objects, and the product of separating the perspectival from the factual, to both memories and plans. But should we postulate only one autobiographical self? We argued earlier that understanding situations can be done in two ways, demonstratively and descriptively, and this suggests that we need two autobiographical selves, one belonging only to human beings, the other shared by humans and other primates. How should we characterize the difference between an autobiographical self that must use verbal descriptions to make sense of situations, from the one that can achieve the same goal using only attention and egocentrically defined action possibilities? And more to the point, do the different ways of understanding situations require postulating separate agents or are they simply different capacities of one and the same agent? Introspection, after all, seems to show that our phenomenal experience is unitary, lived from a single first-person point of view. Some philosophers defend the idea of multiple subjectivities using as evidence the well-known clinical phenomenon of multiple personality disorder.[106] But a less controversial example is that of patients who have undergone surgery to separate their two cerebral hemispheres, preventing the two halves from communicating with each other by normal means.

As everyone knows, each hemisphere governs the contralateral half of the body, the left one specializing on verbal tasks and causal inference, the right one on tasks that involve thinking visually about objects in space. To dissociate these functions, a special apparatus is used after the surgery to stimulate only one half of the patient's body: his right or left visual fields, right or left hands, right or left nostrils. This asymmetric stimulation confirms that the two hemispheres are indeed different: if a word is shown to the right visual field the information goes to the left hemisphere and the patient is able to report what he read, but if it is shown to the left field it goes to the right hemisphere and the patient reports not having seen anything. For those who believe that if a subject is conscious of something he must believe he is so conscious, and be able to report that as a fact, the right hemisphere must appear as an unconscious automaton. But to disprove that, all we need to do is change the way in which the subject indicates what he has seen. We can show a picture to his left visual field so the information goes to his right hemisphere, and then instruct him to use his left hand to find the object represented by the picture from a set of concealed objects. Because in this case neither a verbal input nor a verbal output is required; the subject can display his understanding by picking the correct object, which he invariably does, even as the he verbally insists, using his left hemisphere, that he saw nothing.[107] This dissociation seems to show that there is not a single autobiographical self, but at least two of them, and moreover, that only one of them can understand perceived situations descriptively, thanks to its access to linguistic resources.

But what about the evidence provided by introspection? Does not our own lived experience contradict this conclusion? Perhaps, but we must also ask, *whose introspective experience*? After all, in a multilevel solution to the hard problem, there is not a monolithic phenomenal experience belonging to a single subject, the visual field itself being the emergent result of the consumption activities of many cognitive agents of different complexity. Besides, as we argued in the previous chapter, the subject that can verbally report his experiences also tends to fabricate stories to explain those experiences whenever there are holes in his understanding. We can, therefore, expect this subject to create narratives in order to explain his own past behavior as if a unified person was behind it. Since it is those narratives that will make it into verbal reports, using these as evidence for a unified consciousness can be highly misleading. On the other hand, the belief that there are two fully separate autobiographical selves is called into question by the fact that split brain subjects behave normally in their daily lives, entirely unaware that they are not a single person. Only in a laboratory context, in which the sensory inputs to each hemisphere can be segregated with precision, do the striking dissociations occur. There are several factors promoting this sense of unity: there is only one body inhabited by both hemispheres, so all interoceptive and proprioceptive signs will be shared by them; the two hemispheres also share many unified subcortical structures, including the organs behind the biological value system; and the two must compete for attentional resources that tend to be limited and deployed for a single purpose.[108] Given this uncertainty we may decide to be cautious and draw the conclusion that attribution of a mental activity to a subject does not require us to postulate the existence of a single self, but not the stronger conclusion that there are two selves.[109] Or we can be less cautious and accept two autobiographical selves, one capable of consuming facts demonstratively the other descriptively, and argue that the factors just enumerated make their separate existence *unnoticeable* in ordinary circumstances.

Let's flesh out this account of the three kinds of conscious agents. As we argued when we introduced the idea, populating the intermediate levels with agents like these implies a graded conception of both intentionality and consciousness.[110] We can make the concept of *graded consciousness* more precise by considering two different characteristics of a conscious experience: the temporal scale at which the experience occurs and the kind of awareness it yields. To approach the question of temporal scales it is important to keep firmly in mind the distinction between objective and subjective time, the former being the time measured by clocks, the latter the time of experienced durations. Objective and subjective time may interact in subtle ways to yield phenomenal effects. The way in which we experience the relation of simultaneity between acoustic and visual events, for example, depends partly on the difference between the speed of sound and the speed of light, since this affects the amount of time that natural indices take to travel from their point of origin to our senses: thunder and lightning appear to us as occurring one after the other despite the fact that they take place at nearly the same time. A calculation shows that the distance at which the sources of an acoustic and a visual index must be located in order for us to live them as having occurred simultaneously is about 12 meters. But the actual distance is close to 10 meters because we also have to take into account that visual indices are processed more slowly than acoustic ones.[111] In this example, both traveling and processing time is the time measured by clocks, while the perceived simultaneity refers to phenomenally experienced time. Examples of ordinary temporal experiences, however, are of limited value for our argument. We need well-designed laboratory experiments to assign different temporalities to different kinds of conscious agents.

The simplest case is the perception of properties. In a typical laboratory setup, two lights are flashed to a subject, progressively decreasing the interval of objective time between each flash. As the interval reaches a critical duration, a so-called *threshold of simultaneity*, subjects experience the two lights as flashing at the same time. In other words, while objectively the two lights are separated in time, subjectively they are integrated into a single lived moment. In the case of visual stimuli, this threshold occurs at approximately twenty milliseconds.[112] Other perceived temporal relations also depend on critical thresholds. Take the relation of temporal succession. If the interval between flashes exceeds thirty milliseconds, a *threshold of order*, the two flashes are experienced as having occurred one after the other.[113] Because these two experiences depend on critical thresholds at the scale of tens of milliseconds, and because perceiving flashing lights does not demand binding properties into objects, we may speculate that this is the temporal scale at which protoselves operate. Because in our model core selves are made of interacting protoselves, core selves can use their components' experience of simultaneity and sequencing as part of the perception of objects: properties that belong to a single object will tend to be experienced as existing simultaneously and as moving at the same time when the object moves. But the subjectivity of core selves has its own emergent temporal properties. To measure the temporal scale at which these agents operate requires a different kind of experiment. Subjects may be asked, for example, to estimate the durations of different stimuli. Their judgments tend to coincide with objective time when the duration of the stimulus is approximately three seconds, shorter durations leading them to overestimate, longer ones to underestimate, the actual duration. That this result depends on verbal reports should not mislead us into thinking that we are dealing with more complex agents in this case. The same temporal scale is revealed by various other methods, such as asking the subject to group a regular sequence of stimuli into subjective units (as it occurs during the perception of a melody) or by measuring the amount of time he can attend to one of the two possible versions of an ambiguous stimulus, like a Necker cube, before it spontaneously flips to the other version.[114]

It is important to emphasize that three seconds define only an upper limit, and that faster integrations may occur in different circumstances.[115] Allowing for this variation, the lived present of core selves would come close to the classical concept of a *specious present*. The idea behind this concept is that the phenomenal present is not a point separating past and future but that it has a certain "thickness," a property that emerges from fusing a past that just happened and a future that is about to happen.[116] The past in question cannot be that of memory, and the future cannot be that of plans or projects, since these presuppose autobiographical selves. So past and future for core selves are related to the much shorter temporal scales of protoselves. But what exactly is integrated within the specious present? Unlike the threshold of simultaneity, which varies greatly across modalities, the threshold of order is the same for all modalities.[117] This suggests that the latter is the basic building block of subjective time, the critical duration involved in the integration of information from different modalities. Integrating several of these building blocks into a larger whole could then explain the specific temporal scale at which core selves operate.[118] And similarly for the relation between core selves and autobiographical selves, which is also a part-to-whole relation. The former live in the present and, therefore, exist only in the form of *brief pulses* constantly being emitted. These pulses overlap, giving core selves a sense of continuity, but they are still confined to the here and now. The temporality of autobiographical selves can be built by taking multiple core self pulses and holding the results together within a longer time window.[119] On the other hand, the experience of time proper to the most complex agents must be characterized beyond quantitative differences in temporal durations, because in this case we must take into account memories, both recent and distant.

The idea that memories are crucial to personal identity has a long history dating back to the birth of classical empiricism.[120] But objections to it have also been around for centuries. As early critics pointed out, for example, if recalling a memory is simply being conscious now of what happened to us in the past, then memory presupposes personhood.[121] But this circularity can be avoided if we distinguish different kinds of memory. On the one hand, there is *semantic* memory, involving the storage of the words and sentences heard or read on a particular occasion, and on the other, *episodic* memory, the storing of actually lived scenes. The two kinds can become dissociated by brain lesions, producing different kinds of amnesia.[122] Both forms of memory involve representing past events, but only episodic memory demands that there was an act of *witnessing* at its origin. This can help us break the vicious circle between personhood and memory because having witnessed an event does not presuppose that it was the same person who did the witnessing as the one doing the remembering, only that one and the same living body was involved in both acts.[123] In our terms this can be expressed by saying that witnessing involves only an autobiographical self who can make sense of situations demonstratively, and who can recall lived situations using indexicals. Given that the differences between the kinds of cognitive agents operating at this level are related to the specialization of brain hemispheres, is there evidence that the two kinds of long-term memory are part of this specialization? Yes, at least when it comes to *recall*: recalling lived experiences is done in the right hemisphere while recalling words takes place in the left hemisphere.[124] Lesions that affect the cortical areas involved in the recall of episodic memories affect the ability of subjects to recall past lived events in the correct sequence, and as the construction of a coherent time line is disrupted so is a subject's sense of identity.[125]

But even if we managed to avoid circular definitions by distinguishing kinds of memory, do episodic memories provide enough continuity to personal history to ensure identity? Or to put this differently, if personal history was subdivided into stages, can episodic memory alone give the series of stages enough unity? If we required that every stage possessed memories of all previous stages, then the answer would be negative because some stages (e.g., sleeping) do not possess such memories, and because people tend to forget.[126] A solution to this problem may require weakening our criteria for personal identity, replacing strict identity, which is absolute, with the idea of the *survival* of a person from one stage to another, a relation between stages that varies by degree.[127] In this case what is important is that a subject's defining characteristics have proper successors: their past and future versions should be broadly similar to them and be causally connected to them.[128] Neither of these requirements is absolute. The extent to which a past or future stage of my current personal history is similar to my present one depends on how gradual changes have been—smooth changes yielding a high degree of similarity, drastic changes a low degree. We can survive as persons if we lose limbs in an accident or if a lesion makes parts of our brains cease to function. It will all depend on the degree to which our bodies have been changed—changing our faces may have a more drastic effect on personal identity than other body parts, for example—and the degree to which our brains have continued to function as before, lesions to the prefrontal cortex affecting our sense of identity more than other brain areas. Finally, the extent to which we feel connected to our past selves, and the extent to which we care about our future selves, depends on the intensity of feelings of pride or shame about past actions or feelings of responsibility about future goals.[129]

The phenomenal experience of progressively more complex cognitive agents can also be characterized by the kinds of attentional resources they can deploy. So far we have treated voluntary attention as a capability of the full subject. But now that we have eliminated this unitary subject, we must elaborate the concept a little further. One way to distinguish the different kinds of attention involved is by an analysis of the different uses of the word "consciousness" in ordinary talk. The word is sometimes used for the state of not being in a coma or in dreamless sleep, that is, for *arousal*.[130] Arousal can be defined as the capacity to be stimulated, a capacity that even mindless cognitive agents must possess. Another usage of the term "conscious" refers to a state of awareness that may have greater or lesser focus. When an animal is only vaguely aware of a possible danger, displaying an orienting reaction but without focusing on a definite target, we may speak of a state of *vigilance or alertness*. This can be defined as the capacity to detect signs that are near the threshold of detectability, or what amounts to the same thing, to be in a state of maximum sensitivity to any indications of significant change.[131] Cognitive agents performing a monitoring function of the internal environment, or of the sensory surfaces in contact with the external environment, must be capable of being in a constant state of vigilance, alert to any changes demanding a rapid response. What kind of phenomenal experience can be expected to emerge in a vigilant state? By hypothesis, protoselves consume signs for properties not bound into objects, so what they experience must be diffusion fields, intensity gradients, oscillations, and fluctuations.[132] Or in more subjective terms, waves of sensations washing over the body, intensities reaching critical levels demanding release, as well as feelings of anticipation of consummatory relief.

The kind of attention that emerges at the level of core selves does not have an ordinary language name but does have a technical one: *flow*. As befits an agent that lives in the specious present, this is a highly concentrated form of attention in which the rest of the world disappears as the subject immerses himself on a task involving a skillful interaction with an object. When we learn a new skill we are very aware of our own movements, but as training proceeds these movements take care of themselves, allowing us to direct our limited attention to the effects that our actions have on their targets.[133] This can be expressed in our own terms by saying that at first it is an autobiographical self that monitors the performance of the task but as the level of skill increases it allows a core self to take over the monitoring. The phenomenal effect of this transfer of control is observable in the laboratory. When the target object's affordances are matched by the subject's skills, subjects report a feeling of *effortlessness* and of pleasing *muscular fluidity*. When, on the other hand, skills fail to match the complexity of a task, the result is feelings of anxiety, and when skills are not sufficiently challenged by the task, feelings of boredom.[134] For this type of attention to manifest itself, and for the phenomenally rewarding character of the state of flow to occur, the task being performed has to have clear immediate goals and unambiguous feedback.[135] This is to be expected in the case of core selves who live moment to moment: the final goal of a lengthy action sequence, and feedback acquired after long delays, is bound to have a less pronounced effect on phenomenal experience at this level.

Monitoring the execution of a lengthy task in which the significance of the current action depends on past and future actions is not the same as monitoring an action currently being performed. The former involves keeping track of events in an unfolding situation in which an action may change the very affordances that objects supply for the next action. We have used the preparation of a complex meal by an expert cook as our main example, but the practice of any complex craft would serve equally well. In these cases, a different (but more familiar) form of attention is involved, the nature of which is suggested by a third usage of "conscious": the awareness of the contents of phenomenal experience at a specific location, as when we suddenly become aware of the presence of something in our visual field that had been there all the time but that we had failed to notice. Let's refer to the ability to see details that would escape notice by casual observers as *selective awareness*. The role of this type of attention in the nonconceptual perception of situations was already outlined earlier: what an indexical refers to in demonstrative thoughts is specified by the way attention selects the referent and the way it connects it to possibilities for action. Selecting something for special treatment implies rejecting other things, so selection involves evaluations of what is important and what can be safely ignored, an assignment of value that depends on what has been learned in the past in similar contexts.[136] Selective awareness also plays an important role in directing activity when the information required to perform a task is not all given in the present moment but becomes available in a *temporally discontinuous way*. In this case, our attention must be directed toward the recent past and the near future (at the scale of minutes or hours, not seconds), so we can deal with contingencies separated in time, as when an operation that was performed a few minutes before led to unanticipated results and the current operation must be adapted to take that into account.[137]

Introducing intermediate levels between the brain and a subject who can issue reports does not solve the hard problem but it does break it down into three more tractable problems. And it points to the direction we must follow to find the solution: a methodology that combines analysis and synthesis, starting at the bottom and moving upward. The first step would be to synthesize an artificial protoself, which we can imagine being nothing more complicated than a *sentient measuring device*. If we can imagine a speedometer that can feel the effect of moving slowly or rapidly, we can imagine a protoself. In our model, protoselves are specialist agents, each dedicated to the transformation of a specific measured property into a specific felt property, so each can be synthesized separately, and then allowed to interact with the others. Among the outcomes we can expect from these interactions is the emergence of teams of protoselves to deal with external objects as bundles of properties, much like insects and other simple creatures do. It is also likely that we may have to use simulations of biological evolution, in which populations of synthetic organisms must cope with environmental demands to slowly get the "sentient" part of the measuring device to emerge. If we can solve this problem, and the difficulty of finding a solution should not be minimized, we would be in a much better position to solve the next step: creating an artificial core self. As we mentioned earlier, this would involve another evolutionary process that takes place in parallel with the previous one. Thus, as the first evolution begins to yield sentient measuring devices working in coalitions, the second evolution would consolidate some of these into more permanent wholes with their own properties, taking us from perceived bundles of properties to objects lived as possessing those properties.

Following a synthetic route can generate insights that a top-down analysis of reports from an autobiographical self could never yield. For example, after many failed attempts to get core selves to emerge we may realize that, in addition to protoselves, a core self requires many specialized mindless agents to help in the synthesis of objects. We may also discover that fleshing out the 3D stick figures used by mindless agents to yield the fully rendered objects present in the visual field may require intermediate levels of agency. We may be forced to change the model itself, introducing agents with capacities between those of core selves and protoselves, or even between core selves and autobiographical ones. Novel insights may also be generated about the environments we need to simulate in order to get different agents to emerge. In the case of autobiographical selves we would most likely require a social environment like that of other primates, because the need to recall specific situations from the past, and to take into account possible future situations, has a higher probability of emerging in the context of reciprocating communities.[138] Vervet monkeys, for example, can remember those specific members of their community they have groomed in the past and those members that are expected to groom them in the future, although they do not seem able to monitor failures to reciprocate in order to retaliate. Chimpanzees, on the other hand, do retaliate against conspecifics that have formed alliances against them in the past. And when two chimpanzees enter into an alliance against a third one they behave as if they expected their opponent to enter into alliance against them at some future time.[139]

To synthesize cognitive agents with the social capabilities of monkeys and apes, we would have to extend many of the concepts we have used to explain the workings of bodies, brains, and minds: the concept of attention would have to be changed to include the act of directing other people's attention as well as the act of desiring the attention of others; the concept of an affordance would have to extend to the opportunities and risks with which members of a community supply us; the indexical signs emitted spontaneously or deliberately by others would need to point not only to the causes of their behavior but also to the reasons and motives that are additional determinants of that behavior; the list of emotional responses and the feelings these generate would have to be augmented with social feelings; and to the set of biological values used to select what action is appropriate in a given context, we would have to add social values like reciprocity. Evolving agents capable of living situations demonstratively may seem like an impossible task, but only if we forget that at this point, the existence of agents capable of experiencing properties and objects could be taken for granted. We would also need to take into account that the evolution of protoselves and core selves would continue alongside that of autobiographical selves, and these parallel evolutions would also contribute to the social differentiation of feelings, affordances, indices, values, and other factors affecting experience and behavior.

Solving the hard problem using a synthetic approach would make a science of consciousness look more like chemistry than physics.[140] But as important as this problem is, it should not make us lose sight of the fact that the contributions of the mind to the construction of the visual field must always be considered together with those of the world, the body, and the brain. The three levels of sentient agents we just examined would have nothing to consume if the armies of mindless agents that perform all the representational labor were not constantly at work. The icons and indices these armies produce and consume, in turn, would be useless if they did not belong to causal chains that have their sources in a mind-independent world. For reasons having to do with its history, the world has a definite statistical structure that has been tracked closely during the evolution of sensory organs. And the light that bathes our planet not only transmits information about this statistical structure, which is independent of a subject's location, but also information about the extrinsic relation between the subject and the objects that are visible from a given point of view. This information is objectively present in ambient light, as well as on the retinas that take a slice of it in order to extract natural signs from it and convert them into intentional signs. Finally, those retinas are component parts of eyes which are parts of heads attached to articulated bodies. This implies that the sections of structured light at the start of the visual sensory process are often taken by a body that moves around as it explores its surroundings, generating further signs about the relations between subject and object, such as composite visual and somatic maps that can register the dependencies between a body's motions and the resulting changes in the visual field. This information may sometimes be merely instrumental, moving to a new position to get a better view, but it can also play a role in the synthesis of perceived solid objects. There are still many mysteries surrounding the multiple interactions between these four contributors, but it is already clear that a visual field like ours could not emerge without all of them operating continuously. And this is why it is so important to adopt a materialist approach to phenomenology.

NOTES

Introduction

1 Mario Bunge, *The Mind-Body Problem. A Psychobiological Approach* (Oxford: Pergamon, 1980), 21.

   When writing about the philosophy of mind we may speak with Bunge on "property dualism," since we are making a rough distinction between physics, chemistry, and biology, on the one hand, and the human mind, on the other. But in other fields of philosophy the proper expression would be "property pluralism" because chemical properties cannot be reduced to physical ones, or biological properties reduced to chemical ones.

2 Lynn Rudder Baker, "Non-Reductive Materialism," in *The Oxford Handbook of Philosophy of Mind*, edited by Brian P. McLaughlin, Ansgar Beckermann, and Sven Walter (Oxford: Oxford University Press, 2009), 110–11.

3 Ibid., 112–14.

4 Dealing with the effects of social factors beyond those present in hunter-gatherer communities demands a discussion of social ontology. An ontology that takes into account only two levels of social reality, the individual and society, or the micro and the macro, oversimplifies the explanation. We need to add a *meso-scale*, consisting of communities, organizations, cities, urban regions, and provinces, to bridge the gap between persons and entire countries. And we need to work out in detail how human subjects are incorporated into each of these multiple entities, one at a time. This task has been attempted elsewhere. The interested reader can simply replace the skeletal account of subjectivity given there, with the content of this book. See Manuel DeLanda, *A New Philosophy of Society* (London: Bloomsbury, 2006), 47–52.

Chapter 1

1 Charles Sanders Pearce, "Of Reasoning in General," in *The Essential Pearce*, edited by The Pearce Edition Project (Bloomington: Indiana University Press, 1998), 13–17.

Pearce does not use the term "causality" when defining the relation between an index and its object. Instead he specifies that there must be a "real connection" between the two and that such a connection must force the mind to attend to the object. The problem here is that different ontological positions result in very different definitions of causality. Pearce was an empiricist who accepted a definition of causality as the observed co-occurrence of two events. Given this definition, causality can be reduced to *contiguity* in time, and in some cases (e.g., collisions) contiguity in space. Thus, more recent theorists define indices solely in terms of contiguity, not as in the present book, as involving a productive relation between a cause and its effect that exists independently of any observer and such that the effect carries information about its cause.

2 Thomas A. Sebeok, *Signs: An Introduction to Semiotics* (Toronto: University of Toronto Press, 1994), 48–50.

The author treats different indices separately: animal tracks, clues (e.g., a bullet hole in the wall), and medical symptoms are all taken to be different kinds of signs. The reason for this is that the original formulation has many subdivisions, postulating various kinds of indices and icons, and these may be classified in several ways. In what follows we will stick to the simpler formulation.

3 Ibid., 28 and 85.

Sebeok uses the term "topological similarity," a term closely related to that of "isomorphism" and argues that Pearce acknowledged the distinction between similarity of appearances and similarity of relations.

4 Nicholas Shea, "Millikan's Isomorphism Requirement," in *Millikan and Her Critics*, edited by Dan Ryder, Justine Kingsbury, and Kenneth Williford (Chichester: Wiley-Blackwell, 2013), 64–7.

5 Ibid., 77.

6 The two main philosophers who have rediscovered natural signs are Fred Dretske, who favors indices, and Ruth Millikan, who favors icons. See: Fred Dretske, *Naturalizing the Mind* (Cambridge, MA: MIT Press, 1997), 8. Ruth Garrett Millikan, *Varieties of Meaning* (Cambridge, MA: MIT Press, 2004), 55.

7 Sebeok, *Signs*, 5–14.

Both Pearce and Sebeok conceive of the interpreter (or interpretant) as just another sign. We will disregard this in what follows, as it seems to imply the notion of a self-interpreting representation.

8 William M. Ramsey, *Representation Reconsidered* (Cambridge: Cambridge University Press, 2007), 90.

9 Sebeok, *Signs*, 17.

In what follows the content of both indices and icons will be considered to be the referent of the signs. In the case of symbols and, more specifically, words, the referent is sometimes fixed by the mediation of the signification of the words, acting as an intermediate entity. Since our position is that symbols do not affect perception, we will ignore this difference.

10 Ramsey, *Representation Reconsidered*, 27.

11 Daniel C. Dennett, *Consciousness Explained* (Boston: Little, Brown, 1991), 262.

Dennett uses the term "homuncular functionalism" for this approach to the problem of cognitive agency. The original formulation of the idea can be found in: Daniel C. Dennett, *Brainstorms* (Cambridge, MA: MIT Press, 1981), 123–4.

12 William Bechtel and Adele Abrahamsen, *Connectionism and the Mind*, (Maiden: Blackwell, 2002), 38–9.

This learning rule, called the *Hebbian learning rule*, is actually a bit different. The activations of input and output units are multiplied with each other (and multiplied by a constant representing the learning rate). If the signs of both units are the same (both positive or negative) the connection's strength is increased by an amount proportional to their product; if they are different, it is decreased.

13 Ibid., 30–1.

14 Ibid., 41.

15 Ibid., 42.

The authors argue that although the human user provides semantic content through the choice of training examples, he does not know in advance which *micro-features* of the input-output pairs the neural net will become sensitive to, or which subtle, nonobvious regularities the neural net will extract.

16 Paul M. Churchland, *Plato's Camera, How the Physical Brain Captures a Landscape of Abstract Universals* (Cambridge, MA: MIT Press, 2012), 74–5.

What does it mean to say that a set of input examples has been mapped into a space of *possible* activation patterns? Imagine an abstract space in which each point stands for a possible pattern. Then assign to each point a given *probability* of occurring. At the start of the training the strengths of the connections are set to random values so the possibility space associated with the hidden layer is basically made of equiprobable points; that is, every possibility has the same probability of becoming an actual state. Using a training rule that at every step makes the amount of error between the desired and the actual outcome available to the neural net, the strengths of its connections are adjusted so as to progressively diminish the error, slowly sculpting the possibility space *by breaking the equiprobability* of its possibilities. After the training is over, the correct activation pattern, the one corresponding to the object to be recognized, becomes the most probable outcome. Moreover, points nearby to it will tend to correspond (with high probability) to objects similar to the target, while points away from it will correspond to objects that are different from the target.

17 Ramsey, *Representation Reconsidered*, 121–3.

Ramsey rejects the idea that the sculpted possibility space functions as a representation, and also the idea that the pattern of strengths in the connections function as an *implicit* representation (Ibid., 156–7). It is unclear whether using a self-organizing map to make the iconic classification explicit would satisfy his job description for an internal representation.

18 Teuvo Kohonen, *Self-Organizing Maps* (Berlin: Springer, 2001), 106–19.

In a self-organizing map every unit of the input layer is connected to every unit of the output layer. During training, the activation pattern serving as input is compared to the pattern of strengths of the connections to each of the units in the output layer to assess its degree of similarity to it. (The comparison can be made because an activation pattern and a pattern of strengths are both sets of numbers.) At the beginning of the training the connection strengths are randomly set, so the set with the highest similarity will be found by chance, but the output unit to which they are linked can be selected as a "winner." The connections of the winning unit will then be changed increasing their resemblance to the input, as will those of its neighboring units in the rectangular array, the degree of adjustment decreasing as the units get further away from the winner. The process is repeated many times, each iteration reducing the size of the neighborhood, until only the winner is adjusted. The latter will be an explicit and accessible representation surrounded by a gradient of similar ones. Several philosophers have argued for the need to go from first-order neural nets, in which representations are implicit, to second-order ones that make these representations explicit. If a first-order device can be said to have the skill to navigate a problem domain, the second-order one would make that skill its own problem domain. See: Andy Clark, "Connectionism and Cognitive Flexibility," in *Essays on Nonconceptual Content*, edited by York H. Gunther (Cambridge, MA: MIT Press, 2003), 174–5.

19 The requirement that there be a second neural net capable of using the explicit sign follows from the triadic definition of a sign: the second neural net would play the role of user. Further on we will change the terminology and express this by saying that the two neural nets must play the complementary roles of *producer and consumer* of signs. The terms "producer" and "consumer" were coined by Millikan to refer not to agents with sophisticated capabilities but to relatively simple mechanisms, of which neural nets are an example. See: Ruth Millikan, "Reply to Godfrey-Smith," in *Millikan and Her Critics*, 61.

20 Churchland, *Plato's Camera*, 91.

21 Ibid., 87–9.

Churchland contrasts the Indicator Semantics defended by philosophers like Dretske to his own Domain-Portrayal Semantics. His main argument is that indices without an icon (e.g., a GPS map that has only an indicator dot without a layout of streets and landmarks) are devoid of semantic content (Ibid., 101). In the case of human beings, the perception of color (or any other property) involves both a sculpted possibility space defining the range of colors (an icon) and a current set of activated neurons, indicating the specific color presently causing an experience (an index). But, he argues, if a person were suddenly to lose his color vision and could not produce the index any longer, the semantics of color signs would still be available to him via the icon. What the color-blind person would lack is a way of activating points within the sculpted possibility space containing color categories (Ibid., 93–4). His criticism is echoed by William Ramsey who argues that an icon, but not an index, has sufficient internal structure (due to its being isomorphic with something else) to be used as a representation by mindless agents. He agrees that indices may be mechanically sensed and acted upon, as they are by devices like thermostats, but denies that indices used in that manner are playing a representational role. See: Ramsey, *Representation Reconsidered*, 137 and 141–2.

22 Bechtel and Abrahamsen, *Connectionism and the Mind*, 304.

The authors do not commit themselves to ascribing intentionality to neural nets but do remark that once we give them a robotic body and situate them in a space we would be more inclined to treat them intentionally.

23 William G. Lycan, *Consciousness* (Cambridge: Bradford, 1987), 57–8.

24 Dretske, *Naturalizing the Mind*, 92–3 and 172–7.

25 Millikan, *Varieties of Meaning*, 73.

26 Peter Godfrey-Smith, "Signals, Icons, and Beliefs," in *Millikan and Her Critics*, 45–6.

27 Ibid., 44.

28 Rescorla, "Millikan on Honey Bee Navigation and Communication," in *Millikan and Her Critics,* 90–1.

29 Shea, "Millikan's Isomorphism Requirement," 69–70.

30 Millikan, *Varieties of Meaning*, 76.

31 Fred I. Dretske, *Knowledge and the Flow of Information* (Cambridge, MA: MIT Press, 1981), 156–61.
   Dretske argues that ignoring the information of the possibly many intermediate causal steps when using a sign makes his theory an informational, not a causal, theory of content.

32 James L. Gould, "Ethological and Comparative Perspectives on Honey Bee Learning," in *Insect Learning*, edited by Daniel R. Papaj and Alcinda C. Lewis (New York: Chapman and Hall, 1993), 31–8.

33 Millikan, *Varieties of Meaning*, 81–2.

34 David Marr, *Vision* (Cambridge, MA: MIT Press, 1982), 75.

35 Ibid., 266–7.
   In these pages Marr lists all the assumptions about the statistical structure of the world that we are required to make to constrain the process of recovering an object's geometry.

36 Ibid., 69–70 and 104.

37 Marr considers the signs produced in this process, starting with those that transform a continuous distribution of light intensities into a discrete set of line segments, as involving symbols (Ibid., 67–8). But he seems to derive this conclusion from the type of signs used in his computer model, which are indeed, symbolic (e.g., mathematical). We can disregard this particular theoretical choice and continue to use his ideas as if they involved indices and icons.

38 Millikan, *Varieties of Meaning*, 83.

39 We will be discussing various uses of hybrid signs in the following chapters. In addition to using the icon for types and the index for tokens, the icon can be used to represent the range of values of a property, the index for its current value; or the icon can be used to represent the entire body and the index the part that is being used or monitored.

40 Coupling neural nets with a genetic algorithm would allow us to simulate this coevolution in detail. See: Manuel DeLanda, *Philosophy and Simulation* (London: Continuum, 2011), 86–7 and 91–3.

41 Marr, *Vision*, 265–6.
    Marr emphasizes the importance of including knowledge about the statistical structure of the world as part of the process of designing a computer vision system.

42 Dale Purves and R. Beau Lotto, *Why We See What We Do: An Empirical Theory of Vision* (Sunderland: Sinauer, 2003), 5–8.

43 Ibid., 5.

44 Ibid., 144–5.
    In these pages the authors discuss the relative frequencies of occurrence of line lengths, not surface properties. But the statistical distribution of line lengths and angles depends on the fact that they tend to belong to surfaces. See: Catherine Q. Howe and Dale Purves, *Perceiving Geometry: Geometrical Illusions Explained by Natural Scene Statistics* (New York: Springer, 2005), 33 and 41.

45 Ibid., 15–18.

46 John R. Pani, "Descriptions of Orientation and Structure in Perception and Physical Reasoning," in *Ecological Approaches to Cognition*, edited by Eugene Winograd, Robyn Fivush, and William Herst (Mahwah: Lawrence Earlbaum, 1999), 68–9.

47 Purves and Lotto, *Why We See What We Do*, 147–8 and 155–6.
    The authors analyze various visual illusions and discuss the ways they could be explained by the statistical structure of the world. A well-known phenomenon is the propensity of human subjects to perceive the lengths of projected vertical lines as longer than horizontal ones. Another is the human tendency to overestimate projected acute angles, and underestimate obtuse ones. Both of these phenomena can be explained by the relative abundances of vertical versus horizontal lines in scanned natural scenes, and by the relative abundances of angles subtended by lines in those scanned scenes (Ibid., 147–8 and 155–6). Another well-known phenomenon is the tendency of subjects to judge a brighter surface as being closer to

them. Analysis of scenes performed with a laser range scanner, in which depth and light intensity are co-registered, indicates that there is a real correlation between depth and brightness. The explanation for this correlation depends on the relative abundance of overhead light sources and on the relative abundance of surface layouts, such as the arrangement of leaves in a tree or the arrangement of concavities in a rock, that produce *shadows* with a certain statistical pattern. When lit from above, the outermost leaves of a tree will tend to be fully illuminated while at the same time they will cast shadows on those further inside. Similarly, the exterior of a rock will tend to catch more light than, and cast a shadow on, the interior of its holes and cracks. Finally, from any point of observation, both the outermost tree leaves and the rock's exterior will tend to be less distant. See: Brian Potetz and Tai Sing Lee, "Scene Statistics and 3D Surface Perception," in *Computer Vision: From Surfaces to 3D Objects*, edited by Christopher W. Tyler (Boca Raton: Chapman & Hall, 2011), 5–6.

48 James J. Gibson, *The Ecological Approach to Visual Perception* (New York: Psychology Press, 2015), 60.

49 Ibid., 190–1.

50 James T. Todd, "Formal Theories of Visual Perception," in *Persistence and Change*, edited by William H. Warren and Robert E. Shaw (Hillside: Lawrence Erlbaum, 1983), 88–90.

Todd examines the assumptions behind the concept of structured light as postulated by ecological psychologists. The first three are: light is reflected by surfaces in all directions; its structure can be analyzed by sectioning it with a surface; and this section, cutting through all the solid angles, will possess a certain structure defined by optic elements. As far as the second assumption is concerned the actual shape of the intersecting surface (flat, semi-hemispherical) is immaterial, since the surfaces can be rigorously transformed into one another, but the relative orientation of the incoming rays is important to determine the kind of projection (polar, orthogonal) that we must use in our models.

51 Gibson, *The Ecological Approach to Visual Perception*, 60.

52 Ibid., 96.

53 Todd, "Formal Theories of Visual Perception," 91.

54 Ibid., 96.

55 Gibson, *The Ecological Approach to Visual Perception*, 115–16 and 217–18.

Gibson does not express these ideas in terms of indices. He in fact rejects the idea that light carries signs but this is motivated by his rejection of both symbols and the idea that symbols must be sent and be received (as opposed to broadcasted).

56 G. Johansson, "About Visual Event Perception," in *Persistence and Change*, 38–9.

57 Gibson, *The Ecological Approach to Visual Perception*, 69–72.

58 Ibid., 219.

59 Willard Van Orman Quine, *Word and Object* (Cambridge, MA: MIT Press, 1960), 22–3.

60 Gibson, *The Ecological Approach to Visual Perception*, 47.

Gibson's concept of information is different than the one used in the field of Information Theory. In that field all that matters is the quantity of information that is transmitted through a channel, but in Gibson's usage it refers to the content of what is transmitted not just the amount, and moreover, the concept does not presuppose the existence of a sender and a receiver (Ibid., 56–7). Gibson's concept of information is, therefore, close to that of Millikan's natural signs.

61 Claire F. Michaels and Claudia Carello, *Direct Perception* (Englewood Cliffs: Prentice Hall, 1981), 60–8.

62 In addition to the information provided by solid angles and optic flow, there is another kind of mathematical content that provides ecological psychologists with a reason to deny the need for internal representations: *invariants*. The concept of a property that is invariant under a given transformation is important in the theory of symmetry. A cube's appearance, for example, remains unchanged if it is rotated by exactly 90 degrees. Moreover, it stays invariant under a whole set of rotations, the set containing 90, 180, 270, and 360 degrees. When this set meets several extra mathematical conditions, it is referred to as a *group*. This group captures the identity of all objects shaped as a cube, every bit as much as a description of their properties does, like the property of having six square sides. And it is this intimate relation to the identity of objects that makes invariants a useful kind of informational content. Moreover, the invariant properties of rigid objects like a cube stay invariant when the cube is projected into the retina so information about them is contained in the section of optic array performed by the retina. Gibson argues that invariants fully *specify* the geometrical identity of objects and that they are easy to be picked up directly at the retinal level. But whereas a simple mechanism could learn that rotation by 90 degrees leaves the appearance of a cube unchanged, a single rotation does not specify anything: it is the group as a whole that does that. The problem is that no one has shown how a simple retinal mechanism could extract the group just mentioned without using internal representations. Moreover, some of the invariants used in theories of perception do not meet the required mathematical conditions. Perspective transformations, for example, are a subset of the projective group, but they themselves do not form a group. See: Johan Wagemans, Christian Lamote, and Luc Van Gool, "Shape Equivalence Under Perspective and Projective Transformations," *Psychosomic Bulletin and Review*, Vol. 4, No. 2 (1997): 249.

One attempt to give more rigor to ecological invariants is in terms of dual antisymmetric subgroups. See: William H. Warren and Robert E. Shaw, "Events and Encounters as Units of Analysis for Ecological Psychology," in *Persistence and Change*, 14–17.

63 This description is, in fact, not quite correct. The actual story involves sets, not spaces, and goes like this. In 1662 Pierre de Fermat proposed that light propagates between two points so as to minimize travel time. His basic insight can be explained this way: if we knew the start and end points of a light ray, and if we could form *the set of all possible paths* joining these two points (straight paths, crooked paths, wavy paths), we could find out which of these possibilities is the one that light actualizes by selecting the one that takes the least amount of time. In the eighteenth century, a way to extend this insight into the world of differential functions (the calculus of variations) was created by the mathematician Leonard Euler. Before Euler the main problem was to find a way to specify the set of possible paths so that it was maximally inclusive, that is, so that it contained all possibilities. This was done by parametrizing the paths, that is, by generating the paths through the variation of a single parameter. But there are many physical problems in which the possibilities cannot be parametrized by a discrete set of variables. By tapping into the resources of the differential calculus Euler was able to rigorously specify the set of possibilities and to locate the minimum, maximum, and inflection points (i.e., all the singularities) of the functions that join the start and end points. See: Don S. Lemons, *Perfect Form, Variational Principles, Methods and Applications in Elementary Physics* (Princeton: Princeton University Press, 1997), 17–27.

64 See description and criticism of this way of casting the content of physics, and of the pseudo-problem of the underdetermination of theory by observation created by this, in: Manuel DeLanda, *Philosophical Chemistry: Genealogy of a Scientific Field* (London: Bloomberg, 2015), 136–9.

65 Ronald N. Giere, *Explaining Science: A Cognitive Approach* (Chicago: University of Chicago Press), 65–8.

Giere shows that modern textbooks do not teach physics using linguistically expressed "laws of nature" but rather present us with a large family of equations, called *Hamiltonians*, in which the most stable solution is the one that minimizes the difference between potential and kinetic energy. Hence it is not an exaggeration to say that all of the content of classical physics can be recovered using variational methods. The philosopher who pioneered the return to the actual mathematics used by physicists and who declared that language was largely irrelevant to the study of the way they practice their craft, is Bas Van Fraassen. See: Bas Van Fraassen, *Laws and Symmetry* (Oxford: Clarendon Press, 1989), 222.

66 The extension of variational ideas to more complex cases, and the discovery of a larger variety of singularities, was performed by the mathematician Henri Poincare. See: June Barrow-Green, *Poincare and the Three Body Problem* (American Mathematical Society, 1997), 32.

The terms "attractor" and "repellor" are of more recent coinage. See:
Ralph Abraham and Christopher Shaw, *Dynamics: The Geometry of Behavior. Volume Two* (Santa Cruz: Aerial Press, 1985), 25.

67 Take the example of a counterfactual like "If president Kennedy had not been assassinated the Vietnam war would have ended sooner." We can easily imagine the scenario postulated by the counterfactual, but should we also commit ourselves to the reality of the JKF that survived? And what of other, more trivial, alternative JFK's? The JFK that wore different clothes in Dallas that day, or the one with a different haircut. And if we deny these are real, where do we draw the line? As examples of philosophers that are realists or non-realists about possibilities and possible worlds are, respectively: David Lewis, "Possible Worlds," in *The Possible and the Actual: Readings in the Metaphysics of Modality* (Ithaca: Cornell University Press, 1979), 182–7.

Nicholas Rescher, "The Ontology of the Possible," in *The Possible and the Actual*, 168–9.

68 The inventor of the calculus of variations, Leonhard Euler, expressed this complementarity by distinguishing explanations framed in terms of effective causes from those using maxima and minima that use *final causes*. See Euler's quote in: Stephen P. Timoshenko, *History of Strength of Materials* (New York: Dover, 1983), 31.

69 A sustained discussion of the concept of the structure of a possibility space, and of the differences between explanations using mechanisms and those based on mechanism-independent forms of determination can be found in: DeLanda, *Philosophy and Simulation.*

70 Dennett, *Consciousness Explained*, 39.

Dennett refers to this metaphorical movie screen on which it all comes together simultaneously and consciousness magically emerges in the homuncular audience as *the Cartesian Theatre.*

71 Ibid., 111 and 125.

Dennett refers to this model as *the Multiple Drafts model.* The name seems somewhat inadequate to deal with the visual field, since the latter is not a text that must be edited. But as it turns out, Dennett believes that visual consciousness can be reduced by the ability to verbally report its contents. Hence the name is quite adequate since what is being drafted is the text of these reports (Ibid., 135). We will reject this part of his model, and replace it with something better in Chapter 4. But it should be clear that homuncular functionalism as a theory of how the brain-mind works is independent of the identification of consciousness and reportability.

72 It is not clear from his writing whether Dennett believes that there are internal representations of edges, surfaces, and solids. In one page (Ibid., 112) he accepts that there are processes that work on raw representations to yield enhanced representations, a stance that would be compatible with what we are arguing. But in the very next page he goes on to assert that all that is needed are *distributed discriminations* (Ibid., 113). Onset of stimulus, shape, color, motion, and other properties would in this other view be captured by different discriminative states of the brain (Ibid., 134). Now, mechanical devices like a thermostat can discriminate between degrees of temperature and use these acts of discrimination to guide action (e.g., by triggering the actuator) without using any representation. Dennett believes that such acts are enough for an animal to track a predator while it is in plain sight, but that the same animal would need internal representations if the predator were to hide and be momentarily out of sight (Ibid., 191). So it may be that his position is that there are internal representations but that they are produced only once and used right where they were produced, not re-represented to be delivered to the Cartesian Theatre. This is the position that will be taken in this book.

73 Ibid., 166.

74 Ibid., 114–15.

75 Zenon Pylyshyn, *Computation and Cognition* (Cambridge, MA: MIT Press, 1986), 80.

76 Ibid., 83–4.

Dennett uses a different terminology. One of the earliest implementations of object-oriented programming used the term "demon" to refer to software objects, perhaps because they were not commanded but only invoked into action. The entire population of demons together with their shared workspace was referred to as a *Pandemonium*. See: Dennett, *Consciousness Explained*, 189 and 264.

77 Ibid., 359 and 371.

Dennett argues correctly that the representation of presence, for example, does not imply the presence of a representation, and the representation of absence does not imply the absence of a representation.

78 A critique of the reduction of the brain to a purely syntactic engine can be found in: Bermúdez, *Nonconceptual Content*, 200–10.

79 Dennett, *Consciousness Explained*, 137.

80 Ibid., 81.

Dennett argues that a report about appearances has the same cognitive status as a narrative about fictional characters: just like in a novel the identity of the characters is constituted by statements that describe each of them as possessing certain physical and psychological properties, so reports about appearances would play a constitutive role in defining the identity of the properties that the visual field appears to have for its subject. This can be taken to mean different things. On the one hand, it could mean that we enjoy a direct access to the world (as in naive realism) and that this makes talk of appearances redundant. This is the thesis that we reject. Or it could mean that our visual system automatically separates the perspectival content of perception (the part of its content that depends on point of view) from its factual content, and that it presents us with only the latter to experience. In this case it would take a special training to see appearances (say, the training of a trompe l'oeil painter) to create a new, special representation of that content that captures its perspectival component. This we can accept, but that would still not make these added representations into mere fictions.

What is the overall effect of reducing appearances to fictions? Subscribing to naive realism, the commonsense idea that we see the world as it is. But to espouse naive realism, even if we dress it up to look more sophisticated than its ordinary version, amounts to giving up the task of explaining the genesis of phenomenal experience. Those who follow this path are not dissolving a false problem; they are abandoning any hope of solving a true one. Surprisingly, naive realism (or as it is also referred to, *direct perception*) has been gaining support among philosophers, although each one defends it in a different way. John Searle's conception, for example, is different from that of Gibson or the one implicitly endorsed by Dennett. For Searle perceptual experiences are direct presentations of the conditions that make those experiences veridical: we perceive both the satisfaction conditions and the fact that those conditions are the cause of our experience. See: John R. Searle, *Seeing Things as They Are: A Theory of Perception* (Oxford: Oxford University Press, 2015), 41.

81 Dennett, *Consciousness Explained*, 137.

82 Ibid., 116–24.

The author labels the two possibilities as "Orwellian" and "Stalinesque," respectively.

83 DeLanda, *Philosophical Chemistry*, Chapter 1.

84 John Stuart Mill, *A System of Logic: Ratiocinative and Inductive* (London: Longmans, Green, and Co., 1906), 243.

Mill used the example of water, a compound that has properties and dispositions that cannot be found in either oxygen or hydrogen. He did not use the term "emergence" but the latter was introduced a few decades later on writings referencing his work.

85 David M. Armstrong, *A Materialist Theory of the Mind* (London: Routledge, 1993), 49.

86 Lawrence Sklar, *Physics and Chance: Philosophical Issues in the Foundations of Statistical Mechanics* (Cambridge: Cambridge University Press, 1995), 345–54.

In contemporary philosophy, the uncritical acceptance of reductionist claims is endemic among philosophers of mind, when they pretend to be philosophers of science. But philosophers of physics like Lawrence Sklar who have an actual grasp of the technical details know how difficult it is to defend the supposed reduction of thermodynamics to statistical mechanics. For example, the claim that temperature, a macro-property, was reduced to a collective micro-property, average kinetic energy, is true only for very low-density gases (those that behave like ideal gases) not for solids, plasmas, the vacuum, or even gases in molecular beams.

87 Jaap van Brakel, *Philosophy of Chemistry* (Leuven: Leuven University Press, 2000), 119–33.

The author gives a knowledgeable and technically detailed defense of the irreducibility of chemistry to quantum mechanics.

88 Jaegwon Kim, "Making Sense of Emergence," in *Emergence: Contemporary Readings in Philosophy and Science* (Cambridge, MA: MIT Press, 2008), 149.

Kim is the main proponent of this argument. He asks us to consider the question of if an emergent whole emerges from its causal base condition (i.e., from the properties and relations of its components), why cannot this base displace the whole as the cause of an effect? Why can't the base perform all the explanatory work to account for why the effect occurred? These two questions are not the same, the former being about ontological, the second about epistemological reduction. In what follows we will take Kim as advocating ontological reduction, although not necessarily an eliminative approach to reduction (Ibid., 136).

89 Mario Bunge, *Causality and Modern Science* (New York: Dover, 1979), 47.

90 Jaegwon Kim, "Causation Revisited," in *Supervenience and Mind: Selected Philosophical Essays* (Cambridge: Cambridge University Press, 1993), 11–12.

The events in Kim's model are explicitly conceived as *exemplifications or instantiations* of a generic or universal property. Elsewhere he asserts that a causal relation does not exist between a property and another property but rather that the instantiation of a property causes another property to be instantiated. See: Kim, "Making Sense of Emergence," 152, footnote 16.

This conception of causality, which we reject completely, is referred to as "property causation." See: Paul Noordhof, "Emergent Causation and Property Causation," in *Emergence in Mind*, edited by Cynthia Macdonald and Graham Macdonald (Oxford: Oxford University Press, 2010), 69–73.

91 Ibid., 132.

In this page Kim asserts that being a mechanism that performs a certain causal function is a property. Clearly, the term "property" is being used here in the sense of anything that can be predicated of a thing.

92 Kim, "Causation Revisited," 3.

That Kim believes causality is linear follows from the fact that he subscribes to Hume's conception of causality as the *constant* conjunction of two events. Presumably, as a materialist, he does not subscribe to the idea that the constant conjunction must be actually observed by a human being, as in Hume's original formulation. To us what matters is that he believes that given the logical event "instantiation of components properties" the properties of the whole have *of necessity* to be instantiated. See: Kim, "Making Sense of Emergence," 142.

93 Bunge, *Causality and Modern Science*, 48.

Bunge warns us that too much emphasis on the *logical* form of linear causal statements leads to treating a causal connection as a form of implication, which in turn leads to the belief that the validity of causal statements can be settled *a priori* (Ibid., 242–4).

94 Ibid., 49.

95 Roy Bhaskar, *A Realist Theory of Science* (London: Verso, 1997), 45.

Bhaskar argues that an ontology of atomistic events is inadequate for a theory of causality, and that what is needed is an ontology of generative mechanisms and active objects.

96 Kim, "Making Sense of Emergence," 130.

Kim refers to the set of component properties and relations as the *total micro-structural property* and asserts that the relations among properties give unity and stability to this set. But relations, particularly if conceived as two-place predicates, are not a source of stability that any scientist would accept.

97 Peder Voetmann Christiansen, "Macro and Micro-levels in Physics," in *Downward Causation*, edited by Peter Bøgh Andersen, Claus Emmeche, Niels Ole Finnemann, and Poder Voetmann Christiansen (Oxford: Aarhus University Press, 2000), 52.

98 Claus Emmeche, Simo Køppe, and Frederik Stjernfelt, "Levels, Emergence, and Three Versions of Downward Causation," in *Downward Causation*, 19–29.

The authors consider three types of downward causation: strong, medium, and weak. Strong causation assumes that the whole produces its own parts using efficient causality. They reject this option because it leads to mystifying results. The second option simply says that once boundary conditions are established, once the whole has acquired well-defined spatial boundaries, the latter act on its parts not by creating them but by selecting which interactions will be allowed. Finally, a whole stabilized dynamically by singularities is said to weakly affect its parts by selecting those interactions that are compatible with the stability of the whole.

99 C. Lloyd Morgan, *Emergent Evolution* (New York: Henry Holt, 1931), 8.

Today, that mystified conception has been mostly eliminated. The emergent properties of a whole are now conceived as being fully explainable in terms of the interactions between its parts. This implies that our capacity to analyze a given phenomenon does not entail its epistemological reducibility, and that to discover mechanisms of emergence does not explain emergence away. See: Bunge, *Causality and Modern Science*, 156.

100 Bechtel and Abrahamsen, *Connectionism and the Mind*, 256–7.

101 Ibid., 179–81.

102 Churchland, *Plato's Camera*, 180–2.

As Churchland argues, a recurrent neural net could in principle classify the different types of optic flows that result from different types of motions of the observer: convergent and divergent flow if the observer is moving forward or backward; rotational flow if he is spinning around its center; sideways flow if he moves laterally relative to the direction he is facing.

103 Olcay Kursun and Oleg Favorov, "Cortex-Based Mechanism for the Discovery of High-Order Features," in *Proceedings of the 17th International Symposium on Computer and Information Sciences*, edited by Ilyas Cicekli, Nihan Kesim Cicekli, and Erol Gelembe (Boca Raton: CRC Press, 2003), 287.

104 Dan Ryder, "SIMBAD Neurosemantics: A Theory of Mental Representation," in *Mind and Language*, Vol. 19, No. 2 (Oxford: Blackwell, 2004), 218–20.

Ryder describes a model of one of the most abundant types of neurons in the cortex: a pyramidal cell. These neurons have multiple dendrites that receive inputs from different sources and, according to the model, each dendrite adjusts the way it treats its inputs so as to match the way the other dendrites treat theirs. In other words, each tries to find a mapping between its inputs and its output that matches the mapping performed by the others. If the inputs come from a single source, then this mutual adjustment will zero in the source of the correlations (Ibid., 214–15).

105 Bechtel and Abrahamsen, *Connectionism and the Mind*, 12–13.

In the 1960s, for example, two prominent researchers in artificial intelligence published a book detailing the limited capabilities of two-layer neural nets. In particular, they showed that there existed logical operations (exclusive OR) that were beyond the capabilities of this design. A couple of decades later a three-layer design (with its own training procedure) was shown to be able to perform that function and it nullified the criticism. Since then philosophers have constantly tried to pinpoint limitations in this new design (that its units are labeled semantically; or that the representations in the hidden layer are not explicit) only for new designs to sidestep the criticisms. We may conclude from this that when a scientific field practices analysis and synthesis, it is pointless to criticize its results with arguments directed at particular synthetic products.

106 Gibson, *The Ecological Approach to Visual Perception*, 193–5.

Chapter 2

1 Ruth Garrett Millikan, *Varieties of Meaning* (Cambridge, MA: MIT Press, 2004), 76–9.

This way of stating the definition of descriptive and directive content assumed that all internal signs are icons, which is Millikan's position. They would have to be modified to also incorporate indices.

2 Rolf Pfeifer and Josh Bongard, *How the Body Shapes the Way We Think* (Cambridge, MA: MIT Press, 2007), 109–11.

3 Ibid., 96.

The authors refer to this as *morphological computation*.

4 Ibid., 126.

5 Ralph Abraham and Christopher Shaw, *Dynamics: The Geometry of Behavior. Volume One* (Santa Cruz: Aerial Press, 1984), 13–21.

6 Esther Thelen and Linda B. Smith, *A Dynamical Systems Approach to the Development of Cognition and Action* (Cambridge, MA: MIT Press, 1996), 121–5.

7 Ibid., 264.

8 Pfeifer and Bongard, *How the Body Shapes the Way We Think*, 98–9.

9 Eugene C. Goldfield, *Emergent Forms: Origins and Early Development of Human Action and Perception* (New York: Oxford University Press, 1995), 83–4.

Goldfield argues, for example, that the neck muscles have a long load arm and the fulcrum at the first vertebrate, which makes them a first-order lever. The biceps used to raise a load with the hand has the fulcrum at the elbow making it a third-order lever.

10 J. A. Scott Kelso, *Dynamic Patterns: The Self-Organization of Brain and Behavior* (Cambridge, MA: MIT Press, 1995), 37–8.

To give us an idea of the complexity of the task the brain confronts Kelso gives us some numbers: the human body has 10^2 joints, 10^3 muscles, and 10^4 neurons. The number of possible combinations is huge, and so is the space of possible states. The fact that what we observe is that only a relatively few configurations become actual shows that the dimensionality of the space has been greatly reduced. Or to put this in our terms, that the equiprobability of the possible states has been broken, with the preferred states having become the most probable.

11 Goldfield, *Emergent Forms*, 104.

12 Ibid., 28–9.

13 Timothy van Gelder and Robert F. Port, "It's About Time: An Overview of the Dynamical Approach to Cognition," in *Mind as Motion: Exploration of the Dynamics of Cognition*, edited by Robert F. Port and Timothy van Gelder (Cambridge, MA: MIT Press, 1995), 23.

14 Randall D. Beer, "Computational and Dynamical Languages for Autonomous Agents," in *Mind as Motion*, 130.

Beer refers to the first coupling or mapping as a "sensory function" and to the second as a "motor function."

15 Holists would, of course, reject this requirement, since they view the organism and its perceived environment as forming *an inextricable unit*. See: Evan Thompson, *Mind in Life: Biology, Phenomenology, and the Sciences of Mind* (Cambridge, MA: Harvard University Press, 2010), 13.

16 Andy Clark, *Supersizing the Mind: Embodiment, Action, and Cognitive Extension* (Oxford: Oxford University Press, 2011), 158.

Clark refers to this alternative to holism as the *soft-assembly approach*.

17 Ibid., 116–17.

18 Ibid., 157.

19 Thompson, *Mind in Life*, 60.

In line with his holism, the author conceptualizes emergent properties as involving *co-emergence*, a process in which parts and whole mutually specify one another. We saw in the previous chapter that causal interactions between parts do bring a whole into existence, but that downward causality cannot be like that, because it would be incoherent to say that the whole also brings its parts into existence. Enactivists avoid this incoherence by conceiving of the relations between wholes and parts not as involving efficient causality but relations that constitute the very identity of what they relate. We will tackle this issue below in the main text.

20 Roy Bhaskar, *A Realist Theory of Science* (London: Verso, 1997), 45.

21 James J. Gibson, *The Ecological Approach to Visual Perception* (New York: Psychology Press, 2015), 119–35.

22 William H. Warren and Robert E. Shaw, "Events and Encounters as Units of Analysis for Ecological Psychology," in *Persistence and Change*, edited by William H. Warren and Robert E. Shaw (Hillside: Lawrence Erlbaum, 1983), 11–12.

The existence of these dual dispositions (affordances and effectivities) imply an animal-environment complementarity. But this mutuality does not imply the seamless totalities we rejected earlier. Gibson does not fall into this Hegelian trap, but other ecological psychologists do, arguing that animals and environment are not logically independent entities, and that the abandonment of the animal-environment dualism is a methodological requirement. See: Claire F. Michaels and Claudia Carello, *Direct Perception* (Englewood Cliffs: Prentice Hall, 1981), 100–4.

23 The question of attention, and the special awareness represented by what is noticed by an organism, will play an important role later in this chapter, as well as in the following two chapters.

24 Gibson. *The Ecological Approach to Visual Perception*, 149–50.

Gibson discusses the example of the inborn reaction to precipices shared by many animals, humans included. This tendency is displayed using a laboratory experiment called the "visual cliff." A transparent surface is placed as a bridge between two solid opaque objects to check whether a puppy or an infant will move from the safety of the opaque surface into the apparent danger of the transparent one. An instinctive avoidance behavior is displayed in both cases.

25 Ibid., 125.

26 Thomas A. McMahon and John Tyler Bonner, *On Size and Life* (New York: Scientific American Library, 1983), 195–6.

The ratio of inertial forces to viscous forces is called the *Reynolds's number*. As the authors argue, natural selection favors very different design solutions for locomotion for low and high Reynolds numbers.

27 Mike Hansell, *Animal Architecture* (Oxford: Oxford University Press, 2005).

This is perhaps the best discussion of animal effective environments. As the author argues, animal-built structures serve three purposes: to provide shelter for it, its offspring, and its food; to trap prey; and to communicate with conspecifics. Homes seem to be the most widely used structure, needed to control some property of the environment, such as temperature, oxygen availability, humidity, as well as protection from predation. The last function promotes both the building of small homes and its concealment through camouflage (Ibid., 3–15). Traps are more frequent in invertebrates and involves extending the reach or capture space surrounding the predator, or making sure it is located in an area with high flux of prey (Ibid., 21).

28 Andy Clark, *Being There: Putting Brain, Body, and World Together Again* (Cambridge, MA: MIT Press, 1998), 24–5.

29 Ibid., 45–6.

30 David Kirsh, "The Intelligent Use of Space," in *Computational Theories of Interaction and Agency*, edited by Philip E. Agre and Stanley J. Rosenschein (Cambridge, MA: MIT Press, 1996), 401.

31 Ibid., 422.

32 Ibid., 398, 405, and 425.

33 Clark, *Supersizing the Mind*, 156–9.
    Clark refers to these interfaces as *plug-points*.

34 Defne Kaya and Mahmut Calik, "Neurophysiology and Assessment of the Proprioception," in *Proprioception in Orthopedics, Sport Medicine, and Rehabilitation*, edited by Defne Kaya, Baran Yosmaoglu, and Mahmut Nedim doral (Cham: Springer Nature, 2018), 3–6.

35 Antonio Damasio, *Self Comes to Mind: Constructing the Conscious Brain* (New York: Vintage, 2010), 80.

36 José Luis Bermúdez, *The Bodily Self* (Cambridge, MA: MIT Press, 2018), 39–40.

37 Ibid., 145.

38 Joseph LeDoux, *The Emotional Brain* (New York: Simon & Schuster, 1996), 17–18.

39 David G. Mayers, *Exploring Psychology* (New York: Worth Publishers, 2005), 344–6.

40 LeDoux, *The Emotional Brain*, 45–54.
    LeDoux analyzes the history of the causal sequence inversion. William James was the first to suggest that we do not cry because we feel sad, we feel sad because we cry. Walter Cannon decades later added the connection to internal metabolic processes, in particular, the redistribution of energy to the body parts that would be called into action by an emotional response. Social psychologists then continued to separate emotion from symbolic forms of cognition, to give the former the kind of autonomous function that we now believe it has.

41 Bermúdez, *The Bodily Self*, 185–7.

42 Ibid., 59–64.
    Bermúdez does not use the terminology of icons and indices, but it does very little violence to his argument to frame it like this.

43 Wilder Penfield and Herbert Jasper, *Epilepsy and the Functional Anatomy of the Human Brain* (Boston: Little, Brown, and Co., 1954), 69–72.

44 Bermúdez, *The Bodily Self*, 140–6.

Bermúdez does not mention dynamical systems or preferred states when discussing the advantages of an articulated, proprioceptive map, but he does makes passing reference to limbs as mass-spring systems that have equilibrium positions, and that calculating the latter does not involve complex computations (Ibid., 150).

45 Shaun Gallagher, "Body Schema and Intentionality," in *The Body and the Self*, edited by José Luis Bermúdez, Naomi Eilan, and Anthony Marcel (Oxford: Oxford University Press, 1988), 226–33.

The classical phenomenologists were aware of this fundamental difference, although a clear distinction between body image and body schema was not always made. Gallagher argues that Husserl focused mostly on the body image and that it was only Marleu-Ponty who introduced the body schema into phenomenology. On his side, Bermúdez argues that we can recover most of Merleu-Ponty's insights by replacing his ontological distinction between two types of bodies with two different representations of the space of the body. See: Bermúdez, *The Bodily Self*, 137–8.

He also argues that proprioception, like the vestibular mechanism that gives a body its balance, is a condition for a stable experience of the body as an object in the mirror. Hence, proprioceptive representations do not have the body as their intentional object (as do those related to body image) but are rather *pre-intentional*. We can agree with this, but only if it refers to the complex intentionality of the full subject. If intentionality is graded, as in our account, then even mindless agents can convert natural signs into intentional signs.

46 Lynnette A. Jones, "Motor Illusions: What Do They Reveal About Proprioception," *Psychological Bulletin*, Vol. 103, No. 1 (American Psychological Association, 1988): 72–3.

47 Michael S. Gazzaniga, Richard B. Ivry, and George R. Mangun, *Cognitive Neuroscience: The Biology of the Mind* (New York: W. W. Norton, 2009), 124–5.

48 Chen Ping Yu, William K. Page, Roger Gaborsky, and Charles J. Duffy, "Receptive Field Dynamics Underlying MST Neuronal Optic Flow Selectivity," *Journal of Neurophysiology*, Vol. 103 (The American Physiological Society, 2010): 2795–6.

49 Giacomo Rizzolatti and Corrado Sinigaglia, *Mirrors in the Brain: How Our Minds Share Actions and Emotions* (Oxford: Oxford University Press, 2006), 53–62.

50 Ibid., 72–6.

51 Marie Martel, Lucilla Cardinali, Alice C. Roy, and Alessandro Farnè, "Tool-Use: An Open Window into Body Representation and Its Plasticity," *Cognitive Neuropsychology*, Vol. 33, No. 1–2 (Taylor and Francis, 2016): 83–4.

52 Rizzolatti and Sinigaglia, *Mirrors in the Brain*, 23–5.

53 Ibid., 34–8.

54 Paul Bach-y-Rita, "Sensory Substitution and Qualia," in *Vision and Mind*, edited by Alva Noë and Evan Thomson (Cambridge, MA: MIT Press, 2004), 500.

55 Susan L. Hurley, *Consciousness in Action* (Cambridge, MA: Harvard University Press, 1998), 345.

56 Alva Noë, *Action in Perception* (Cambridge, MA: MIT Press, 2004), 61–4.

57 Ibid., 50–1.
   Noë refers to accessibility as constituting the content of what he calls *virtual representations*. But these are not internal representations that can be manipulated during the processing that produces phenomenal experience, but the very content of that experience. The fact that when looking at a scene we are not capable of being aware of it in its entirety (some is out of focus, some undifferentiated, some hidden) implies to him that phenomenal experience is *virtual all the way in*: we cannot break down the contents of the visual field into an actual and a virtual part, because even visible surfaces have detail of which we may not be aware (Ibid., 215–17).

58 Marc Jeannerod, *The Cognitive Neuroscience of Action* (Oxford: Blackwell, 1997), 97–8.

59 Ibid., 109.

60 In addition to providing an extra input to the mostly unconscious process that generates phenomenal experience, the brain's ability to simulate may have more conscious effects: the same cortical areas that become active during planning and execution also become activated when *imagining* an action. And the effect of this conscious simulation can be quite dramatic: in some cases mentally practicing skills using motor imaging can lead to the same changes in the size of peripersonal receptive fields normally caused by actually practising those skills (Ibid., 117).

61 David Marr, *Vision* (Cambridge, MA: MIT Press, 1982), 30.

62 Noë, *Action in Perception*, 2.

63 Gilbert Ryle, *The Concept of Mind* (New York: Barnes and Noble, 1949), 27–32.

64 Noë, *Action in Perception*, 84–6.

65 Thompson, *Mind in Life*, 52–4.

Thompson rejects the concept of information as being "objectivist," a pejorative introduced by Husserl for those who believe in the mind-independence of the objective world. But this is yet another source of incoherence for the enactivists: they help themselves to all the results of objectivist scientific research (nonlinear dynamics, self-organization, embryology, catalysis, symbiosis) as if their own rejection of objectivism did not matter.

66 Jean-Michel Roy, Jean Petitot, Bernard Pachoud, and Francisco J. Varela, "Beyond the Gap: An Introduction to Naturalizing Phenomenology," in *Naturalizing Phenomenology*, edited by Jean Petitot, Francisco J. Varela, Bernard Pachoud, and Jean-Michel Roy (Stanford: Stanford University Press, 1999), 6.

67 The ambiguity of the term "meaning" exists in most European languages. But in English the term is even more ambiguous. In addition to signification and significance it can refer to *intention*, as when people say, "What do you mean?" to say "What's your point?" or "What are you getting at?" It can also refer to *implication* as when someone responds to the complement "You look good in black" by saying, "Do you mean I am fat?" In most philosophical contexts the word "meaning" is used without the required qualification to eliminate its ambiguity, and that makes the word particularly misleading.

68 The concept expressed by the term "significance" has been neglected in Anglo-American philosophy partly because of this tradition's reliance on logic. While no one can deny the importance of the invention of logical systems like the predicate calculus, and their direct relation to contemporary computer languages, the notion of significance is conspicuously absent from them: these logical calculi deal with the transmission of truth from one proposition to another, regardless of whether the truth in question is important or trivial. The debate over the underdetermination of theory by observation, for example, was made possible by this neglect. A notable exception is the philosopher Adrian Cusssins for whom cognitive significance (in the case on nonconceptual knowledge) plays the same role as the notion of truth conditions in conceptual knowledge. See: Adrian Cussins, "Content, Conceptual Content, and Nonconceptual Content," in *Essays on Nonconceptual Content*, edited by York H. Gunther (Cambridge, MA: MIT Press, 2003), 139.

69 Thompson, *Mind in Life*.

Thompson, a leader in the enactive movement, exemplifies this confusion perfectly. He uses the word "meaning" as synonymous with significance in one page (Ibid., 27) and then as synonymous with the word "sense" in another page (Ibid., 32). The word "sense" comes from the logician Gotlob Frege, whose theory of reference (now mostly refuted) greatly influenced Husserl. In Frege's work the term "sense" refers to signification, that is, to the semantic content of phrases like "the morning star." Thus, Thompson is using the word "meaning" as if it had a unitary signification. This confusion pervades the entire enactive approach as well as its assessment of classical phenomenology. See for example: Jean-Luc Petit, "Constitution by Movement: Husserl in Light of Recent Neurobiological Findings," in *Naturalizing Phenomenology*, 228–9.

70 Thompson, *Mind in Life*, 428.

Thompson refers to this as *relational holism*: the enactive whole does not merely influence its parts, it subsumes their independent existence into a relational structure.

71 For a defense of extrinsic relations in emergent wholes see: Manuel DeLanda, *Assemblage Theory* (Edinburgh: Edinburgh University Press, 2016), 9–10.

72 Thompson, *Mind in Life*, 13.

In this page Thompson defines the enactive approach in basically these terms. The only part of the definition left out in this section is his (and Varela's) conception of the brain, a topic we will tackle in the next chapter.

73 It is true that some byproducts of bacterial metabolism (oxygen) did go on to accumulate and then affect the evolution of respiration, but this simply implies that the activities of animals can modify their effective environment (quite a large one in this case) and create new opportunities and risks for other animals. And clearly oxygen was not the product of a skillful engagement with the world but a waste product with absolutely no intentional content.

74 Ibid., 191–2.

The need to revise well-established theories, such as Darwin's, to fit the *a priori* needs of a philosophy should surely count as a cost of accepting enactivist views.

75 Anthony Chemero, *Radical Embodied Cognitive Science* (Cambridge, MA: MIT Press, 2009), 29.

76 Abraham and Shaw, *Dynamics*, 19.

The authors make clear distinction between two components of state space diagrams: the vector field (obtained through differentiation) and the trajectories (obtain through integration). The former represents the potential (or virtual) part of the model, the latter the actual part.

77 Beer, "Computational and Dynamical Languages for Autonomous Agents," 131.

78 Chemero, *Radical Embodied Cognitive Science*, 35 and 185-6.

79 Tim Van Gelder. "What Might Cognition Be, If Not Computation?" *The Journal of Philosophy*, Vol. 92, No. 7 (New York: Columbia University, 1995): 348.

80 Ibid., 349.

81 Ibid., 356-7.

82 William Bechtel and Adele Abrahamsen, *Connectionism and the Mind* (Cambridge: Basil Blackwell, 1991), 273-5.

  The authors argue that the angle of the arms does represent speed for the valve, but do not express this in terms of iconic-indexical content.

83 Gelder, "What Might Cognition Be, If Not Computation?" 353.

  Van Gelder rejects the idea that the angle of the arms represents speed because the angle is correlated with the engine's speed only when the entire system has reached its stable equilibrium point. Any sudden change in load, for example, can destroy the correlation by affecting the angle and speed differently. But this is incorrect. The height of the mercury column in a thermometer must correlate with the temperature of the body with which the thermometer is in contact, else it would not be a useful measuring instrument. But the correlation only obtains once the thermometer and the body are in thermal equilibrium, hence the need to wait a few minutes to allow them to reach the singularity. There is nothing wrong with the idea that an index can point to what it represents only when sign and referent have both reached a stable state.

84 Chemero, *Radical Embodied Cognitive Science*, 71-7.

85 Lawrence Shapiro, *Embodied Cognition* (New York: Routledge, 2011), 133-7.

  Shapiro argues convincingly that we need both a dynamical and a mechanistic explanation of coupled systems. The need to complement dynamic accounts with causal mechanisms is also defended by Andy Clark, but for different reasons. Without the latter we cannot *build robots* that implement a particular dynamic. We need to know both that a pattern of behavior will emerge and be stable, and that particular causal interactions between components will cause that behavior to emerge and then maintain it in existence. See: Clark, *Being There*, 119-22.

86 Thompson, *Mind in Life*, 68-9.

  In these pages Thompson tries to recover causality as an intrinsic relation by arguing that only linear causality is extrinsic while nonlinear causality is intrinsic. But this argument is mistaken. Nonlinear causality does force us to consider both capacities to affect and capacities to be affected, as well as whether one is matched to the other, but this leaves the entities that possess these capacities fully logically independent from each other. A tool that can cut requires an object that can be cut, but this relation between capacities does not constitute the identity of the tool or the object. So why then does Thompson believe that nonlinearity implies mutual constitution? Because he is confusing nonlinear causality with the nonlinearities that enter into dynamical systems theory, and in particular, the nonlinear coupling of two dynamical systems. But we have already seen that this line of argument confuses facts about the math with facts about the reality that math is supposed to model. To give one more example: everyone knows that two solutions to a linear equation (one without feedback among variables) can be added into a new solution. And conversely, one solution may be separated into two. Nonlinear equations do not display this additivity or separability. But this does not make them an example of an intrinsic relation: the relations between variables, even with feedback added, are extrinsic. And this is even more true of the real system modeled by the equation: even if its properties are related to each other in complex ways, with as much feedback and circularity as we want, their relations do not constitute their very identity.

87 The inverted causal sequence (I feel sad because I cry, rather than I cry because I feel sad) is accepted today by most materialist philosophers. See for example: David M. Armstrong, *A Materialist Theory of the Mind* (New York: Routledge, 1993), 320–1.

88 Damasio, *Self Comes to Mind*, 120–1.

89 Jaak Panksepp, *Affective Neuroscience: The Foundations of Human and Animal Emotion* (Oxford: Oxford University Press, 1998), 48–9.

Panksepp does not classify hunger and fear together because they do not use the same kind of neural circuitry. Rather, hunger, thirst, and other appetites share a common emotional response: the drive to seek rewards (Ibid., 51). For ease of exposition we will continue to refer to both types of response as interoceptive, much as before we grouped together what is properly proprioceptive with what may be called kinesthetic.

90 Jaak Panksepp, "The Basic Emotional Circuits of Mammalian Brains: Do Animals Have Affective Lives?" *Neuroscience and Biobehavioral Reviews*, Vol 35 (Elsevier, 2011): 1795.

In this page Panksepp gives a summary of all the circuits that have been found so far, complete with the brain areas and the neuromodulators involved.

91 Ibid., 1794.

92 Antonio Damasio, *The Feeling of What Happens: Body and Emotion in the Making of Consciousness* (San Diego: Harcourt, 1999), 71–5.

93 One way to tackle the question of social feelings like pride or shame is to complement the account of a private self as given in this book, with a discussion of our *public persona*. See: DeLanda, *A New Philosophy of Society*, 52–5.

94 Carrol E. Izard, Brian Ackerman, Kristen M. Schoff, and Sarah E. Fine, "Self-Organization of Discrete Emotions, Emotion Patterns, and Emotion-Cognition Relations," in *Emotion, Development, and Self-Organization: Dynamic Systems Approaches to Emotional Development* (Cambridge: Cambridge University Press, 2000), 15–19.

   This approach is called *Differential Emotion Theory*. But, as we saw earlier, dynamic approaches can be combined with an anti-representationalist philosophy. An example of this error in this volume is: Freeman, "Emotion Is Essential to All Intentional Behaviors," in Ibid., 232.

95 Lewis, "Emotional Self-Organization at Three Time Scales," in Ibid., 43.
   The three timescales referred to in the title are short-lived emotional episodes, longer-lived moods, and enduring personality traits.

96 Mascolo, Harkins, and Harakal, "The Dynamic Construction of Emotion," in Ibid., 128.

97 Lewis, *Emotional Self-Organization at Three Time Scales*, 42.

98 Panksepp, "The Basic Emotional Circuits of Mammalian Brains," 1793.

99 Damasio, *The Feeling of What Happens*, 284–5.

100 Harold E. Pashler, *The Psychology of Attention* (Cambridge, MA: MIT Press, 1998), 224.

101 Christopher Chabris and Daniel Simons, *The Invisible Gorilla* (New York: Crown Publishers, 2009), 5–7.

   In a famous experiment conducted by the authors, subjects were asked to carefully watch a group of people play with a ball and count the number of times the ball had changed hands. As the subjects were attending to the ball, tracking it as it moved from one player to the next, a woman on a gorilla suit walked into the scene, standing right in the middle of the game, and hence, the middle of the visual field of the subjects. Despite its prominent position and its salient appearance, half the subjects reported that they did not see the gorilla. This phenomenon is referred to as *inattentional blindness*.

102 Panksepp, "The Basic Emotional Circuits of Mammalian Brains," 1795.

Panksepp argues that while emotions may have a subcortical basis, homologous in all mammals, they are re-represented in nested hierarchies all the way up to the cortex.

103 Noé, *Action in Perception*, 166–7.

Dennett also uses realist painters to illustrate the point that habits of attention can override the normal perpetual process to capture appearances pictorially. See: Dennett, *Consciousness Explained*, 53.

104 Damasio, *Self Comes to Mind*, 201–2.

In Damasio's model of a nested hierarchy the levels are constituted by signs that are re-represented. Thus, he refers to the intentional signs that represent emotions as "maps" and uses the word "image" for the representations that reach phenomenal experience as primordial feelings. (Ibid., 106–8). For that reason, the protoself is not conceived as an agent, let alone a *kind of agent* as we do in this book, but rather as a collection of maps (interoceptive maps, among others) that somehow generate felt images. In what follows we will be adapting Damasio's model to the multi-homuncular model of Dennett, so we will avoid referring to "the protoself" and speak instead of multiple protoselves.

105 Ibid., 22–4.

106 Ibid., 196.

107 Ibid., 214–20.

108 Ibid., 218.

Damasio refers to these other feelings as feelings of knowing and saliency.

109 Ibid., 179–80.

Chapter 3

1 Jonathan J. Nassi and Edward M. Callaway, "Parallel Processing Strategies of the Primate Visual System," *Nature Reviews. Neuroscience*, Vol. 10 (Macmillan, May, 2009): 361.

2 Ruth Garrett Millikan, *Varieties of Meaning* (Cambridge, MA: MIT Press, 2004), 83.

3 The first philosophical treatment of the laminar and columnar organization of cortical areas was given by: Patricia Smith Churchland,

Neurophilosophy: Toward a Unified Science of the Mind-Brain (Cambridge: Bradford, 1986), 117–20 and 131–7.

A discussion of the imagining techniques used to locate the boundaries of retinotopic maps may be found in: Alyssa A. Brewer and Brian Barton, "Visual Field Map Organization in Human Visual Cortex," in *Visual Cortex: Current Status and Perspectives*, edited by Stéphane Molotchnikoff and Jean Rouat (Rijeka: InTech, 2012), 30–7.

4 Ibid., 38.

5 Jean-Pierre Changeux, *Neuronal Man* (New York: Pantheon Books, 1985), 59–62.

What we are referring to as "location columns" are more appropriately called "ocular dominance columns," since their neurons' receptive fields do not only indicate location in general but also location in a particular eye. Because there are two V1 areas, one in each hemisphere, the retinotopic map in the left V1 contains the right fields of both eyes, the right V1 contains both left fields. Since we are ignoring binocular vision we will disregard the complications in the mapping that this involves.

6 Michael S. Gazzaniga, Richard B. Ivry, and George R. Mangun, *Cognitive Neuroscience: The Biology of the Mind* (New York: W. W. Norton, 2009), 182–3.

7 Rodney J. Douglas and Kevan A. C. Martin, "Mapping the Matrix: The Ways of Neocortex," *Neuron*, Vol. 56 (Elsevier, 2007): 234–5.

8 Changeux, *Neuronal Man*, 56–8.

9 Gazzaniga, Ivry, and Mangun, *Cognitive Neuroscience*, 180.

10 David Marr, *Vision* (Cambridge, MA: MIT Press, 1982), 270–2.

11 Ibid., 75.

12 Ibid., 42, 268 and 298.

Marr is not always consistent in his assignment of coordinate systems, sometimes referring to both the primal sketch and the $2^{1/2}$ D sketch as using viewer-centered coordinates.

13 The first derivative of the function used by Marr yields a curve with a single peak when fed a discontinuity, while the second derivative yields a curve named a *zero-crossing* (Ibid., 54). Zero-crossings are used to mimic center-surround fields (Ibid., 64–5). Receptive fields tuned to different orientations are simulated by two center-surround fields with opposite signs (one on-center, the other off-center) linked together by a simple And gate (Ibid., 66).

14 Ibid., 71–3 and 91–2.

Marr represents the properties of linear segments symbolically, as lists of numbers, and of course, representing receptive fields by mathematical functions also implies the use of discrete symbols. It is unclear whether he believes that the brain itself uses symbols. On our side we will continue to exclude symbols and use icons instead. But what about the equations? These we can replace in our minds by neural nets taking advantage of the fact that the latter have been shown to be *universal approximators*. Just about any mathematical function that has practical applications can be given an approximate, nonsymbolic, form by a suitably designed neural net, the degree of accuracy of the approximation being dependent on the number of units in the hidden layers. For the general proof of this see: Kur Hornik, Maxwell Stinchcombe, and Halber White, "Multilayer Feedforward Networks Are Universal Approximators," *Neural Networks*, Vol. 2 (Oxford: Pergamon Press, 1989): 359–66.

To approximate the differential equations used in computational approaches to vision, see: Neha Yadav, Anupam Yadav, and Manoj Kumar, *An Introduction to Neural Network Methods for Differential Equations* (Dordrecht: Springer, 2015), Ch. 4

15 Marr, *Vision*, 215–16.

16 Ibid., 220.

Marr refers to the objective set of points corresponding to a contour as a "contour generator."

17 Ibid., 235–7.

18 Ibid., 277–8.

19 John R. Pani, "Descriptions of Orientation and Structure in Perception and Physical Reasoning," in *Ecological Approaches to Cognition*, edited by Eugene Winograd, Robyn Fivush, and William Herst (Mahwah: Lawrence Earlbaum, 1999), 63–70.

20 Marr, *Vision*, 299–306.

Marr does not use elongated cylinders for his stick figures but what he calls *generalized cones*: shapes generated by moving a cross section of the same shape but variable size along an axis (Ibid., 223). Many shapes that are generated by growth process (tree trunks and branches, animal limbs) can be approximated by generalized cones. Thus, the shape of a horse can be modeled by eight cones, four for the legs, and one for the head, tail, neck, and body.

21 Because Marr's model is intended for machines, all that matters is that they can successfully perform visually guided tasks not that they can experience the world like we do. But Marr does touch briefly on a topic that bears on phenomenology. As we argued in the main text, different places in the visual field are rendered with different amount of detail, the fovea having full resolution while the periphery has almost none. Hence, we can imagine that objects being foveated are generated using 3D models as a starting point, while peripheral objects would need only a $2^{1/2}$ D sketch (Ibid., 354).

22 Kai von Fieandt and Ib Kristian Moustgaard, *The Perceptual World* (London: Academic Press, 1977), 106.

23 Clyde L. Hardin, *Color for Philosophers: Unweaving the Rainbow* (Indianapolis: Hackett, 1988), 33.

This description of retinal ganglia is itself a simplification. In reality, there are not just three outputs (black-white, blue-yellow, and red-green) but up to twenty specialized visual pathways using eighty different ganglion cell types. See: Dennis Dacey, "Origins of Perception: Retinal Ganglion Cell Diversity and the Creation of Parallel Visual Pathways," in *The Cognitive Neurosciences III*, edited by Michael S. Gazzaniga (Cambridge, MA: MIT Press, 2004), 281–3.

24 The cells in the LGN specialized in color and form, and motion and depth, are referred to as *magnocellular* and *parvocellular*, respectively. (There is also a third kind, *koniocellular*, that also contributes to color perception.) Each of the six layers of the LGN is made of one of these types, and receives specialized inputs from retinal ganglia also composed of specialized cells (midget and parasol cells). See: Dacey, *Origins of Perception*, 282–5.

25 J. C. Horton and L. C. Sincich, "A New Foundation for the Visual Cortical Hierarchy," in *The Cognitive Neurosciences III*, 234.

26 Gerald M. Edelman and Giulio Tononi, *A Universe of Consciousness: How Matter Becomes Imagination* (New York, Basic Books, 2000), 106–7.

27 Alessandra Angelucci and Jean Bullier, "Reaching beyond the classical receptive field of V1 neurons: Horizontal or feedback axons?" *Journal of Physiology*, Vol. 97 (Elsevier, 2003): 141–2.

28 Melvyn A. Goodale, "Transforming Vision into Action," *Vision Research*, Vol. 51 (Elsevier, 2011): 1571–2.

Originally, the two streams were labeled "What" and "Where," until it was understood that the dorsal stream is involved not just in the determination of location but any spatial property that affects the way we interact with an object. Hence a better label would be "How."

29 Vonne van Polanen and Marco Davare, "Interactions Between Dorsal and Ventral Streams for Controlling Skilled Grasp," in *Neuropsychologia*, Vol. 79, Part B (Elsevier, 2015): 186–91.

The task of recognizing an object, for example, can be performed in different ways: if the targets are abstract geometrical objects then their ventral stream information about shape is used for identification, but if the objects are tools, so that their shape is related to their function, then dorsal stream information about how we can interact with them is used to identify them.

30 The names for the visual areas (V1–V6) refer to the macaque monkeys' brains. Human brains have corresponding areas, but these are sometimes referred by a different name. Area V5, for example, is referred to as MT in humans.

Causal interactions between oscillators in which they affect one another are required for synchronization: if a population of oscillators goes through their cycles at different speeds, they must adjust to one another, some slowing down, some accelerating, so they can all end up oscillating in synchrony.

31 Horton and Sinich, "A New Foundation for the Visual Cortical Hierarchy," 234–5.

32 The traditional view posited strict separation of channels. Disregarding color for the time being, the model can be described like this: layers 4Ca and 4B of V1 get their input from magnocellular layers in the LGN and project motion information to the thick stripes in V2, while layers 2, 3, and 4Cb in V1 receive input from parvocellular layers in the LGN, and project shape information to the pale stripes of V2. But new techniques have shown a more complex relation between V1 layers and V2 stripes (Ibid., 239–40).

End-stopped cells (also referred to as "hypercomplex") were originally thought to exist only beyond V1. But further research has shown that they exist also in some layers of V1 itself. See: Martin J. Tovée, *An Introduction to the Visual System* (Cambridge: Cambridge University Press, 1996), 80–1.

33 Isabel Gauthier, Michael J. Tarr, Jill Moylan, Pawel Skudlarasky, John C. Gore, and Adam W. Anderson, "The Fusiform 'Face Area' is Part of a Network that Processes Faces at the Individual Level," *Journal of Cognitive Neuroscience*, Vol. 12, No. 3 (Cambridge, MA: MIT Press, 2000): 495–504.

34 Claudio Galletti and Patrizia Fattori, "The Dorsal Visual Stream Revisited: Stable Circuits or Dynamic Pathways?" *Cortex*, Vol. XXX (Elsevier, 2017): 3.

35 Chen Ping Yu, William K. Page, Roger Gaborski, and Charles J. Duffy, "Receptive Field Dynamics Underlying MST Neuronal Optic

Flow Selectivity," *Journal of Neurophysiology*, Vol. 103 (The American Physiological Society, 2010): 2794–807.

36 Gyorgy Buzsáki, *Rhythms of the Brain* (Oxford: Oxford University Press, 2006), 137.

The state that results from the coupling of oscillators is called *entrainment*, and may be visualized as many limit cycles wrapping around a state space shaped like a torus. See: Ralph H. Abraham and Christopher D. Shaw, *Dynamics: The Geometry of Behavior. Part One: Periodic Behavior* (Santa Cruz: Aerial Press, 1984), 175–89.

37 Buzsáki, *Rhythms of the Brain*, 138.

38 Steven Strogatz, *Sync: The Emerging Science of Spontaneous Order* (New York: Hyperion, 2003), 52–4.

Causal interactions between oscillators in which they affect one another are required for synchronization: if a population of oscillators goes through their cycles at different speeds, they must adjust to one another, some slowing down, some accelerating, so they can all end up oscillating in synchrony.

39 Buzsáki, *Rhythms of the Brain*, 150–1.

40 Ibid., 152–3.

41 Risto Miikkulainen, James A. Bednar, Yoonsuck Choe and Joseph Sirosh, *Computational Maps in the Visual Cortex* (New York: Springer, 2005), 9–10, 23, and 33–5.

42 Buzsáki, *Rhythms of the Brain*, 238–40.

43 Francis C. Crick and Christof Koch, "A Framework for Consciousness," in *The Cognitive Neurosciences III*, 1136.

The oscillations behind the entrainment effect belong to what is called the Gamma range (30–60 Hertz). At one point the authors believed that a subset of these oscillations (40 Hertz) was the hallmark of a conscious state. They no longer believe that, but they continue to emphasize their importance for the recruitment of neurons and the formation of coalitions (Ibid., 1139).

44 W. A. Freiwald and N. G. Kanwisher, "Visual Selective Attention: Insights from Brain Imaging and Neurophysiology," in *Cognitive Neurosciences III*, 576.

45 Crick and Koch, "A Framework for Consciousness," 1139.

46 Gazzaniga, Ivry, and Mangun, *Cognitive Neuroscience*, 513.

47 Freiwald and Kanwisher, "Visual Selective Attention," 583–4.

48 Zenon W. Pylyshyn, *Things and Places: How the Mind Connects with the World* (Cambridge, MA: MIT Press, 2007), 12.

Pylyshyn agrees that the visual field has pictorial content but he seems to equate this with descriptive content in a language of thought (Ibid., 20–1). Elsewhere in his book, however, he seems to allow for a distinction between icons and symbols (Ibid., 99–100).

49 Ibid., 18–19.

50 Pylyshyn, *Things and Places*, 21.

Pylyshyn cites psychophysical evidence that focal attention can be used to track a maximum of four or five different objects at a time (Ibid., 51).

51 Thomas Metzinger, "Faster Than Thought," in *Conscious Experience*, edited by Thomas Metzinger (Thorverton: Imprint Academic, 1995), 443–4.

52 Andy Clark, *Supersizing the Mind: Embodiment, Mind, and Cognitive Extension* (Oxford: Oxford University Press, 2011), 187–9.

53 Millikan, *Varieties of Meaning*, 177–8.

54 Susan L. Hurley, *Consciousness in Action* (Cambridge, MA: Harvard University Press, 1998), 180–1.

55 Michael S. Gazzaniga, Richard B. Ivry, and George R. Mangun, *Cognitive Neuroscience: The Biology of the Mind* (New York: W. W. Norton, 2009), 101–2.

56 Samuel Harding-Forrester and Daniel E. Feldman, "Somatosensory Maps," in *Handbook of Clinical Neurology,* Vol. 151. The Parietal Cortex, edited by Giuseppe Vallar and H. Branch Coslett (Amsterdam: Elsevier, 2018), 73–7.

57 Andrew H. Fagg and Michael A. Arbib, "Modeling Parietal–Premotor Interactions in Primate Control of Grasping," in *Neural Networks*, Vol. 11 (Pergamon, 1998), 1296–7.

58 Goodale, "Transforming Vision into Action," 1568.

59 Fagg and Arbib, "Modeling Parietal–Premotor Interactions in Primate Control of Grasping," 1281.

60 Polanen and Davare, "Interactions between Dorsal and Ventral Streams for Controlling Skilled Grasp," 188.

61 Fagg and Arbib, "Modeling Parietal–Premotor Interactions in Primate Control of Grasping," 1280 and 1287.

62 Ibid., 1296.

63 Ibid., 1285.

64 Ibid., 1291.

The simulation is called "FARS," the acronym derived from the last names of the researchers who contributed to the model. Besides the two authors (Fagg and Arbib) these are Giacomo Rizzolatti, who discovered premotor neurons that fire in association with specific types of manual action, such as precision grip, finger prehension, and whole hand prehension, as well as tearing and holding (Ibid., 1280), and Hideo Sakata, who developed the experimental protocol for the study of macaque monkeys, the data from which forms the basis for the model (Ibid., 1279).

65 Ibid., 1285.

66 Bevil R. Conway, "The Organization and Operation of Inferior Temporal Cortex," *Annual Review of Vision Science*, Vol. 4 (September, 2018, Online journal): 386.

Some authors subdivide IT into two areas, the temporal occipital cortex (TEO) and the anterior temporal cortex (TE). Others perform a three-way classification (a posterior, a central, and an anterior area). Some add another nearby area, the superior temporal sulcus (STS), that specializes in recognizing biological motion (animal gaits).

67 Ibid., 387–9.

68 Ibid., 391.

69 Churchland, *Neurophilosophy*, 131.

70 Gazzaniga, Ivry, and Mangun *Cognitive Neuroscience*, 261.

71 Emilio Bizzi and Ferdinando A. Mussa-Vivaldi, "Toward a Neurobiology of Coordinate Transformations," in *The Cognitive Neurosciences III*, 416.

The data comes from studies of the frog and rat spinal motor systems. The authors do not use the term "emergent property" but "muscle synergies," but it can be argued that the terms "synergetic" and "emergent" are synonymous.

72 Gazzaniga, Ivry, and Mangun *Cognitive Neuroscience*, 265 and 269.

73 Ibid., 273.

74 Ibid., 276.

75 Ibid., 277–8.

The main obstacle to the use of this procedure with human beings is that the subjects are typically already injured before the experiment can begin and this precludes the calculation of a "healthy" population vector associated with a given action. On the other hand, the sensory-motor dependencies between thinking about an action and perceiving its motor consequences can be learned through training. This allows patients to successfully move a cursor on the screen simply by intending to do it.

76 Michael S. A. Graziano, *The Intelligent Movement Machine: An Ethological Perspective on the Primate Motor System* (Oxford: Oxford University Press, 2009), 125–9.

77 Ibid., 134–6 and 152–60.

78 Ichiro Fujita, "The Inferior Temporal Cortex: Architecture, Computation, and Representation," *Journal of Neurocytology*, Vol. 31 (Kluwer, 2003): 364–6.

The author proposes that IT contains a kind of *visual alphabet* that can combinatorially generate an infinite number of "sentences." Thus, with something between 1,300 and 2,000 columns per agent, and one column per object's distinctive feature, it has room for millions of objects.

79 Richard A. Andersen, Lawrence H. Snyder, Chiang-Shan Li, and Brigitte Stricanne, "Coordinate Transformations in the Representation of Spatial Information," *Current Opinion in Neurobiology*, Vol. 3 (Elsevier, 1993): 171.

80 John O'Keefe and Lynn Nadel, *The Hippocampus as a Cognitive Map* (Oxford: Clarendon Press, 1978), 201–5.

81 Emilio Salinas and Larry F. Abbott, "Coordinate Transformations in the Visual System: How to Generate Gain Fields and How to Compute with Them," *Progress in Brain Research*, Vol. 130 (Amsterdam: Elsevier, 2001): 177.

82 Ibid., 182.

83 Lawrence H. Snyder, "Coordinate Transformations for Eye and Arm Movements in the Brain," *Current Opinion in Neurobiology*, Vol. 10 (Elsevier, 2000): 747.

84 Ibid., 750.

Neural net models of the agent pair 7a and LIP have been created to simulate the first coordinate transformation: the devices were trained to map a visually located target to head-centered coordinates using as inputs any arbitrary pair of eye and retinal positions. Interestingly, the hidden layer of the neural net developed an activation pattern that resembled the gain fields measured in primate brains. See: David Zipser and Richard A. Andersen, "A Back-Propagation Programmed Network that Simulates Response Properties of a Subset of Posterior Parietal Neurons," in *Nature*, Vol. 331 (Springer, 1988): 679–84.

85 Churchland, *Neurophilosophy*, 78–80.

There are four criteria for a neurotransmitter: it must be synthesized by presynaptic neurons, released from the presynaptic terminal, bind with a postsynaptic receptor to cause either depolarization or hyperpolarization of its membrane, and be removed promptly from the site.

86 Leonard K. Kaczmarek and Irwin B. Levitan, *Neuromodulation: The Biochemical Control of Neuronal Excitability* (New York: Oxford University Press, 1987), 8.

More exactly, changes in the electrical properties of a neuron can be produced in one of three ways: by the action of chemicals at the synaptic junction, by chemicals released at a distance from the target neuron, and by the action of hormones. A neuromodulator would be defined as a neurotransmitter of the second kind, or more specifically, as a transmitter that acts on receptors to trigger the formation of second messenger substances that can go on to influence many other processes indirectly (Ibid., 9–10).

87 A. Graybiel and E. Saka, "The Basal Ganglia and the Control of Action," in *The Cognitive Neurosciences III*, 496.

88 Ibid., 499.

89 Gary A. Lucas, *Emergence, Mind, and Consciousness: A Bio-Inspired Design for a Conscious Agent* (Bloomington: iUniverse, 2011), 95–8.

Lucas argues that the areas in the parietal and premotor cortex that engage in action planning are mere promoters of plans, the actual selection of plan which will be sent to the motor cortex for execution being performed by the basal ganglia, and this makes the latter the actual decision-maker.

90 Jeremy D. Schmahmann and Deepak N. Pandya, "The Cerebrocerebellar System," in *The Cerebellum and Cognition*, edited by Jeremy D. Schmahmann (San Diego: Academic Press, 1997), 35–7 and 55.

91 O'Keefe and Nadel, *The Hippocampus as a Cognitive Map*, 77.
Lucas, *Emergence, Mind, and Consciousness*, 142–4.

92 The role of the hippocampus in affective modulation seems to be largely inhibitory. Lesions to this structure result in a greater willingness to engage in novel behavior, as well as a general increase in exploratory activities. See: Robert L. Isaacson, *The Limbic System* (New York: Plenum, 1978), 161–6.

93 Edelman and Tononi, *A Universe of Consciousness*, 42–6.

94 Isaacson, *The Limbic System*, 63–72.

95 Lucas, *Emergence, Mind, and Consciousness*, 141.

The amygdala and its immediately adjacent areas (stria terminalis, septal area, etc.) are referred to as the "extended amygdala." It is the entire complex, not just the almond-shaped collection of nuclei, that performs the function of controlling emotional reactivity, given information about internal and external states.

96 Ralph Adolphs, "Processing of Emotional and Social Information by the Human Amygdala," in *The Cognitive Neurosciences III*, 1019–20.

97 Ibid., 1026–7.

98 Hans C. Breiter and Gregory P. Gasic, "A General Circuitry Processing Reward/Aversion Information and Its Implications for Neuropsychiatric Illness," in *The Cognitive Neurosciences III*, 1044–5.

99 Ibid., 1046.

On the topic of reinforcement learning and the interactions between the different nuclei of the amygdala, the hypothalamus, and other components of the circuit, see also: Lucas, *Emergence, Mind, and Consciousness*, 142–4.

100 Xiaosi Gu, Patrick R. Hof, Karl J. Friston, and Jin Fan, "Anterior Insular Cortex and Emotional Awareness," *The Journal of Comparative Neurology*, Vol. 521 (Wiley Periodicals, 2013): 3373.

101 Antonio Damasio, *Descartes' Error* (New York: Penguin, 1994), 140–2.

102 Joseph M. Erwin and Patrick Hof, "The Anterior Cingulate Cortex," in *Annals of the New York Academy of Sciences* (New York: NYAS, 2001): 2–5.

103 Thomas A. Sebeok, *Signs: An Introduction to Semiotics* (Toronto: University of Toronto Press, 1994), 30.

104 William G. Lycan, *Consciousness* (Cambridge, MA: MIT Press, 1995), 38–9.

Lycan is very critical of the two-level approach defending instead the same multi-homuncular model we have taken from Dennett.

105 Timothy D. Wilson, *Strangers to Ourselves: Discovering the Adaptive Unconscious* (Cambridge: Belknap Press, 2002).

Wilson's discussion is not limited to priming and confabulatory phenomena. He deals with unconscious learning (Ibid., 24–7), unconscious feelings (Ibid., 124–5), and other intriguing phenomena.

106 Ibid., 30.

107 Ibid., 95.

108 Michael S. Gazzaniga, *Who's in Charge* (New York: Harper-Collins, 2011), 83.

109 Wilson, *Strangers to Ourselves*, 186.

110 Gazzaniga, *Who's in Charge*, 76–7.

111 Stanislas Dehaene, "Conscious and Nonconscious Processes," in *Better Than Conscious?* edited by Christoph Engel and Wolf Singer (Cambridge, MA: MIT Press, 2008), 27.

112 Robert Kurzban, "The Evolution of Implicit and Explicit Decision Making," in *Better Than Conscious?* Ibid., 159–60.

113 Wilson, *Strangers to Ourselves*, 49–54.

114 Walter J. Freeman, *Neurodynamics: An Exploration in Mesoscopic Brain Dynamics* (London: Springer–Verlag, 2000), 1–2.

115 Andrew A. Fingelkurts and Alexander A. Fingelkurts, "Mapping of Brain Operational Architectonics," in *Focus on Brain Mapping Research*, edited by F. J. Chen (New York: Nova Science Publishers, 2006), 70–1.

116 Susan A. Greenfield and Toby F. T. Collins, "A Neuroscientific Approach to Consciousness," in *The Boundaries of Consciousness*, edited by Steven Laureys (Amsterdam: Elsevier, 2005), 11–12.

117 Fingelkurts and Fingelkurts, "Mapping of Brain Operational Architectonics," 72.

We must be careful of how we characterize the content of the signs produced and consumed by the agents embodied in these transient assemblies. The authors argue that this content is not defined by information linked to sensory inputs but rather by *temporal patterns* in the activity of distributed neurons with sensory content: raw data from the senses is deleted and only self-organized amplitude modulation patterns are kept. In our terms this would imply that the signs that agents consume do not stand for external objects and events, but for the temporally coherent behavior of thousands of neurons within the area over which the integration is performed. But if all signs standing for objects and events is deleted, how can conscious agents transform the simple 3D stick figures that mindless agents produce into the fully rendered objects we experience?

118 Ibid., 73–4.

119 Ibid., 77–8.

Such a recursive combinatorial process is exactly what is needed to generate the mesoscale levels of the brain. Among philosophers, the first author to use these ideas was Mario Bunge. He emphasized the need for neuron systems that are plastic, that is, uncommitted by their anatomy to certain functions and, therefore, capable of self-organization, and referred to them as *psychons*. Animals with a nervous system in which everything is hard-wired, or that possess neural plasticity but only at the level of synapses, would lack psychons and, therefore, a mental life. See: Mario Bunge, *The Mind-Body Problem: A Psychobiological Approach* (Oxford: Pergamon, 1980), 56–7.

120 Olaf Sporns, *Networks of the Brain* (Cambridge, MA: MIT Press, 2011), 152–3.

121 Duncan J. Watts and Steven H. Strogatz, "Collective Dynamics of Small-World Networks," in *The Structure and Dynamics of Networks*, edited by Mark Newman, Albert-Lázló Barabási, and Duncan J. Watts (Princeton: Princeton University Press, 2006), 310.

122 Steven H. Strogatz, *Sync: The Emerging Science of Spontaneous Order* (New York: Hyperion, 2000), 249.

123 Sporns, *Networks of the Brain*, 116–20.

124 Ibid., 121–2.

125 Ibid., 36–7.

126 Ibid., 262–3.

127 Ibid., 152–3.

128 Humberto R. Maturana and Francisco J. Varela, *Autopoiesis and Cognition* (Boston: D. Reidel, 1980), 127.

129 Ibid., 128.

130 Hurley, *Consciousness in Action*, 2–3.

131 Ibid., 343.

Hurley does not put it this way. Rather she argues that once the relation input-output is drawn for processes inside the brain, it becomes fuzzy, some sensory inputs becoming part of personal volitions, and some outputs (via proprioceptive signs) becoming part of personal perceptions. This breaks any kind of one-to-one mapping between input-output and perception-action. On the other hand, Hurley is ambivalent about the question of content at the subpersonal level. She asserts that the subpersonal is all about the vehicles of signs, while all the content belongs at the personal level (Ibid., 17–18). This is, of course, the position held by Dennett, which we rejected in the first chapter. But she accepts the existence of subliminal content and the priming or biasing effects this can have on behavior, even accepting that the personal level can make passive use of these effects, which implies that content can exist at the subpersonal level (Ibid., 147–8).

132 William Bechtel and Robert C. Richardson, *Discovering Complexity: Decomposition and Localization as Strategies in Scientific Research* (Princeton: Princeton University Press, 1993), 25–7.

133 Evan Thompson, *Mind in Life: Biology, Phenomenology, and the Sciences of Mind* (Cambridge, MA: Harvard University Press, 2010), 420–2.

Thomson grants that near decomposability is compatible with closure, but not when it comes to the brain as a whole, in which case we must classify it as undecomposable. Varela and Maturana also argue that operational closure implies it is intrinsically impossible to localize functions. See: Maturana and Varela, *Autopoiesis and Cognition*, 129.

134 Maturana and Varela, *Autopoiesis and Cognition*, xix–xx.

In these pages Maturana argues that the relations between components constitute the identity of the composite whole, and that the properties of the components do not matter except to the extent they enter into these relations.

135 Francisco J. Varela, "Patterns of Life: Intertwining Identity and Cognition," *Brain and Cognition*, Vol. 34 (Academic Press, 1997).

This surplus of meaning is variously characterized as surplus of significance (value, relevance) as well as a surplus of signification (content). Varela uses the terms "meaning" (85), "signification" (79), and "significance" (84) as if they were synonymous.

136 There are many parallels between the enactive and empiricist approaches, including the fact that both pretend to be midway between realism and idealism, or as enactivists put it, between "objectivism" and "subjectivism." The main difference between the two positions seems to be that while empiricists use extrinsic relations, and their perceptual objects are mere bundles of properties, the enactivists use intrinsic relations to pretend they can go beyond that and synthesize these properties into true perceptual objects. We, of course, do not have to pick between these two bad options: the concept of emergence (as opposed to the enactivist co-emergence) can help us conceive of objects (not mere bundles) arising from extrinsic relations (causal interactions) between components.

Chapter 4

1 Alvin I. Goldman, "Consciousness: Folk Psychology and Cognitive Science," in *The Nature of Consciousness*, edited by Ned Block, Owen Flanagan, and Güven Güzeldere (Cambridge, MA: MIT Press, 1997), 111–13.

2 Ibid., 120.

3 Daniel C. Dennett, *Consciousness Explained* (Boston: Little, Brown, 1991), 371–3.

Dennett defends the relational option in the case of visual properties along these lines: objects in the world possess properties some of which are primary (shape, motion), while others are secondary, like their power to produce color sensations; human brains also possess primary properties, like the connectivity of their neurons, and secondary properties, like their power to cause appropriate responses to color experiences, such as uttering the sentence "that object is red." The properties of the visual field are constituted by the relation between an object's secondary properties, our discriminative neural states, and our verbal reports.

4 Richard Rorty, "Holism, Intrinsicality, and the Ambition of Transcendence," in *Dennett and His Critics*, edited by Bo Dahlbom (Oxford: Blackwell, 1993), 185–6.

Rorty claims that Dennett is a holist using the old strategy of replacing intrinsic properties with relational ones. Dennett, on his part, argues that the properties of a visual space are really properties of a logical space, and that the properties of this other space are relationally constituted by judgments and beliefs. See: Dennett, *Consciousness Explained*, 131.

5 Ibid., 132.

Dennett can be taken to mean two different things: that appearances are literally fictions, created by their descriptions much like the identity of the characters in novels are; or that noticing appearances takes special training (like that of realist painters) and that, therefore, when we do notice how a thing appears we create an additional representation, one that did not exist before we extracted it. If his intention is the latter, we can agree with him, but this still does not imply that noticing X demands having the explicit and reportable belief that we have created a separate representation.

6 Fred Dretske, "Conscious Experience," in *The Nature of Consciousness*, 774.

Dretske is concerned with all kinds of perceptual awareness, not only visual: our awareness of someone playing piano, of a piece of bread burning, and so on. All modalities, however, are subjected to the same treatment. Someone who has never heard a piano, or smelled burning toast, can hear the sounds and smell the aroma, although he would not be able to form factual beliefs about them.

7 Dennett, *Consciousness Explained*, 354–5.

8 Patricia S. Churchland and Viyalanur S. Ramachandran, "Filling In: Why Dennet Is Wrong," in *Dennett and His Critics*, edited by Bo Dahlbom (Oxford: Blackwell, 1993), 44.

9 Daniel C. Dennett, "Back from the Drawing Board," in *Dennett and His Critics*, 209.

Dennett acknowledges that a mechanism in terms of receptive fields is an improvement over phenomenological explanations and that the brain may in fact use information from one area as if it came from another. Yet, he insists that this operation need not involve duplication (of represented properties) but *pinching off*: the area from the blind spot is not filled in but folded over. Arguing over *a priori* neurophysiology, however, seems pointless. And the lack of evidence for the premise that all perception is perception of facts weakens the conclusion that intrinsic properties are fiction. Indeed, as some philosophers argue, this conclusion is a presupposition of the argument. See: Ned Block, "Begging the Question against Phenomenal Consciousness," in *The Nature of Consciousness*, 175–7.

10 Fred Dretske, *Naturalizing the Mind* (Cambridge, MA: MIT Press, 1997), 2–3.

More exactly, Dretske's definition is as follows: a phenomenal property X stands for an objective property Y if X possesses *the function of indicating* the presence of Y.

11 This version of Dretske's theory is, in fact, an adaptation. Dretske does not think of representations as hybrids of icons and indices, but simply as indices. Rather than saying that the mapping of a range of objective intensities into a range of representational states specifies the type that a given index (the result of a given measurement) is a token of, he argues that the index acquires its representational function by being embedded in the whole system: the instrument itself (Ibid., 12).

A description of how a range of speeds is mapped into a range of needle positions is a fact about a representational system but is not a representational fact (Ibid., 3). The problem with ignoring the role of icons, however, is that Dretske leaves himself open to criticisms by philosophers like William Ramsey. Ramsey argues that the representational content of indices (the information that an effect carries about its cause) is minimal and that a richer content, such as that provided by icons, is required. For Ramsey mental representations are to be conceived as simulations, which fall under the category of icons. See: William M. Ramsey, *Representation Reconsidered* (Cambridge: Cambridge University Press, 2007), 80–2 and 194–200.

12 Dretske, *Naturalizing the Mind*, 25.

13 Fred I. Dretske, *Knowledge and the Flow of Information* (Cambridge, MA: MIT Press, 1981), 157–8.

14 Dretske, *Naturalizing the Mind*, 6–7 and 92–3.

15 Ibid., 90–1.

16 Ibid., 13.

Metamerism gives us a good reason to believe that the mapping that yields color space is not between light wavelengths and colors. We will argue further that the actual mapping is between surface reflectances and colors. The problems created by a many-to-one mapping can then be dealt with by a more detailed analysis of the mapping process itself. Let's examine one possible way this analysis could be carried out. In the laboratory, reflectance is represented as a curve plotting the amount of light reflected by a surface against the different wavelengths of the light illuminating it. This curve is known as a *reflectance profile*. In these terms, the problem of metamerism arises from the fact that a set of reflectance profiles with entirely different geometrical properties correlates with the same phenomenal color, and from the fact that the set of profiles does not seem to have any internal order. This apparent randomness, however, disappears if we transform the set following a precise procedure. A reflectance profile is basically a two-dimensional plot in a piece of paper, so we can imagine that we can roll each of the plots in the set corresponding to a given color, gluing their two ends to form a cylinder. Next, we section the resulting tubes with a plane making sure the cut fully samples the curves plotted on each of them. Finally, we create the three-dimensional space formed by all the elliptical sections. This space, the dimensions of which are the altitude relative to the cylinder at which the slice was made, the inclination of the sectioning plane, and the degree of rotation of the elliptical section relative to the cylinder, can be shown to be isomorphic with the hue, brightness, and saturation dimensions of color space. See: Paul M. Churchland, "On the Reality (and Diversity) of Objective Colors: How Color-Qualia Space Is a Map of Reflectance-Profile Space," in *Color Ontology and Color Science*, edited by Jonathan Cohen and Mohan Matthen (Cambridge, MA: MIT Press, 2010), 43–8.

17 Matthew Soteriou, "The Perception of Absence, Space, and Time," in *Perception, Causation, and Objectivity*, edited by Johannes Roessler, Hemdat Lerman, and Naomi Eilan (Oxford: Oxford University Press, 2011), 187.

Soteriou considers several positions on this question, including the one that perceiving absences is a variety of perceiving the fact that there are absences (Ibid., 189).

18 Thomas Metzinger, *Being No One: The Self-Model of Subjectivity* (Cambridge, MA: MIT Press, 2003), 186–8.

19 Christopher Peacocke, "Sensation and the Content of Experience," in *The Nature of Consciousness*, 341–3.

Peacocke draws a sharp line between the sensational and the representational content of experience, the latter being concerned with objects, and through its links to judgment and belief, being inherently conceptual. But why draw such a sharp line between properties and objects? One reason may be that developmental psychologists of the empiricist tradition used to think that infants prior to the acquisition of linguistic abilities perceived the world in constant flux, a realm of surfaces without depth or stable identity, that randomly appeared and disappeared from view. But more recent studies have shown that infants as young as three months old can see a world composed of bounded objects that behave coherently, as shown by their surprise when one object passes through another, or when an object that just disappeared behind a screen emerges on the other side as a different object. See: Alan Slater, "Visual Organization and Perceptual Constancies in Early Infancy," in *Perceptual Constancy: Why Things Look as They Do*, edited by Vincent Walsh and Janusz Kulikowsky (Cambridge: Cambridge University Press, 1998), 6–7.

20 Tyler Burge, *Origins of Objectivity* (Oxford: Clarendon Press, 2010), 396–9.

21 Ibid., 408–10.

22 Ross and Plug, "The History of Size Constancy and Size Illusions," in *Perceptual Constancy*, 501.

The authors argue that size constancy was already described by Ptolemy in the second century AD, and discussed in detail by Ibn al-Haytham in the eleventh century. The experimental approach to the question begins with Helmholtz in the nineteenth century.

23 Kai von Fieandt and Ib Kristian Moustgaard, *The Perceptual World* (London: Academic Press, 1977), 380.

The ratios are traditionally expressed as a simple linear relation, so that changes in apparent size and apparent distance are assumed to remain proportional at all times, but that may be an oversimplification.

24 Dretske, *Knowledge and the Flow of Information*, 164–5.

Dretske thinks that we are visually sensitive not only to objects acting as a stimuli but also to various relations between them like ratios, gradients, and rates of change, and that these higher-order percepts may be used to explain perceptual constancy effects.

25 McKee and Smallman, "Size and Speed Constancy," in *Perceptual Constancy*, 377–9.

26 Collett and Parker, "Depth Constancy," in Ibid., 426.

27 James J. Gibson, *The Ecological Approach to Visual Perception* (New York: Psychology Press, 2015), 153–4.

28 The use of any of these indices presupposes the existence of the required mathematical operators to calculate ratios, gradients, or rates of change. If these operators were represented explicitly they would involve the concepts of distance, size, or angle, but all that is required is that the operators be implemented in the hardware of the brain without any explicit representation. See: Burge, *Origins of Objectivity*, 488–9.

29 Dorothy L. Cheney and Robert M. Seyfarth, *How Monkey's See the World* (Chicago: University of Chicago Press, 1990), 102–3.

30 Dretske, *Naturalizing the Mind*, 17–18.
   Dretske uses the opposition between discrete (or digital) signs and analog (or continuous) signs to distinguish two ways in which facts can be perceived. The difference can be illustrated by comparing two speedometers. The design we have been considering maps a continuous range of vehicle speeds into a continuous range of needle positions. This analog mapping allows a driver to assess that a given position of the needle indicates a speed that is higher than that indicated by another position, but not to judge by exactly how much the two speeds differ. A different design can be created by placing numerical markings on the display, each denoting a different speed. By subdividing a continuous range of needle positions into a set of discontinuous values, we have, thereby, transformed an analog sign into a digital one. And this, in turn, allows the driver to make *quantitative judgments*, such as those involved in comparing the current speed of the vehicle to the speed limit in that highway. Those judgments would involve concepts.

31 Ned Block, "Introduction: What Is Functionalism?" in *Readings in Philosophy of Psychology*, Vol. 1, edited by Ned Block (Cambridge, MA: Harvard University Press, 1980), 177–80.

32 Hilary Putnam, "Philosophy and Our Mental Life," in *Philosophical Papers*, Vol. II (Cambridge: Cambridge University Press, 1979), 291–3.
   Putnam does not use a mere metaphor but makes a more sophisticated analogy, using automata theory. Thus, instead of "hardware" he writes about Turing Machines and instead of "software" he uses the concept of a Turing Machine's table that describes the states of the hardware solely by their relations. Since as a mathematical entity a Turing

machine can be realized in many different computer designs, the relations specified by the machine table are indifferent to their realization, and can, therefore, be *functionally isomorphic* with mental states.

33 Patricia Smith Churchland, *Neurophilosophy: Toward a Unified Science of the Mind-Brain* (Cambridge: Bradford, 1986), 355.

34 Thomas W. Polger and Lawrence A. Shapiro, *The Multiple Realization Book* (Oxford: Oxford University Press, 2016), 30.

One reason why some functionalists accept an unrestricted view of multiple realization is that for them a valid realization of a program can be a computer made out of *different materials*, and the latter could be anything at all (copper, cheese, or soul). But as the authors point out, the concept of multiple realizations must apply not to multiple material compositions but to *multiple mechanisms* realizing one and the same function. The authors add further restrictions on multiple realizability. First, the evidence must go beyond demonstrating than the same effect (a given psychological state) can be produced by multiple causes (Ibid., 46). Second, even when we confine ourselves to functions realized by the brain, the evidence must be that different areas of the brain realize the same function, not that the same area can perform different functions (Ibid., 93–7). And third, the use of neuronal plasticity or convergent evolution in arguments for multiple realization must be qualified (Ibid., Ch 7).

35 Clyde L. Hardin, *Color for Philosophers: Unweaving the Rainbow*, (Indianapolis: Hackett, 1988), 2–3.

Refection, emission, and transmission are in fact only a subset of the ways in which light with different spectral composition can be produced. Hardin gives a fuller list of the objective phenomena involved in the production of phenomenal color.

36 Dennett, *Consciousness Explained*, 378.

37 Dale Purves and R. Beau Lotto, *Why We See What We Do: An Empirical Theory of Vision* (Sunderland: Sinauer, 2003), 102–4.

38 Hardin, *Color for Philosophers*, 82.

39 Churchland, "On the Reality (and Diversity) of Objective Colors," 37.

40 Hardin, *Color for Philosophers*, 111.

Hardin asserts that colors are illusions but not unfounded ones. This seems to imply that they are effects, not mere illusions like a mirage. There is no problem considering colors as effects, since most indexical signs are effects carrying information about their causes, as long as we add that, unlike natural indices, colors have acquired the function of indicating one of their causes through an evolutionary process.

41 Rolf G. Kuehni, "Color Spaces and Color Order Systems: A Primer," in *Color Ontology and Color Science*, edited by Jonathan Cohen and Mohan Matthen (Cambridge, MA: MIT Press, 2010), 5–6.

42 Hardin, *Color for Philosophers*, 31.

43 Donald I. A. MacLeod, "Into the Neural Maze," in *Color Ontology and Color Science*, 159–60.

44 Hardin, *Color for Philosophers*, 34–5.
   Hardin discusses the various ways in which this model is too simple: it disregards nonlinear (nonadditive) interactions; the choice of color label for activations below or above the base rate are conventional (although the need to give them opposite signs is not); and it lacks the means to represent other important causal factors in the process, like the relative efficiencies of different cones or their different proportions in different parts of the retina. There is no consensus yet about the right model for retinal ganglia, with several proposals being considered that cover the complete range of alternatives. See: Dennis Dacey, "Origins of Perception: Retinal Ganglion Cell Diversity and the Creation of Parallel Visual Pathways," in *The Cognitive Neurosciences III*, edited by Michael S. Gazzaniga (Cambridge, MA: MIT Press, 2004), 286.

45 Hardin, *Color for Philosophers*, 56–8.
   It can be shown by simulating retinal ganglia with an artificial neural net, that the space of possible activation patterns of the neural net has a sufficiently close topology to that of the spindle-shaped phenomenal color space, that one can conceivably be mapped into the other. The neural net model is referred to as the Hurvich-Jameson model. See: Churchland, "On the Reality (and Diversity) of Objective Colors," 44–5.

46 MacLeod, "Into the Neural Maze," 162–3.
   MacLeod argues convincingly that any simple psychoneural isomorphism (e.g., a one-to-one mapping of retinal ganglia outputs and phenomenal colors) is put into question by the multiple ways in which wavelength information is used in the cortex (e.g., neurons with receptive fields sensitive to both color and shape). But if in addition to the sensory analysis performed by earlier processing stages we consider the perceptual synthesis performed by later stages, and add feedback from the latter to the former, a more stable mapping between reflectances and colors may be achieved (Ibid., 170–1).

47 Kuehni, "Color Spaces and Color Order Systems," 8.
   The mathematical procedure is known as principal component analysis. This procedure reveals which components of a spectral function

are present more often. Using the first three of these components (which explain most of the variability in the function) as the axes of a space of possible reflectance functions, one can find patterns that correspond to features of phenomenal color space such as circular arrangements of points that correspond to the color wheel at the center of the spindle (Ibid., 6).

48 Jonathan Cohen, *The Red and the Real: An Essay in Color Ontology* (Oxford: Oxford University Press, 2011), 178.

Cohen argues that the color red must be thought of as having the *functional role* of disposing its bearers to look red to an observer under some viewing conditions, and that this makes it a relational property. He defines "relationalism" about colors as the claim that they are constituted by the relation subject-object (Ibid., 8). Yet, he fails to distinguish between intrinsic relations from extrinsic ones. And once all relations are put into the same category, an intrinsic property can be defined as a property that is what it is regardless of the relations its bearer may have to other things. But we can defend intrinsic properties without having to commit ourselves to this isolationism. The very real variation in perceptual experience caused by changes in illumination, contrast effects between nearby objects, angle of view, and other relations, which Cohen views as evidence of a relational nature, can be acknowledged to exist as long as the relations involved are conceived as extrinsic.

49 Joseph Levine, "Qualia: Intrinsic, Relational, or What?" in *Conscious Experience*, edited by Thomas Metzinger (Thorverton: Imprint Academic, 1995), 284.

50 Cohen, *The Red and the Real*, 46–9.

Cohen defends his metaphysical conclusion (all variants are veridical) only against accounts that place colors in the world. In the present account the only property about which questions of veridicality can be raised is reflectance (and its categorical basis) not the intrinsic properties of phenomenal signs which can vary widely without disrupting their evolutionary function.

51 Hardin, *Color for Philosophers*, 101.

Hardin discusses this in more quantitative terms using degrees. If the visual field of the right eye is taken to extend 110 degrees to the right of center, then red and green disappear past 40 degrees, and all color beyond 65 degrees.

52 Alva Noë, *Action in Perception* (Cambridge, MA: MIT Press, 2004), 135–6.

Noë argues that any apparently actual qualia (say, a color currently foveated) has further qualia potentially in it, in the sense that with better discriminatory skills we would get to see that what seems to be just one color is actually two. We can grant this point but argue that the mere mention of skills, without any attempt at explaining their neural and bodily implementation, does not explain anything phenomenal. Skills matter, and perceptual skills can certainly have a very real effect on what we perceive (by affecting the way we deploy attention and notice things) but they do not explain perception itself.

53 We will not deal in the main text with what philosophers find objectionable about qualia: being *ineffable, atomic, private,* and *directly graspable.* The problem with arguments against these four properties is that they only hit their target if we assume that the properties are necessary, that is, if we take them to be part of the *essence* of what qualia are. Let's consider them one by one. To be ineffable means to be inexpressible in language. Thus, the fact that we can see many more colors than we have words for them is taken by some to prove that we could not possibly give an exhaustive description of our experience of color. But is it really that impossible to imagine a culture that places so much value on colors (perhaps because of the role they play in their religion or technology) that it has developed an extensive vocabulary for all shades and saturations of phenomenal colors? There is, in fact, a recursive method to generate color terms that shows this to be possible. See: Hardin, *Color for Philosophers,* 183–6.

To be atomic means to be unanalyzable: we cannot acquire knowledge about qualia by dissecting them into components. This may be taken to mean two different things. We may require qualia to be analyzable into their *ingredients,* much like pigments or lights can be analyzed in the case of colors like orange or purple. In this case, the primary or unmixed colors would indeed be unanalyzable. But there is another possible target for analysis: not the color but the process of which the color is an emergent consequence. The more we know about their production and consumption the closer we get to analyzing qualia as emergent properties caused by the interaction between components, their apparent atomicity being contingent on our knowledge of the mechanisms of emergence. Finally, both being private and being apprehensible in a direct way imply that qualia can only be studied from a first-person, as opposed to a third-person, point of view. We cannot, for example, ever know what it is like to be a bat, only bats can. See: Thomas Nagel, "What Is It Like to Be a Bat?" in *The Nature of Consciousness,* 521.

It is, however, surprising how much we can learn about the phenomenal experience of an animal using echolocation by analyzing its hunting strategies, the nature of the sonar signal at different stages of a hunt, the way in which the organs send and receive the signal are meshed together, and the brain mechanisms used to process the signal. When we approach the space of possible mental states for a bat using only our imagination, the space seems to have no structure, and hence to afford us no entry point into it. But once hunting behavior, the nature of the signal, the relation between sender and receiver organs, and the underlying brain events are brought into the picture, the space becomes sufficiently constrained that it no longer seems so forbidding. In other words, before the constraints are in place the possibility space seems to be essentially unknowable, whereas afterward it seems merely contingently so. See: Kathleen A. Akins, "What Is It Like to Be Boring and Myopic?" in *Dennett and His Critics*, 133–45.

54 Hardin, *Color for Philosophers*, 101.

The gradient of determinacy we discussed in the main text depends not only on retinal location but also on the size and speed of the object being perceived. The color and shape of a small object in the periphery of the visual field will tend to be indeterminate, but if the object is large enough both of these properties become determinate. Similarly, we can perceive a rapidly moving car flashing across our visual field, and distinguish it from the background, without being able to perceive either its color or its shape which are indeterminate in these conditions, but become determinate if the vehicle slows down.

55 Burge, *Origins of Objectivity*, 397.

56 J. M. Troost, "Empirical Studies in Color Constancy," in *Perceptual Constancy*, 275–7.

The two different viewing conditions are referred to as *surface* and *aperture* modes, respectively. Phenomenal experience correlates with surface reflectance only in the former case, when a scene is viewed in its full complexity. Any factor that impoverishes the information reaching the eye can result in the loss of the effect. This fact, the author argues, suggests that color constancy cannot be due solely to processes occurring at the retina (chromatic adaptation, lateral inhibition) but must involve the higher-level processes involved in object perception.

57 H. Komatsu, "The Physiological Substrates of Color Constancy," in *Perceptual Constancy*, 359–63.

58 Makoto Kusunoki, Konstantinos Moutoussis, and Semir Saki, "Effect of Background Colors on the Tuning of Color-Selective Cells in Monkey

Area V4," *Journal of Neurophysiology*, Vol. 95 (American Physiological Society, 2006): 3048.

59 Gibson, *The Ecological Approach to Visual Perception*, 129.

The dependency of object perception on affordances has left linguistic traces. In ordinary language the number of surfaces that a given object is said to have varies considerably depending on how we interact with it: paper and cloth are typically thought as having two surfaces; rounded rocks as having only one surface; and rainbows, shadows, and clouds as having zero bounding surfaces. In some cases, what we call a surface depends on the kinds of operations we can perform on it, such as painting or polishing. See: Avrum Stroll, *Surfaces* (Minneapolis: University of Minnesota Press, 1988), 19–20 and 28–35.

And a similar point applies to depressions, hollows, fractures, and grooves. These are discontinuities in a host surface that are causally significant in relation to their affordances: an object with a hole but just one opening affords transportation of water or grain, while a hole with two openings is basically a tunnel that affords passage, as long as it is of the right size relative to our bodies. See: Roberto Casati and Achille C. Varzi, *Holes and Other Superficialities* (Cambridge, MA: MIT Press, 1994), 63–4.

60 Gibson, *The Ecological Approach to Visual Perception*, 130.

61 Ibid., 133–4.

62 Andrew H. Fagg and Michael A. Arbib, "Modeling Parietal–Premotor Interactions in Primate Control of Grasping," *Neural Networks*, Vol. 11 (Pergamon, 1998): 1280.

63 Giacomo Rizzolatti and Corrado Sinigaglia, *Mirrors in the Brain: How Our Minds Share Actions and Emotions* (Oxford: Oxford University Press, 2006), 166–74.

The authors argue that the main function of mirror neurons may not be to allow for imitative learning but to anticipate the action of others, when engaged in a cooperative task, by guessing their goals. Being able to anticipate conspecific actions by guessing their intentions is a way to bridge the first- and the third-person point of view (Ibid., 175). Such a bridge would also be important in the separation of the perspectival from the factual in the case of social affordances: the opportunities and risks for interaction supplied by other members of a community.

64 Mark Wagner, *The Geometries of Visual Space* (New York: Psychology Press, 2006), 19–24 and 30–49.

The history of attempts to discover the nature of visual space is interesting but we cannot go into it here. Wagner argues that in the past most attempts to conceptualize the geometry of visual space were performed in mathematical terms, picking an existing metric geometry—a geometrical system in which properties like length, area, and volume are the basic notions—and using it to explain spatial perception. Some researchers even tried to test their choice of metric geometry (flat, convex, or concave) using psychophysical experiments. But the data coming from their laboratories tended to conflict with the axioms of those geometrical systems. But there are other ways to approach this question that do not rely on axiomatized geometries: we simply assign coordinates to locations in visual space so we can make systematic predictions about the metric judgments subjects make in the course of an experiment, that is, judgments about the volume of space occupied by a perceived object or about the distance that separates two perceived objects.

65 John Campbell, *Past, Space, and Self* (Cambridge, MA: MIT Press, 1995), 27–9.

66 Ibid., 20–3.

Campbell provides an excellent discussion of the interplay between egocentric and allocentric frames of reference.

67 John O'Keefe and Lynn Nadel, *The Hippocampus as a Cognitive Map* (Oxford: Clarendon Press, 1978), 75–6 and 82–4.

68 Ibid., 51–2 and 72–3.

69 Ibid., 93–6.

An allocentric map may have many unrepresented places and missing connections between them, and may need the help of route and landmark signs to fill the holes and discontinuities.

70 Campbell, *Past, Space, and Self*, 24.

71 O'Keefe and Nadel, *The Hippocampus as a Cognitive Map*, 78.

To understand the expression "cognitive map" as used by the authors we need to keep in mind the distinction we made in the previous chapter between a cognitive agent and the icons and indices it produces and consumes. The authors do not use the agent-sign terminology we have used here, but they make similar distinctions. First, maps as signs are not considered to be icons capturing similarity of appearances (pictures) but similarity of relations. And second, the hippocampus itself is not considered to be a cognitive map (despite the book's title) but an information structure from which maps (as signs) can be generated.

72 Ibid., 220.

The three modules are the known as *fascia dentata, CA3, and CA1.*

73 Ibid., 93.

74 Robert Muller, "A Quarter of a Century of Place Cells," *Neuron*, Vol. 17 (Cambridge: Cell Press, 1996): 813.

Interconnected places in the environment are represented by assemblies of place cells that remain stable over long periods of time. That is, the assemblies remain invariant if the distribution of objects in a place changes, and they change as a whole when a new environment is explored and mapped (Ibid., 816). In our terms, an active assembly constitutes the iconic component of the internal sign, while those cells which are currently firing indicate the place in the map that the animal is presently occupying. On the other hand, the transformation between egocentric to allocentric iconic signs is more complex than this. In particular, the input to the hippocampus is not *raw* egocentric data. Rather the cortical area that projects to it (the entorhinal cortex) has its own specialized neurons that prepare the material for further processing: *grid cells*, assembled together in a regularly spaced triangular grid; *border cells*, responding to geometric boundaries; and *head direction cells*. See: May-Britt Moser, David C. Rowland, and Edvard I. Moser, "Place Cells, Grid Cells, and Memory," *Perspectives in Biology*, Vol. 7, No. 2 (Cold Spring Harbor, 2015): 7–10.

75 Alexander A. Skavenski and Ronald M. Hansen, "Role of Eye Position Information in Visual Space Perception," in *Eye Movements and the Higher Psychological Functions*, edited by John W. Sanders, Dennis F. Fisher, and Richard A. Monty (Hillsdale: Lawrence Erlbaum, 1978), 25–32.

76 Churchland, *Neurophilosophy*, 433–4.

The author does not discuss perceptual stability but a related phenomenon, the so-called *vestibulo-ocular reflex*, which endows viewers with the capacity to fix their gaze on an object as their head moves left and right or up and down. To keep the object in focus the rotation of the eyes must be precisely controlled so the brain can exactly compensate for the movements of the head, a trick performed using vector transformations. Alternative mechanisms that also postulate using eye position information to counteract the apparent motion due to self-movement are discussed in: Marc Jeannerod, *The Cognitive Neuroscience of Action* (Oxford: Blackwell, 1997), 167–74.

77 Thomas Metzinger, "Faster Than Thought," in *Conscious Experience*, 443–4.

78 Gareth Evans, *The Varieties of Reference*, edited by John McDowell (Oxford: Clarendon Press, 1982), 143–6.

Evans uses the terms "demonstrative" and "descriptive" for different kinds of thoughts not for different kinds of understanding. Nothing much hangs on this difference.

79 Campbell, *Past, Space, and Self*, 42.

80 Ibid., 11–15.

81 John Campbell, *Reference and Consciousness* (Oxford: Clarendon, 2002), 29.

82 Evans, *The Varieties of Reference*, 147–9.

The requirement that the object be directly visible is meant to distinguish cases of ordinary, unmediated perception, from those in which the informational link involves technology, as when we point to a football player while watching a television screen, or when the informational link involves a long delay, as when pointing to a star in the sky. When the link does not provide the subject with the means to locate the object, then concepts (as well as beliefs and judgments) are required. So Evan's two conditions for a successful demonstrative identification are that there is an informational link between object and subject, and that the link *endures through time*, as it does when we track an object as it changes. Evans also agrees that the referent of an indexical is linked to behavioral possibilities (Ibid., 153–4).

83 Max A. Freund, *The Logic of Sortals* (Cham: Springer, 2019), 9.

84 Campbell, *Reference and Consciousness*, 70.

Campbell argues that we can single out an object even if we use the wrong sortal concept, as when we point to a plastic plant and say "That's a beautiful plant." Campbell uses a very similar model of the effect of attention on internal feature maps (Ibid., 32–3). Unfortunately for us, he later on declines to consider this fact as demanding a representational theory of perception. He subscribes to a relational theory in which the qualitative character of visual experience is constituted by its relation to the qualitative character of the scene perceived (Ibid., 155). He claims that representational theories must be rejected because they assume that the brain creates a representation independently of what the world is like (Ibid., 119). But we have shown in the previous chapter that this is true only of representational theories that postulate raw sense data as an impoverished input that must be enriched by inferences operating on symbols. In the end, as in the cases of Dennett, Searle, Gibson, and others, a relational approach leads Campbell to accept naive realism.

85 Paul Churchland, *The Engine of Reason, the Seat of the Soul* (Cambridge, MA: MIT Press, 1996), 27–34.

86 William Bechtel and Adele Abrahamsen, *Connectionism and the Mind* (Maiden: Blackwell, 2002), 342–3.

87 Giulio Tononi, Olaf Sporns, and Gerald M. Edelman, "Reentry and the Problem of Integrating Multiple Cortical Areas: Simulation of Dynamic

Integration in the Visual System," *Cerebral Cortex*, Vol. 2, No. 4 (Oxford Academic, 1992): 315.

Areas V1 and V2 are modeled as a single structure, but each of their three channels (shape, color, motion) is modeled separately. On the ventral stream, V3 and V4 are included, one processing shape information (oriented corners, line terminations) the other one color. The dorsal stream is represented by area V5, specializing in the detection of coherent motion in whole patterns, such as the movement of extended contours. In addition to these topographically organized areas, two additional cortical areas are included: IT (inferior temporal cortex) and PG (parietal cortex). IT is assumed to be the place where ventral information about edges and contours is converted into representations of objects, which in this case are flat geometric figures of different colors. PG stands for a cortical area in which synthesis is performed, this time of visual and haptic information and their relation to spatial locations. The motor output is restricted to control of the rotation of the eyes in their sockets, which allows simulating the exploratory movements of the gaze. The simulation can achieve *figure-ground segregation*: when presented with a simple object which moves against a background of differently moving objects, units in the motion channel of V1/V2 partition themselves into two correlated subsets, those responding to the figure in the foreground having the same phase, while those responding to the background having a different phase. More complex objects and motions can be segregated from the background using the reciprocal connections between the motion channel of V1/V2 and V5. (Ibid., 316–17.)

88 Gerald M. Edelman, *The Remembered Present: A Biological Theory of Consciousness* (New York: Basic Books, 1989), 54–6.

Edelman refers to the whole made by two different maps (say, one visual and one tactile) linked by reentrant connections as a *classification couple*. But as he argues a couple (or even an n-tuple) is not enough for perceptual categorization: we need as global map linking sensory, motor, and value information, the activity of which is stabilized dynamically. (Ibid., 143) The global map would link perceptual "sortal" concepts not only to similarities in the tokens of a type but to behavioral and evaluative information about the type.

89 Andy Clark, *Being There: Putting Brain, Body, and World Together Again*, (Cambridge, MA: MIT Press, 1998), 45–6.

90 Campbell, *Past, Space, and Self*, 43–6.

91 Ibid., 48.

Campbell argues that nonhuman mammals must be thought as capable of using causal indexicals: a squirrel does not need words to perceive nuts as edible and as surrounded by a crackable shell, and to deal with them in different ways depending on the task: eating them now or storing them for winter. The squirrel can identify the natural signs that indicate that the nut can be eaten (its shape, its color) as well as the obstacles preventing it from eating directly (the hard shell) and have a practical grasp of the significance of these indices: it must work hard to break the shell to reach the edible center.

92 John R. Searle, *Seeing Things as They Are: A Theory of Perception*, (Oxford: Oxford University Press, 2015), 41.

Searle defines phenomenal experience as a direct presentation of satisfaction conditions lived *as caused* by those satisfaction conditions.

93 Burge, *Origins of Objectivity*, 292

Burge refers to the idea that satisfaction conditions are explicitly represented as the *hyper-intellectualization* of perception (Ibid., 116–17).

94 Evans, *The Varieties of Reference*, 170–1.

95 Campbell, *Reference and Consciousness*, 28.

96 Evans, *The Varieties of Reference*, 158.

97 Campbell, *Reference and Consciousness*, 30.

98 David J. Chalmers, "The Conscious Mind," in *Search of a Fundamental Theory* (Oxford: Oxford University Press, 1996), 24–31.

99 These two approaches are referred to as HOT and HOP, for higher-order thought and higher-order percepts, respectively, the former defended by Lycan the latter by Rosenthal. See: William G. Lycan, "Consciousness as Internal Monitoring," in *The Nature of Consciousness*, 762.

David Rosenthal, "A Theory of Consciousness," in *The Nature of Consciousness*, 741.

100 Uriah Kriegel, "The Same-Order Monitoring Theory of Consciousness," in *Self-Representational Approaches to Consciousness*, edited by Uriah Kriegel and Kenneth Williford (Cambridge, MA: MIT Press, 2006), 143–5.

101 Making phenomenal experience a matter of consumption of signs rather than their production eliminates the idea that the visual field is like a veil separating us from reality, as well as the idea that the transparency of this veil must be accounted for. The very real question of why we tend to see objects and not appearances is then answered by the way we deploy our attention. Without any training we attend to what matters to carry on activities, but we can train our attention (as many visual artists do) to notice the perspectival content instead. For a treatment of the genesis of subjectivity as a form of *voluptuous consumption of residues*, which may be seen as a materialist rendering of the phenomenological concept of passive synthesis, see: Gilles Deleuze and Félix Guattari, *Anti-Oedipus*, (London: Continuum, 2004), 42 and 92–8.

102 Antonio Damasio, *Self Comes to Mind: Constructing the Conscious Brain* (New York: Vintage, 2010), 140.

These brain areas are the pariaqueductal gray, the parabrachial nucleus, and the nucleus tractus solitarius. As we noted in a note in Chapter 2, Damasio does not write about agents consuming visceral content to produce primordial feelings but rather about interoceptive maps becoming visceral images that are *spontaneously felt* at the level of the brain stem. This implies that for him the emergence of a protoself is a matter of a transformation of signs, from maps to images, and that the latter are, in a sense, self-interpreting. On the other hand he grants that brain centers have dispositions to act in certain ways, that they have *dispositional knowledge* (Ibid., 200). If dispositions are thought of as capacities to affect and be affected by information produced in other centers then this is just another way of talking about cognitive agents producing and consuming signs. Similarly, the concept of voluptuously consumed signs need not clash with his ideas, since it may be taken to refer to the same thing as his spontaneously felt images, a special type of sign consumption being what transforms maps into images.

103 Nicholas Humphrey, A *History of the Mind* (New York: Simon & Schuster, 1992), 42–3.

Humphrey does not write about the perception of properties and objects but about raw sensations and percepts. We avoid this terminology because it can cause confusion between sensory inputs and phenomenal perceptions. On the other hand, he considers only two kinds of content, raw sensations and world perceptions, instead of four—properties, objects, facts represented demonstratively, and facts represented descriptively—so mapping his categories into ours is problematic. In particular, some characteristics of experience that we keep apart are lumped together in his account. Thus, for him representing a sensation involves making a copy of the stimulus, but representing a percept requires a *story* about the source of the stimulus (Ibid., 101). But in our own account, narratives content are not part of the perception of objects. Similarly, signs for sensations are taken by him to be analog, while those for percepts to be digital (Ibid., 102). For us the conversion from continuous to discrete takes place only at the level of facts. Finally, affective content is taken by him to characterize only sensations, percepts being affectively neutral (Ibid., 73 and 94). For us, different kinds of affect accompany all four kinds of perception.

104 Ibid., 47 and 98.

105 Ibid., 77–8.

106 Dennett, *Consciousness Explained*, 419–22.

107 Michael S. Gazzaniga, *Who's in Charge* (New York: Harper-Collins, 2011), 56–7.

108 Ibid., 54.

109 Thomas Nagel, "Brain Bisection and the Unity of Consciousness," in *Personal Identity*, edited by John Perry (Berkeley: University of California Press, 1975), 242.

110 William G. Lycan, *Consciousness* (Cambridge: Bradford, 1987), 45.

111 Ernst Pöppel, *Mindworks. Time and Conscious Experience* (Boston: Hardcourt Brace Jovanovich, 1985), 29–30.

112 Ibid., 16.
Because the actual threshold varies in different conditions it is not given as an absolute value but rather as a range of values. Pöppel refers to these ranges as *windows of simultaneity.*

113 Ibid., 19.

114 Ibid., 61.

115 Ibid., 65–6.

116 William James, *The Principles of Psychology* (New York: Henry Holt, 1918), 630. See also: Edmund Husserl, *Ideas I* (Indianapolis: Hacket Publishing, 2014), 140.

117 Pöppel, *Mindworks*, 12.
The window of simultaneity for acoustic stimuli, for example, is considerable lower than that for visual stimuli, a difference explained by the slower processing speed for the latter. The window in this other case is 2,000 to 5,000 of a second. But the window of order, which is 30,000 to 40,000 of a second, is the same for acoustic, tactile, and visual stimuli (Ibid., 20).

118 E. Ruhnau, "Time Gestalts and the Observer," in *Conscious Experience*, 167–8.

119 Damasio, *Self Comes to Mind*, 225.

120 John Locke, "Of Identity and Diversity," in *Personal Identity*, edited by John Perry (Berkeley: University of California Press, 1975), 45.

121 Joseph Butler, "Of Personal Identity," in *Personal Identity*, 100.

122 Daniel L. Schacter and Endel Tulving, "What Are the Memory Systems in 1994?" in *Memory Systems 1994*, edited by Daniel L. Schacter and Endel Tulving (Cambridge, MA: MIT Press, 1994), 28.

The dissociation between episodic and semantic forms of memory is well documented: subjects may be incapable of recalling specific autobiographical events while remembering what was said in those same events, or vice versa, recall actually lived scenes but unable to remember what was said to them. It is this possibility of double dissociation that shows that the two types of memory are distinct.

123 John Perry, "Personal Identity, Memory, and the Problem of Circularity," in *Personal Identity*, 144–7.

124 Reza Habib, Lars Nyberg, and Endel Tulving, "Hemispheric Asymmetries of Memory: The HERA Model Revisited," *Trends in Cognitive Sciences,* Vol. 7, No. 6 (Elsevier, 2003): 241–4.

125 Antonio R. Damasio, "Remembering When," *Scientific American*, Vol. 287, No. 3 (New York, 2002): 68–9.

126 John Perry, "The Problem of Personal Identity," in *Personal Identity*, 16–20.

Perry argues that the problem of discontinuities in the sequence of stages may be solved by relaxing the requirement that each stage should contain a memory of the entire sequence of past stages, and requiring only that each stage possess a memory of the immediately preceding one. On the other hand, the problem of forgetting becomes more acute if we imagine persons that live much longer than we do. For such a Methuselah, the discontinuities between events occurring at a young age and those at an older ager may be too large to bridge. See: David Lewis, "Survival and Identity," in *The Identities of Persons*, edited by Amélie Oksenberg Rorty (Berkeley: University of California Press, 1976), 30.

127 Derek Parfit, "Personal Identity," in *Personal Identity*, 206 and 214–15.

128 Lewis, "Survival and Identity," 17–18.

129 T. Penelhum, "Self-Identity and Self-Regard," in *Identities of Persons*, 272.

The empiricist philosopher David Hume, who famously denied the unity of the person as it regards to thought, accepted it with respect to some feelings. While some pleasant and unpleasant feelings have only causes, others (pride, humiliation, sympathy) have both causes and an intentional object: a person with enduring identity. A favorable fact may cause us to have joy, but not pride (or love) because the latter involves in addition the Idea of oneself (or of a loved person). And similarly for humiliation and hatred (Ibid., 256–8).

130 Monte Jay Meldman, *Diseases of Attention* (Oxford: Pergamon Press, 1970), 140.

The author approaches the attentional system as involving a hierarchy of complexity, the levels of which he labels "atomic," "molecular," and "molar." These correspond to the three levels which we are referring here to as "arousal," "vigilance," and "selective awareness."

131 Ibid., 7.

132 Ibid., 48–39.

133 Mihaly Csikzentmihaly and Jeanne Nakamura, "Effortless Attention in Every Day Life: A Systematic Phenomenology," in *Effortless Attention*, edited by Brian Bruya (Cambridge, MA: MIT Press, 2010), 186.

The term for an intrinsically rewarding experience which simultaneously excludes self-conscious thoughts and fears of social evaluation is *autotelic*. The state of consciousness itself is referred to as *flow*.

134 Ibid., 187.

135 Fredrik Ullén, Örjan de Manzano, Töres Theorelll, and László Harmat, "The Physiology of Effortless Attention: Correlates of State Flow and Flow Proneness," in *Effortless Attention*, 205.

136 Meldman, *Diseases of Attention*, 66–7.

137 Joaquín M. Fuster, *Cortex and Mind* (Oxford: Oxford University Press, 2003), 167–9.

138 Manuel DeLanda, *Philosophy and Simulation* (London: Continuum, 2011).

Chapter 10 explores the transition from primate to human societies, modeled as a transition from a two-person iterated prisoners dilemma to the N-person case. Simulations of the evolution of language are discussed in chapter 12.

139 Cheney and Seyfarth, *How Monkey's See the World*, 70–1.

140 Chalmers, "The Conscious Mind," 213–18.

Chalmers proposes to model a science of consciousness on physics, as conceived by philosophers ever since the model was put forward by the Vienna Circle: physics is the search for fundamental laws that are ultimately expressed as general statements, the truth of which has no exceptions. This model was based on the axiomatizations of classical physics, a format that reduces its content to propositions linked logically. Thus, Chalmers proposes a search for psychophysical laws as the foundation for a science of consciousness. The problem is, physics as portrayed by its axiomatic versions is not how physics is actually practiced. And more importantly, to identify science with physics is another mistake philosophers have made ever since Kant put forward this erroneous idea. For a vision of what the philosophy of science could be without dragging around these historical errors is put forward in: Manuel DeLanda, *Philosophical Chemistry: Genealogy of a Scientific Field* (London: Bloomsbury, 2015).

INDEX